AUTOCOURSE
INDY CAR ™
1993-94

HAZLETON PUBLISHING

PPG MAKES RACING A LOT MORE COLORFUL.

The colorful paint finish on every Indy Car race machine
is supplied by PPG, a world leader in automotive finishes and
sponsor of the PPG Indy Car World Series.

**A world leader
in automotive
finishes.**

CONTENTS

PUBLISHER
Richard Poulter

EDITOR
Jeremy Shaw

EXECUTIVE PUBLISHER
Elizabeth Le Breton

ART EDITOR
Steve Small

PRODUCTION MANAGER
George Greenfield

HOUSE EDITOR
Peter Lovering

CHIEF PHOTOGRAPHER
Michael C. Brown

Additional photographs
have been contributed by
IndyCar
Jori Potiker
Sutton Photographic
Steve Swope
John Townsend

US Advertising Representative
Barry Pigot
12843-A Foothill Boulevard
Sylmar, California 91342
Telephone: (818) 365-2936
Fax: (818) 365-1238

INDY CAR 1993-94
is published by
Hazleton Publishing,
3 Richmond Hill,
Richmond, Surrey
TW10 6RE, England.

Color reproduction by
Barrett Berkeley Ltd, London, England.

Printed in England by
Butler and Tanner Ltd,
Frome.

ISBN: 1-874557-45-4

Michael C. Brown

ACKNOWLEDGEMENTS
The publishers wish to thank William Stokkan, Scott Johnson, Randy Dzierzawski, Kirk Russell, Tim Dolman,
John Chuhran, Jeff Kowalczyk and Dave Elshoff for their assistance.

DISTRIBUTORS

UNITED KINGDOM
Bookpoint Ltd
39 Milton Park
Abingdon
Oxfordshire OX14 4TD

NORTH AMERICA
Motorbooks
International
PO Box 1
729 Prospect Ave.
Osceola
Wisconsin 54020, USA

AUSTRALIA
Technical Book and
Magazine Co. Pty
289-299 Swanston
Street
Melbourne
Victoria 3000

NEW ZEALAND
David Bateman Ltd
'Golden Heights'
32-34 View Road
Glenfield
Auckland 10

SOUTH AFRICA
Motorbooks
341 Jan Smuts Avenue
Craighall Park
Johannesburg

Nigel Mansell,
1993 PPG Indy Car World Series
Champion (Newman-Haas Racing)

Raul Boesel
(Dick Simon Racing)

The success of Cosworth engines in international motor racing is legendary.

Continuous research, development and new manufacturing technology form the centre of our race ethic. Our commitment to excellence ensures that Cosworth will continue to achieve the competitive edge vital for tomorrow's success.

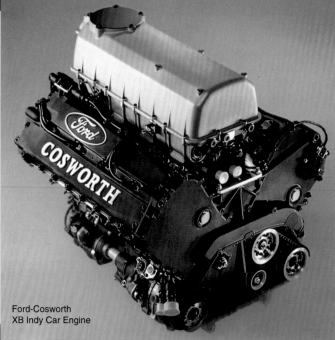

Ford-Cosworth
XB Indy Car Engine

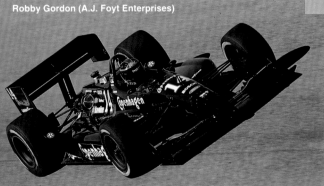

Robby Gordon (A.J. Foyt Enterprises)

Scott Goodyear (Walker Motorsport)

Arie Luyendyk (Chip Ganassi Racing)

COSWORTH®

Cosworth Engineering, St James Mill Road, Northampton NN5 5JJ, UK.
Telephone: (0) 604 752444/ Fax: (0) 604 580470
Cosworth Engineering Inc., 3031 Fujita Street, Torrance, CA90505-4004, USA. Telephone: (0) 310 534 139
Fax: (0) 310 534 263
A division of Vickers PLC

FOREWORD
by NIGEL MANSELL

Coming to America to race in the PPG Indy Car World Series has been a wonderful experience for the family and myself. The atmosphere at the circuits is much more friendly and relaxed than what I found in Formula One. Rosanne and I had a marvelous time traveling with the children to the summer races.

For this, I give full credit to the two men who made this championship season possible: Paul Newman and Carl Haas. Paul has supported us tremendously and is a great presence within the team. As for Carl, the biggest compliment I can pay is to say I rate him with the late, great Colin Chapman.

Newman-Haas Racing is second to none. My thanks to team manager Jim McGee, engineer Peter Gibbons, number one mechanic Tom Wurtz and all the boys for a fantastic effort. And to Kmart, Texaco, Lola, Ford/Cosworth and all the other sponsors.

Indy Car is an incredible series. The officials are first-rate, the best I have worked with. It's amazing to me you can have ten or more teams, with the same chassis and engine, which can win on any weekend. The competition – especially on the ovals – is pure racing at its best. That makes this championship extremely satisfying.

Together with the Newman-Haas team, we've achieved things never done in the 82-year history of the series. To win the championship is a fantastic feeling, which I hope each of you will share through the pages of this book.

THE NEW M3 IN YELLOW.

Would it be going too far to describe the new BMW M3 as the understatement of the year? BMW think not.

There is little in its appearance to hint that, yet again, BMW has totally redefined the sports car. Spoilers are nowhere to be seen. (As with the legendary Z1, they're underneath the car.)

Here is a machine launched, some might imagine, in the shadow of the most successful sports car ever built.

The previous M3 notched up 1500 victories on the track, one for almost every day of its life.

Yet the performance of the new M3, with 286 bhp, eclipses its forerunner. At idle speed, it delivers virtually the same torque as its predecessor achieved at full revs.

This was made possible by BMW Motorsport's revolutionary continuously variable valve timing system.

Thus for the new M3, there is no such thing as a torque curve. From idle, the torque climbs to 236 ft.lbs at 3600rpm. From there, it's a straight line all the way to 6500 rpm.

As a result, power is available in any situation, even when 5th gear is engaged at 1000 revs.

0-62 takes 6 seconds. 62-0 a mere 2.8.

OR INCOGNITO.

Yet to BMW, what makes the M3 revolutionary is not merely its exceptional responsiveness and performance but something more down to earth.

This is the first sports car to put fuel efficiency top on the agenda with performance. Its normally aspirated 24 valve, 3 litre engine is more fuel efficient than many a production 2 litre engine. And it exceeds the world's toughest emission regulations by 50%.

Two quotes sum up the new M3's achievements.

'Point to point, this is probably the fastest car BMW has built.' Autocar & Motor, 9th December 1992.

And 'Considering the strength of its performance, the M3's average fuel consumption of 30.9mpg is sensationally low.' Car, January 1993.

In other words, in the BMW M3, response and responsibility go together. But then, that's BMW.

THE ULTIMATE DRIVING MACHINE

Nigel Mansell with the PPG Cup. The 1992 Formula 1 World Champion has created tremendous worldwide interest in Indy Car racing as well as providing a bench-mark for all aspiring drivers to aim at.

Opposite: The traditional season-opener at Surfers Paradise; rookie Gary Brabham pits himself against the seasoned Danny Sullivan. The great strength of Indy Car racing lies in the opportunity it provides for both drivers and teams to compete on more of an equal footing than in Formula 1.

DIFFERENT STROKES . . .

These are interesting times for the PPG Indy Car World Series. This season there has been virtual parity between the leading teams, and an influx of extremely talented drivers. There has been a healthy rivalry between chassis manufacturers Lola and Penske as well as intense competition between the leading engine suppliers, Ford/Cosworth and Chevrolet/Ilmor.

The match-ups have helped to raise the profile of the category significantly. Furthermore, the addition of the reigning Formula 1 World Champion Nigel Mansell has helped to generate enormous, and unprecedented, public and media interest, not only in North America but around the world.

The euphoria surrounding Mansell's arrival was to a degree unexpected, not least by Mansell himself, who had become used to such overt adulation during his Formula 1 days but had anticipated a distinctly less fervent reception on 'the other side of the pond'. Not so. In spite of that, Mansell has adapted well to the different surroundings. His on-track achievements speak for themselves, of course, and the Englishman has displayed an entirely positive attitude . . . which to many people has come as something of a surprise after all that had been written about him in Formula 1.

Mansell will happily relate how much he has enjoyed being a part of the Indy Car scene. It is, he says, more relaxed but no less professional or demanding than the world from which he came. Indeed it is more difficult in many ways. The complex race strategies, for example, require a whole new train of thought. He finds the diversity of the race tracks both intriguing and immensely challenging.

His sentiments are echoed by all who have been drawn to the series, either through curiosity or with a genuine desire to participate. Many interlopers from For-

mula 1 have visited the series at one time or another this season, and without exception they have been impressed by what they have seen.

The biggest difference between Formula 1 and Indy Car racing is not necessarily the financial outlay involved, although even the most lavishly equipped Indy Car teams do not spend anything like the outlandish figures quoted in Formula 1. Any driver with a couple of million dollars to spend will be able to buy a drive in either of the two series (and let's face it, the notion of paying drivers is nothing new). But whereas in Formula 1 the investment might, at best, bring the possibility of a top-ten finish – assuming significant attrition among the leaders – the same stake would ensure a much more competitive proposition in the PPG Cup environment.

The real point here is that in Formula 1, with the best will in

the world – or the most talent or an unlimited budget – a 'wannabe' driver cannot even hope to compete with the established front-runners. After all, he can't even buy the equipment necessary for success. The Williams-Renaults are not for sale. Period. Conversely in Indy Car racing anyone with the cash can purchase a Lola chassis and a Ford/Cosworth or Chevrolet/Ilmor engine and go racing. Furthermore he will have an excellent opportunity to win, because, after all, he will have virtually identical equipment to the other leading contenders.

Of course, it's not quite as simple as that. Success cannot be guaranteed. The recipe for victory is complex, the ingredients many and varied . . . as several teams have found, some to their surprise, this season. Countless other factors have to be included in the equation, such as ongoing devel-

opment, team personnel, engineering expertise and testing. All cost money.

But at least the costs are not outrageous. The level of technological sophistication is kept firmly in check by the system of democratic government which controls the sport of Indy Car racing. It's the way the Indy Car folks want it to be.

While Formula 1 indubitably represents the pinnacle of technical achievement, Indy Car racing, arguably perhaps, represents the zenith of driver-to-driver, team-to-team competition. Pit stops and race strategy are of paramount importance. Items such as traction control, automatic gearboxes, active suspension and anti-lock braking, which have been pioneered – at least in terms of auto racing – in Formula 1, are expressly prohibited, banned from the PPG Cup series. They are not missed. The high-tech gizmos

Jori Potiker

Indy Car races can be won or lost in the pits. The Newman-Haas crew who await this scheduled stop by Nigel Mansell are drilled to preserve every second he has gained out on the track.

have taken a huge financial toll on many Formula 1 teams and they have not been seen to benefit the cause of competition.

An Indy car is nonetheless a potent piece of equipment. The chassis themselves, like Formula 1 cars, are constructed from state-of-the-art composite materials which provide an impressive degree of structural integrity. They are even stronger, able to withstand greater impacts, than their Formula 1 cousins. They have to be, since no Formula 1 car is required to withstand the staggering g-forces generated, for example, by an accident on one of the high-speed ovals which comprise almost one-third of the PPG Cup series.

Great advances have been made in recent years in terms of safety. The growing trend toward minimal cockpit dimensions, which reached almost ludicrous proportions in the 1990 March-Porsche which was designed exclusively for the diminutive Teo Fabi and John Andretti, was halted with

new regulations aimed at ensuring a relatively comfortable seating position for drivers up to at least six feet tall.

Other mandatory changes have included stronger, and longer, structures in the footbox area, designed to minimize the kind of extensive lower leg injuries suffered by two drivers at Indy in 1992 alone. The latest cars are undoubtedly more robust and safer than their predecessors, while even the integrity of older chassis has been improved by a modification to the nosecone assembly penned last winter by design engineer Julian Robertson.

There have also been changes to

the aerodynamic specification of the cars aimed at curbing the continual increase in speeds on the superspeedways. In 1992, Roberto Guerrero claimed the pole at Indianapolis at a four-lap average in excess of 232 mph, while this year at Michigan, Mario Andretti established a new world closed-course record of more than 234 mph. Even Mario, one of the bravest souls around, agrees that's too fast.

The problem, however, is paradoxical. At Indianapolis, a reduction in downforce will result in less grip through the corners, which in concert with the revised track is sure to decrease corner-

ing capabilities and lap speeds. We have seen evidence of that already this season, and the proposed changes to be introduced over the next two years are likely to produce similarly effective results. At MIS, though, the same changes will reduce drag and maybe even increase straightaway speeds slightly, while cornering speeds, due to the steep banking, will in all likelihood not be affected much at all. And the mind boggles at what speeds might be achieved should the place ever be resurfaced . . .

The good news, at least, is that the technical powers-that-be are attempting to address the issue.

The PPG Cup series itself, meanwhile, continues to thrive. More teams are expected to join in next season and the overall quality of the drivers will continue to improve. Michael Andretti will be back after a disappointing foray into Formula 1. He will be anxious to prove his talent once again – not that anyone in the Indy Car ranks doubts his capabilities.

Intriguingly, Andretti, the 1991 series champion, will be responsible for dialing in the brand-new Reynard 94I chassis for Chip

---

In Memoriam

Roger McCluskey, Executive Vice President and Chief Operating Officer of the United States Auto Club, passed away August 29, following a three-year battle with cancer. Prior to becoming a highly respected official, McCluskey was an accomplished race driver, the winner of five Indy Car races as well as the 1973 USAC National Championship. He also won two sprint car titles and a pair of USAC Stock Car championships during his 30-year career. Among his innovative ideas was the Rookie Orientation Program, introduced at Indianapolis in 1981. McCluskey was 63.

Duane Carter, a well-known competitor even before World War II, who later became the first Director of Competition upon the formation of USAC in 1956, died March 7 at the age of 79.

IN A MATTER OF SECONDS, IT CREATES A HIGHER STANDARD.

It takes only seconds to appreciate the full performance capabilities of its 295-hp Northstar System.

Northstar System: 32-Valve, 295-HP V8 • Road-Sensing Suspension • Traction Control • ABS • Plus Dual Air Bags • Call 1-800-333-4CAD

Imagine you just stepped on the accelerator of an Eldorado Touring Coupe with the Northstar System by Cadillac.

As you reach 60 mph in 7.5 seconds, the Road-Sensing Suspension is actually reading every inch of the road.

The Speed-Sensitive Steering grows firmer as you quickly pass 100 mph. Of course, you wouldn't really do this because you're not a professional driver on a closed track. But if you were, you'd be approaching 150 mph.

ELDORADO TOURING COUPE
CREATING A HIGHER STANDARD

Cadillac

Main photo left: The legendary A.J. Foyt chose Indianapolis 1993 to announce his retirement from the cockpit, 35 years after his first race at The Speedway.

Left: Rick Mears, looking unfamiliar with a beard, offers the benefit of his enormous experience to Marlboro Penske's brilliant young Canadian driver Paul Tracy.

Below: The men behind the Chevrolet Indy Car engines, Ilmor's Paul Morgan *(left)* and Mario Illien, watch anxiously from the infield at Indianapolis. Their latest V8s will be racing again next season, but not as Chevys.

Photos: Michael C. Brown

A Salute To Two Champions

Things were different at Indianapolis in 1993 – and not just because the historic track itself had undergone distinct change. Two of Indy Car racing's most accomplished and widely respected champions, A.J. Foyt and Rick Mears, were present as usual but, for the first time since 1958, neither one was among the 33-car starting field.

Mears had announced his surprise retirement at the Penske team's annual dinner last December. Foyt, meanwhile, as befitting his brash Texan style, departed the scene – to the astonishment of his peers, and even his team – rather more publicly at Indianapolis, on the morning of Pole Day.

Between them Mears and Foyt earned 93 poles and 96 victories, as well as ten National Championship titles. They shared eight Indianapolis 500 wins. Both are among the most recognized sports personalities in North America, despite their entirely disparate styles.

Happily, they remain an integral part of the sport, Foyt as a team owner and Mears as a team advisor/race engineer for Roger Penske, for whom he drove exclusively from 1978 until the conclusion of the 1992 season. Their legacies and influence have been quite apparent. Mears has assisted enormously this year in developing Paul Tracy's prodigious talent, smoothing out some of the rough edges, while Foyt has worked toward a similar goal with his own protégé, Robby Gordon.

Their styles, not surprisingly, have varied. Mears favored quiet encouragement, while Foyt tended to be rather more vocal. A case in point was in April at Phoenix, where Gordon drove superbly through the field to third place, only to spin into the wall. Afterward Gordon explained he had 'lost the air' from his front wings, causing the crash. Foyt wasn't impressed. 'S**t, boy,' he retorted. 'I was racin' before we had air!'

Ganassi's team. That promises to be an exciting combination, and it will be interesting to see how the car shapes up against the established marques. Judging by Reynard's previous track record in other categories, plus the fact Bruce Ashmore has jumped ship from Lola, Adrian Reynard's latest project is likely to represent a formidable challenge.

Nigel Mansell, of course, will be back with Newman-Haas Racing, and Lola Cars will produce a new design featuring a Penske-style transverse, sequential-shift gearbox. There is no doubt Eric Broadley's Huntingdon, England-based concern is highly motivated to repel the onslaught from Reynard and maintain its position as the primary supplier of customer chassis.

In opposition, the already imposing Penske operation is sure to be up to scratch. Nigel Bennett has been hard at work in ensuring the 1994 model is even better than this year's PC22, while the signing of 1990 PPG Cup champion Al Unser Jr to the driving strength will add another string to Roger Penske's bow.

In terms of engines, Chevrolet confirmed toward the end of the 1993 season it will not renew its association with Ilmor Engineering in development of the new 'D' specification motor. Certainly that is sad news, since the Ford vs. Chevrolet storyline provided an appealing facet to the sport. Nevertheless, Ford and Cosworth are

John Townsend

working ceaselessly to improve the capabilities of their XB engine, while Ilmor is proceeding apace with its program; and the chances are high that a fresh manufacturer name will appear on the cam covers ere long.

Honda, too, will bring grist to the mill, supplying its new V8 motors to Rahal/Hogan Racing and one other team yet to be nominated. The Japanese giant has been hard at work in developing the engine in partnership with American Honda. Most insiders believe it is sure to be competitive virtually from the get-go, and the perennially competitive Bobby Rahal will doubtless be able to extract its maximum potential.

Toyota is also in the midst of an extensive 'feasibility study' and is expected to join the fray, adding still further to the series' depth and credibility.

The organization of the series itself is not immune from change, with current IndyCar Chairman and Chief Executive Officer Bill Stokkan having announced he will not stand for re-election once

his term expires. A new regime is likely to be installed, with a firm emphasis placed on increasing market awareness and establishing more solid relationships within the corporate community of North America. This area of responsibility has long been lacking, one of the perennial shortfalls endured by the sport and one which has surely restricted its ability to grow.

Stokkan, though, has been responsible for many positive changes during his three-year tenure, and the new figurehead of the sport has a firm basis from which to work – assuming he is able to overcome some of the con-

flict of interests that has pervaded the sport to some degree.

A broadening of the appeal of Indy Car racing is already in progress, while expansion of the PPG Cup series into new markets, notably Texas and the South-East, and perhaps even Europe and/or Japan, is possible within the next couple of years.

Above all, the series remains stable in terms of technical regulations and venues, with the now traditional – and extremely popular – high-visibility season-opener on the Gold Coast of Australia confirmed again for 1994.

The future prospects for Indy Car racing are distinct and

bright. Next season Bridgestone/ Firestone will take steps to challenge the might of Goodyear by developing tires which are due to be introduced on a fulltime basis in 1995. The ramifications of that renewed rivalry will be felt in due course, although Goodyear has publicly welcomed the advent of competition, since it will provide an opportunity at last to compare its own technology with a worthy adversary.

And competition, after all, is what auto racing is all about. The 1993 season has been, arguably, the best in the history of Indy Car racing. But 1994 promises to be so much better.

Top: Red 5 to Red 1. Newly crowned as PPG Cup champions, Carl Haas and Nigel Mansell celebrate their triumph at the season's-end gala dinner.

Left: Mike Groff tries Rahal/Hogan Racing's Honda-engined test car. The 1994 season should see the debut of this exciting combination, yet another boost for the competitiveness of Indy Car racing.

Steve Swope

When Nigel Mansell's not driving
Indy cars, he's driving a Sunseeker.

DETROIT DIESEL
Marine Power

Sunseeker Florida
Hideaway Marina
599 S Federal Highway
Pampano Beach
Florida 33062
Tel: (305) 943 3200 Fax: (305) 786 8985

Head Office
Sunseeker International (Boats) Ltd,
27 - 31 West Quay Road, Poole ,
Dorset, BH15 1HX England.
Tel: (0202) 675071 Fax: (0202) 681646

Sunseeker powerboats - a seventeen boat
range built and equipped to exceptional
levels, bringing together the finest in
American marine engines - Detroit with the
DDEC system for even greater performance
- and the best of 'total - boat' design and
technology from Britain.

1994 PPG INDY CAR WORLD SERIES SCHEDULE

March 20	AUSTRALIAN INDY CAR GRAND PRIX	Surfers Paradise Street Circuit, Queensland, Australia
April 10	PHOENIX 200	Phoenix International Raceway, Phoenix, Arizona
April 17	GRAND PRIX OF LONG BEACH	Long Beach Street Circuit, Long Beach, California
May 29	INDIANAPOLIS 500	Indianapolis Motor Speedway, Speedway, Indiana
June 5	MILWAUKEE 200	Milwaukee Mile,Wisconsin State Fair Park, Milwaukee, Wisconsin
June 12	DETROIT GRAND PRIX	Belle Isle Park Circuit, Detroit, Michigan
June 26	PORTLAND 200	Portland International Raceway, Portland, Oregon
July 10	THE GRAND PRIX OF CLEVELAND	Burke Lakefront Airport Circuit, Cleveland, Ohio
July 17	MOLSON INDY TORONTO	Exhibition Place Circuit, Toronto, Ontario, Canada
July 31	MICHIGAN 500	Michigan International Speedway, Brooklyn, Michigan
August 14	MID-OHIO 200	Mid-Ohio Sports Car Course, Lexington, Ohio
August 21	NEW ENGLAND 200	New Hampshire International Speedway, Loudon, New Hampshire
September 4	MOLSON INDY VANCOUVER	BC Place, Vancouver, British Columbia, Canada
September 11	ROAD AMERICA 200	Road America, Elkhart Lake, Wisconsin
September 18	NAZARETH GRAND PRIX	Nazareth Speedway, Nazareth, Pennsylvania
October 2	MONTEREY GRAND PRIX	Laguna Seca Raceway, Monterey, California

How many oils won the Indy 500?

Just **.**

Racing at speeds over 200 mph, Emerson Fittipaldi won America's greatest motor race – the Indianapolis 500. His Penske-Chevrolet V8 enjoyed 100% engine reliability with Mobil 1, as the team recorded its ninth victory in this tough 500-mile classic event.

Whatever car you drive, from 200 mph Indy car to Formula 1 flyer to family hatchback, you can enjoy the same unbeatable engine protection with fully synthetic Mobil 1.

The world's most advanced motor oil

For further information, call free on 0800 585995

ANOTHER C

NIGEL MANSELL • 1993 PPG INDYCAR WORLD SERIES CHAMPION

ALAIN PROST • 1993 FIA F1 WORLD CHAMPION

GOODYEAR

Goodyear

Eagles winners on road and track

electronic laps at speed, a staggering amount of data must be entered to produce the digitized models of tracks, cars and drivers. A single model can take 20 hours to process.

Where Goodyear outshines any tire competition is its edge at the other end of the process: analyzing results and applying a variable 'real world' correc-

Goodyear reigns number one in racing around the globe with its Eagle racing tires the choice of drivers and teams in all major forms of the sport, including Indy Car, Formula 1 and Winston Cup.

The commitment continues with the same unshakable will to win that began 30 years ago, in 1963, when a call from driver A.J. Foyt inside the famed Gasoline Alley confines at the Indianapolis Motor Speedway implored Goodyear to 'get some tires out here'. The company did. Just four years later, Goodyear and its tires rolled into Victory Circle with A.J. in 1967 for his second Indy 500 win and Goodyear's first since winning the 1919 race and exiting the sport. With A.J.'s victory, Goodyear began its climb to the pinnacle of motorsports.

Today, Goodyear's Indy Car winning streak is nearing the magic 300 mark, with 290 wins at the end of the

1993 season. Goodyear has 295 Formula 1 wins and is approaching the 1,000 win milestone in NASCAR Winston Cup racing.

Foyt has played an important role in developing Goodyear racing tires, so it was an especially poignant moment this past May when the Texan announced to a hushed crowd at the Indianapolis Motor Speedway that he was hanging up his helmet for good, though he continues as a team owner.

As for future challenges and any challengers, Goodyear welcomes them – for the health and excitement of the sport and for the innovations that Goodyear successfully transfers from the track to the street in its high-performance Eagle passenger tires.

The Akron, Ohio, world headquarters of Goodyear houses the 700,000 square foot Technical Center where all of the company's race tires have been produced since 1983, along with prototype and experimental tires.

Included in the race tire lineup are Eagles for Indy Car and Formula 1, as well as drag racing, sprints, sports cars and stock cars. Off-road truck racing is done on Wrangler tires.

Is it art or magic, the wizardry that takes place in this computerized Tech Center?

Actually, advancing the technological state of the art of tires is what CAE (Computer Assisted Engineering) is all about, as engineers test racing tires on tracks around the world, while sitting at their computer workstations.

To do so, they program the configurations and characteristics of various racing circuits into the computer, add a race car complete with suspension and aerodynamics, and a close-to-perfect driver. But, before beginning those

tion factor gained by ongoing regular test programs with teams all over the world, and interpreting the data, then integrating it into the manufacturing process.

In the motorsports world, any performance advantage is a moving target – but Goodyear engineers shoot straight to create advantages and then transfer them to the track and street.

Growing audiences around the globe watch the results. Driven by some of the closest championship competitions in motorsports history, attendance at events in 15 different North American auto racing series increased by more than a half million spectators in 1992, drawing a record 13,123,706 fans for 273 events, up 5 percent over 1991. Indications are the trend continued in the 1993 season, with added international interest focused on 1992 Formula 1 Champion Nigel Mansell as he charged relentlessly in his first Indy Car season to capture the 1993 championship title, and, in the process, became the first in history to hold both titles consecutively. Goodyear tires recorded 375 wins out of 492 major events in North America (in 1992), as well as 16 of 16 races in the international Formula 1 circuit, making Goodyear the number one winning tire in the world for 23 consecutive years.

Though the NASCAR Winston Cup stock car racing series leads the attendance chart, the PPG Indy Car World Series, including the USAC-sanctioned Indianapolis 500, drew nearly three million spectators in 1992, up 4.9 percent from the prior year. On Indy 500 race day, an estimated 400,000 fans packed the grounds and an additional 14 million watched on television as Al Unser Jr edged Scott Goodyear by 0.043 seconds in the closest finish in the race's history – on newly introduced yellow-lettered Goodyear Eagle Racing Radials. In 1993, Emerson Fittipaldi drove the yellow logo tires into Victory Circle for his second Indy 500 win.

Goodyear Eagles were the common denominator of the 1993 Indy Car season, in which Mansell joined Mario Andretti and Fittipaldi as the only dri-

uses about 100 tires for practice, qualifying and the race. On many other circuits, the teams are limited to seven sets per car, in the interest of economy, so the engineers are challenged to produce a safe and reliable tire.

Goodyear rubber streaking around the Indianapolis Motor Speedway is watched, measured, probed, pondered – and judged – like no other in the race world.

Leo Mehl, director of racing worldwide, explained that 'the complex construction and advanced materials used in today's high performance Eagle passenger tires have filtered in from the ultimate test bed – the race tracks of the world. And none is like Indianapolis.'

There, Goodyear's Indy Car tires are subjected to more than 3.5g of force when cornering and can reach temperatures topping 250 degrees. Traveling at 230 mph, the tires rotate at more than 3,000 rpm and the car itself travels the distance of a football field in less than one second. Such demands make tire uniformity a major challenge.

Equally challenging is the drag race

Mansell's departure to the Indy Car racing scene and the 33-year-old Londoner quickly settled into the swing of full-time F1, adding the Belgian and Italian Grands Prix to that initial success at Budapest.

Damon's proven aptitude for test and development work, combined with a refusal to become ruffled under pressure when racing, made him an impressive teammate for Alain Prost as the Frenchman sped towards his fourth World Championship.

The 1993 title represents the latest milestone for Goodyear in a run of almost unbroken success which began when the company supplied its first purpose-made F1 racing tires to the Brabham and Honda teams in 1965. Goodyear's first World Championship was secured by Jack – now Sir Jack – Brabham in 1966, but Goodyear only really started to dominate F1 after forging a partnership with Jackie Stewart and the Tyrrell team in 1971 which yielded two drivers' titles for the Scot in three seasons.

Thereafter Goodyear's successes came thick and fast. In 1977 Niki

racing continues to provide Goodyear with a consistently effective and demanding testing ground. If a component or material functions satisfactorily in a highly stressed racing environment, it can generally be assumed that it will work under normal operating conditions in a road environment with a significant safety margin.

Thus comes Goodyear's high-speed tire technology transfer from track to street – an enviable success when considering that today's Goodyear high-performance Eagle street tire is better than the race tire of 30 years ago.

Over several decades, racing has contributed such technological improvements to Goodyear auto tires as graduated stiffness sidewalls, bias-belted construction, contoured tread shoulders, wraparound treads, heat-resistant carcass compounds, stronger reinforcing materials, performance-specific tread patterns and improved wet-weather tread rubber compounds. Many of the transfers go unseen, hidden inside, such as new advances in materials, fibers, reinforcements, polymers and construction techniques.

Slick pit work by the Penske team contributed to Emerson Fittipaldi's momentous win at Indy.

vers to win both Formula 1 and Indy Car series titles. En route to the crown, Mansell won five races and seven poles. Andretti scored a win for his 52nd in Indy Car competition and 100th in his overall career and announced he would retire after the 1994 season.

When the dust settled, Goodyear had produced more than 20,000 tires for the circuit that year, including more than 4,000 for the Indy 500 alone. For that race, a typical team

scene, where Goodyear's Top Fuel dragster tires travel more than 300 mph in a quarter mile, powered by a 5,000 hp machine.

The only new name to be added to the distinguished roll call of Goodyear's Grand Prix winners during 1993 was Damon Hill, whose victory in the Hungarian Grand Prix earned him the unique distinction of becoming the first second-generation winner in F1 history some 24 years after his late father Graham posted his final career victory at Monaco.

Hill gained promotion from his position as Williams-Renault test driver to fill the vacancy caused by Nigel

Lauda scored Akron's 100th Grand Prix win when he steered his Ferrari to victory in the German Grand Prix. Two years later, Alan Jones posted the 125th such success in Canada and, in 1983, René Arnoux took the tally to 150 when he won the Montreal race. By 1987 Gerhard Berger's victory in Australia had lifted the tally to 200 wins and Ayrton Senna's triumph in the 1991 Brazilian Grand Prix marked a landmark 250th win for the company. After two further successful seasons, the total number of Grand Prix wins stands at 295 at the end of 1993.

By pushing components to the outer limit of their performance, motor

Rather than direct, the transfer is more evolutionary and often bears little resemblance to the original. However, one visible track-to-street link was in 1983 when the company introduced the Eagle VR 'Gatorback' high-performance tire with a directional tread pattern adapted from Goodyear's Formula 1 race rain tire. In 1991, the newest Eagle, the asymmetrical, directional GS-C ultra-high-performance tire again was patterned after a Formula 1 rain tire. Even airplane tire and truck tire designers get technology transfer from NASCAR Winston Cup stock car racing, due to the combination of heavy vehicles and high speeds encountered

by the Eagle radials that resemble the forces on airplane tires during taxiing and takeoff.

Goodyear has received many recent awards and recognition for tire advancements. Among them was the Discover Award for Technological Innovation for the second consecutive year, the first time any company has earned repeat honors. The Discover magazine award honors 'breakthrough technologies and the visionary scientists and engineers who shape the future.' This year, the Goodyear Eagle GS-C EMT (extended mobility tire) was recognized as the world's first run-flat tire to be fitted on conventional wheels. It can operate effectively up to 200 miles at 55 mph with zero inflation pressure, and will be an option on the 1994 Chevrolet Corvette. Last year the award went to Goodyear's Aquatred all-season radial, a tire known for its wet-traction and hydroplaning-resistance capabilities.

With racing's tremendous technological benefits coupled with a passenger tire marketing edge that's the envy of all imitators, no wonder storm clouds of tire competition are brewing on the horizon for an assault on the Eagles' domain in 1994 and beyond.

To that, Racing Director Leo Mehl says, 'we welcome race tire competition once again. There was plenty around the globe when Goodyear re-entered major racing in the 1960s, and, fortunately, Goodyear's racing edge is sharper than ever. Major capital investments are completed and our chain of technical centers is linked to transfer technology and maintain our leadership position. And, as always, our number one concern will continue to be the safety of the drivers.'

Left: **Refueling for Nigel Mansell and his car – and a fresh set of Goodyear Eagles to keep them firmly on the road to victory.**
Below left: **Some of the hundreds of sets of Goodyear tires carefully prepared for each Indy Car race.**
Below: **Sensation of the Grand Prix season – Damon Hill and his Canon Williams-Renault on Goodyear's latest F1 Eagles.**

LIFE IS GOOD

One year ago, Nigel Mansell departed the Formula 1 scene with bittersweet memories. In his own words, it had been his life for the past 13 years. It had been his passion. And finally, after several crushing disappointments, he had achieved his lifetime goal: he had won the Formula 1 World Championship.

Yet following a breakdown in negotiations with team owner Frank Williams, Mansell did not renew his contract.

'I don't really want to go into all the details,' says Mansell, 'but let's just say there was a period of time where I thought we had a deal on the table for 1993 that would give me the opportunity to defend the World Championship in the manner that I was afforded in winning it.

'Then I was told that I wasn't required, basically, and I had the option, effectively, of going to a lesser team, or retiring.'

Mansell insists he wasn't ready to retire. The thrill of competition still coursed through his veins; he enjoyed driving and racing. He wanted to continue. So he began to look around. Before long he was approached by Carl Haas, co-owner with movie star Paul Newman of Newman-Haas Racing.

A deal was quickly agreed for Mansell to take on an entirely fresh challenge in the PPG Indy Car World Series. It was a prospect he relished.

'My motivation comes from hav-ing the opportunity to compete at the highest level,' says Mansell. 'I feel very fortunate that Carl and Paul were prepared to give me that opportunity. The Newman-Haas team is one of the best in the business. The caliber of people is second to none. There's no question in my mind they're on a par with the best in Formula 1.

'So I knew coming into the [1993] season I would have good equipment; and my motivation was to win some races and try to

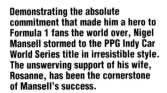

Demonstrating the absolute commitment that made him a hero to Formula 1 fans the world over, Nigel Mansell stormed to the PPG Indy Car World Series title in irresistible style. The unswerving support of his wife, Rosanne, has been the cornerstone of Mansell's success.

Photos: Michael C. Brown

win the championship – to try to be the first Englishman ever to achieve that.'

Mansell knew he faced an uphill struggle. First of all, he had no experience of driving an Indy car. It was heavier than a Formula 1 car, with a turbocharged as opposed to normally aspirated engine, steel brakes compared to the far more efficient carbon brakes of Formula 1, and with a manual gear-shift, which in itself took some getting used to. Even

Mansell's road cars had been automatic. He didn't know any of the race tracks, nor most of the people, and he had never so much as seen an oval track until this past January.

Yet he approached the task with a sense of professionalism that had a profound effect on his team.

'I hadn't worked with him before,' said Bruce Ashmore, then chief Indy Car designer for Lola, immediately following Mansell's first test at Phoenix. 'He's great.

Not a bit as I expected – only because I think of the way they portrayed him in the press and on television from Formula 1 – but the man behind the scenes, the one you engineer with, is very positive. He has excellent feedback. I mean, he was quick and he knew just what to do, and he adapted to the circuit so quickly, just from talking to the drivers and watching some film. And he was a great character, a great laugh, good fun to be around.'

Race engineer Peter Gibbons was similarly impressed at that initial test: 'I probably wasn't quite ready for such good feedback. He was fantastic. He picked it up right away. It was like he'd been driving over here for ten years. He had the confidence to drive it deep into Turn One right away, which to me was just astounding.'

Mansell was able to establish an immediately productive rapport with both Gibbons, who had

Relaxed and confident, Mansell has risen to the challenge presented by his first season in Indy Car racing with the assurance of a true champion. Carl Haas and Paul Newman *(below)* **gave him the tools, and the Englishman did the job.**

worked previously with Rick Mears and Michael Andretti, and former Tyrrell engineer Brian Lisles. The result was a cohesive effort which rarely failed to extract maximum potential from the car. Mansell was consistently fast, and especially so on the oval tracks.

Mansell was a raw rookie at the start of the season, and his inexperience betrayed him on his first run in anger at Phoenix in April. No one was faster than the Englishman, but Mansell was not on the starting grid. Instead he was *en route* to his home in Florida, nursing a concussion and an extremely sore back following a heavy crash during practice.

Nevertheless, Mansell learned from the error and came back with a vengeance on the ovals. He very nearly won at Indianapolis in a sensational oval track race debut, and one week later at Milwaukee he set the record straight with a superbly judged, come-from-behind triumph. Amazingly, Mansell remained undefeated on the ovals thereafter. He scored a dominant victory at Michigan, where his Ford/Cosworth engine clearly had the legs of everything else, while at New Hampshire and Nazareth his successes were the consequence of dazzling displays of controlled aggression rather than any mechanical advantage.

Those results provided the key to Mansell's PPG Cup crown. 'We didn't know what to expect of Nigel when he first came over,' says veteran team manager Jim McGee, who Mansell now hails as the best he has ever worked with. 'He was new to all of us and we were new to him. After just a couple of tests we knew he was special. He really is unbelievable. The way he is in and out of traffic is fantastic. He's just fantastic.'

And bear in mind the fact McGee is not one for hyperbole. Make no mistake, Mansell is a worthy champion, having impressed equally with his trade-mark flair and tenacity on the track as well as his new-found cool demeanor off it.

There's no question Mansell has enjoyed his first season of Indy Car racing. He has relished the open camaraderie, which, sadly, has long since disappeared from Formula 1, and has appreciated the close competition which is virtually assured by the tight technical regulations governing the sport.

'I've learned an awful lot this year,' he says. 'It's a new way of driving; it's a new way of operating. It's been fun – and fascinating to experience the different culture in America. We think we speak the same language but there are a lot of words in English which mean totally different things in America, and vice versa. We have to be very careful at times, so there's been a lot of laughs along the way.'

No question, life is good – good enough for him to renew his agreement with Newman-Haas for a further two years. Mansell does not hanker after a return to Formula 1. He regards himself now as a fully fledged Indy Car driver. Proudly. And rest assured there will be more successes to come.

Photos: Michael C. Brown

The eyes of a racer. The heart of a champion. The products he trusts.

Nigel Mansell 1993 Indy Car Champion. Texaco and Havoline congratulate Nigel Mansell on winning the 1993 Indy Car World Championship. We're proud of the fact he did it running on Texaco Havoline Motor Oil. The same Havoline he relies on in his family cars. And at Texaco stations, you can fill up with Texaco Gasoline, the gasoline Nigel uses in his everyday driving. Again, congratulations to Nigel, team owners Paul Newman and Carl Haas, and the rest of the Kmart/Texaco/Havoline Racing Team on a great championship season.

**TEXACO GASOLINES
HAVOLINE MOTOR OILS**

TEAM *by* TEAM
REVIEW *by Jeremy Shaw*

Indy Car racing is comparable to any other form of top-line motorsport. In order to compete at the highest level, to challenge for the PPG Cup crown, a team must have assembled all the ingredients necessary for success.

From the beginning of the campaign it was apparent this year's championship would feature a battle between two such teams: Newman-Haas Racing and Penske Racing. Make no mistake, this year at least, these were the two best teams in the business. They employed the finest drivers and had access to the best equipment, in terms of both chassis and engines. They were well-organized, and composed of experienced top-line personnel. They had positioned themselves to ensure adequate financial resources with which to support their crusades.

It turned out to be a fascinating contest. It was Lola vs. Penske. It was Ford and Cosworth vs. Chevrolet and Ilmor. It was experience vs. youth. It was all these things and more. And most of all it was fun to watch.

Center: Paul Tracy scored five wins with the Penske PC22, which enjoyed a clear advantage on the road courses.

The Rahal/Hogan 001 proved to be a severe disappointment, although Mike Groff (bottom) managed to score points in three of his four starts with the updated Truesports chassis.

THE CHASSIS

Lola

Production base: **Huntingdon, Cambridgeshire, England**
Number of cars built in 1993: **33**
Wins: **8**; *Pole positions:* **12**

Three distinct versions of the Lola T93/00 family were produced this season. In addition to catering to the Ford/Cosworth XB (internally designated T93/06) and the Chevrolet Indy V8/C engines (T93/07), Lola also produced a T93/04 derivative which was developed exclusively for the Buick V6 at Indianapolis.

The cars feature different aerodynamic and suspension configurations as decreed by the various engine packages, although all three are based squarely on the successful '92 designs.

Bruce Ashmore, who started the season as chief Indy Car designer for Lola Cars before defecting to the fledgling Reynard project, is a firm advocate of 'evolution rather than revolution' in terms of chassis manufacture. He learned the credo from Nigel Bennett, his predecessor at Lola who now heads up the Penske design team in Poole, England.

The most obvious differences from the '92 car include a longer monocoque which meets the latest regulations and extends an additional ten inches in front of the previous forward-most bulkhead. Accessibility to the inboard front suspension is improved, with the pushrod-activated spring/damper units now located above the driver's legs and reached via a removable panel atop the nose section.

Nigel Mansell's Ford-powered Lola nestles in the Newman-Haas Racing transporter. Once again the Indy Car entry lists were dominated by the Huntingdon company's products. The T93/00 was not always a match for the Penskes but nevertheless won half the season's 16 races.

Penske

Production base: **Poole, Dorset, England**
Number of cars built in 1993: **8**
Wins: **8**; *Pole positions:* **4**

Nigel Bennett says his latest PC22 represents the most radical departure from an evolutionary concept which began with his first Penske design, the PC17, in 1988. As with the Lola, new regulations have mandated a longer and substantially stiffer tub which is a little over 20 lb heavier than last year's version. The engine cover is lower than on the PC21, due to the smaller dimensions of the Chevy/C engine for which the new car has been exclusively constructed.

The six-speed transverse gearbox features many improvements,

including a new casing and a motor cycle-style sequential shift, which was tried last year and has proven very successful following a few glitches early in its development.

Front suspension features pushrod-activated spring/dampers which, like on the Lola, are now mounted above the driver's legs. Revisions also have been made to the rear suspension, which also employs pushrods and spring/dampers mounted atop the transaxle.

Rahal/Hogan

Production base: **Hilliard, Ohio**
Number of cars built in 1993: **0**
Wins: **0**; *Pole positions:* **0**

When Bobby Rahal and Carl Hogan decided to move their team from Indianapolis to the old Truesports facility on the outskirts of Columbus, Ohio, they also took over the 'Made in America' chassis project which had been commissioned by Steve Horne in 1989.

Perhaps unwisely, the team opted to begin its 1993 season with a mildly updated version of last year's 92C chassis, renamed the Rahal/Hogan 001. New roll-centers were tried along with a switch to the new Chevy/C engine, while the original plan called for construction of an all-new chassis which was scheduled for completion in June. Unfortunately for designer Don Halliday, the project was shelved following Rahal's embarrassing failure to qualify for the Indianapolis 500.

Galmer

Production base: **Bicester, Oxfordshire, England.**
Number of cars built in 1993: **0**
Wins: **0**; *Pole positions:* **0**

Galmer Engineering, formed by team owner Rick Galles and design engineer Alan Mertens, did not produce any new cars this year as a result of the decision by Galles to order Lolas for his team. Nevertheless, one of the genre of 1992 Indianapolis 500-winning chassis was run on a customer basis by Dominic Dobson.

The tub received minor changes to meet the new regulations, whereupon Dobson qualified comfortably at Indianapolis despite both a bare minimum of practice time and the fact he was using one of the out-dated Chevy/A engines. Dobson also raced the car for a new team, PacWest Racing, later in the season. The ambitious new outfit produced an updated version of the car, complete with one of the latest Chevy/C engines, which may yet lead to renewed interest in the project.

Left: **Carl Haas took most observers by surprise when he lured the reigning Formula 1 World Champion to Indy Car racing. His bold initiative was to be richly rewarded.**

Bottom: **As Mansell was quick to acknowledge, his championship triumph was the result of a concerted effort by the whole Newman-Haas team. The Englishman soon developed a close rapport with team manager Jim McGee *(below left)*, while his hugely experienced teammate, Mario Andretti *(below)*, provided dependable support.**

THE TEAMS

Newman-Haas Racing

Base: **Lincolnshire, Illinois**
Drivers:
Nigel Mansell, Mario Andretti
Sponsors: **Kmart, Texaco/Havoline**
Chassis: **Lola T93/00**
Engine: **Ford/Cosworth XB**
Wins: **6** *(Mansell **5**, Andretti **1**)*
Pole positions: **8**
*(Mansell **7**, Andretti **1**)*
Points: **308**
*Mansell **191** (1st), Andretti **117** (6th)*

Nigel Mansell lost no opportunity this season to praise his crew for their support and unfailing effort. Indy Car racing is, after all, very much a team sport. Much more so in many ways than Formula 1. Race strategy, for example, is far more complex. Fuel consumption, tire wear, caution flags, pit stops and umpteen other variables come into play and the crew has to be perfectly synchronized to minimize time spent in the pit lane.

Mansell credits veteran team manager Jim McGee as the best he has ever worked with. It is McGee who makes most of the calls concerning pit stops. Race engineers Peter Gibbons and Brian Lisles handle the responsibilities for extracting maximum potential from the team's Lolas, while crew chief Tom Wurtz takes charge of the mechanical aspects. The result is a well coordinated effort that has triumphed in the face of stern opposition from Penske Racing.

The team struggled to be competitive in Toronto, and also, in the race at least, in Vancouver, but otherwise Mansell was always at the forefront of the action, with Andretti usually not too far behind. The team developed new components for its Lolas during the season and moved closer to the Penskes, which appeared to be a little more consistent and easier to tune to the various tracks. One of the key ingredients may well have been the Swedish-built Ohlins dampers used exclusively by Newman-Haas.

Photos: Michael C. Brown

Michael C. Brown

Right: Retired from the cockpit after a distinguished driving career, Rick Mears *(left)* continued to make an influential contribution to Roger Penske's standard-setting team.

Below right: Neatly packaged around the new Chevy Indy V8/C engine, Nigel Bennett's Penske PC22 displayed exemplary handling. The compact rear suspension *(center right)* typifies the attention to detail that characterises the design.

Penske Racing

Base:	**Reading, Pennsylvania**
Drivers:	
Emerson Fittipaldi, Paul Tracy	
Sponsor:	**Marlboro**
Chassis:	**Penske PC22**
Engine:	**Chevrolet Indy V8/C**
Wins: **8**	(*Tracy* **5,** *Fittipaldi* **3**)
Pole positions: **4**	
(*Tracy* **2,** *Fittipaldi* **2**)	
Points: **340**	
Fittipaldi **183** (2nd),	*Tracy* **157** (3rd)

Roger Penske's team came up short in its quest for a ninth PPG Cup championship to go with the record ninth Indianapolis 500 crown earned by Fittipaldi. (Penske, incidentally, also holds the records for wins, 79, and poles, 104.)

The PC22 was unquestionably the best car in the field, especially on the road courses. It displayed excellent traction and turn-in capabilities which even the best-tuned Lolas were unable to match. The team was equally strong, bolstered still further by the wealth of knowledge supplied by Rick Mears, who hung up his helmet last winter but remained with the team as a technical advisor.

Mears was able to assist race engineers Nigel Beresford and Grant Newbury in discovering valuable information during the second week of practice at Indianapolis, which helped to transform the PC22 from merely a top-five contender to one with a legitimate chance of victory. Fittipaldi did the rest. The team also benefited from a close relationship between the engineers and drivers.

Ultimately, though, some plain misfortune, a couple of dubious calls by officialdom (including the jump-start penalty imposed on Fittipaldi in Detroit) and too many driver errors cost a chance at the title.

Left: **Bobby Rahal and his team endured a traumatic time at Indianapolis, the reigning PPG Cup champion failing to qualify for the 500. Following that setback, Rahal and his partner Carl Hogan** *(below)* **took the difficult decision to set aside the disappointing Rahal/Hogan chassis and acquired a pair of Lolas** *(bottom).*

Rahal/Hogan Racing

Base:	**Hilliard, Ohio**
Drivers:	
	Bobby Rahal, Mike Groff
Sponsor:	
	Miller Genuine Draft/MGD Light
Chassis:	**R/H 001** and **Lola T93/00**
Engine:	**Chevrolet Indy V8/C**
Wins:	**0**
Pole positions:	**0**
Points:	**141**
Rahal **133** (4th), *Groff* **8** (23rd)	

Michael C. Brown

Winter test sessions at Laguna Seca and Phoenix left Rahal full of optimism about his prospects of successfully defending his PPG Cup crown. Unfortunately, those hopes proved unfounded.

It is impossible to know whether the requirements of developing a successful interim car while at the same time laying down the groundwork for a new chassis and establishing a test program for the new Honda engine provided too many distractions, but it became clear some people within the team had misgivings about proceeding with the R/H chassis project. Ultimately, following a dismal month at Indy, the decision was made to shelve the new car and concentrate on development of a couple of Lolas. The team then lost more time accumulating data on the Lolas before returning to full competitiveness.

New team member Groff assisted Rahal in the Honda test program in addition to contesting six races. He showed promise on several occasions, earning points in three out of four starts with the R/H chassis, and also raced the Lola twice.

The tightly knit team jointly owned by Dick Simon *(far right)* and his wife Dianne *(center right)* made dramatic progress in 1993. Raul Boesel *(below)* enjoyed the most competitive season of his intermittent Indy Car career at the wheel of a Lola T93/00 demonstrating specially developed aerodynamic refinements, but Scott Brayton *(right)* was less impressive with the Amway/Northwest Airlines-backed Lola-Ford *(bottom center)*. Australian Gary Brabham showed well at Surfers Paradise *(below center right)*, while Formula 1 refugee Mauricio Gugelmin *(bottom right)* showed his class in a handful of outings at the end of the season.

Dick Simon Racing

Base: Indianapolis, Indiana

Drivers:

Raul Boesel, Jimmy Vasser, Scott Brayton, Stephan Gregoire, Gary Brabham, Lyn St James, Bertrand Gachot, Eddie Cheever, Mauricio Gugelmin, Didier Theys

Sponsors: **Duracell/Mobil 1/Sadia, Kodalux Processing/STP, Amway/Northwest Airlines, JC Penney/Nike, Hollywood American Blend, Kinko's**

Chassis: **Lola T93/00 and T92/00**

Engine: **Ford/Cosworth XB**

Wins: **0**

Pole positions: **1** *(Boesel)*

Points: **207**

Boesel **132** (5th), *Brayton* **36** (15th), *Vasser* **30** (16th), *Cheever* **8** (of 21 total – 17th), *Gachot* **1** (34th)

Dick and Dianne Simon almost achieved the impossible in 1993. They ran a minimum of two cars (for Boesel and Brayton), sometimes as many as five, and for much of the season harbored hopes of lifting the PPG Cup crown from under the noses of Newman-Haas or Penske.

The husband-and-wife team managed their limited resources well. Dick still has a habit of interfering in strategic decisions when perhaps he might be better advised to allow his hired experts to do the job, but that criticism stems merely from his infectious enthusiasm and an overwhelming desire to succeed.

The team earned one pole – although it should have been two, as Boesel was unlucky at New Hampshire – and came close to victory several times. Much of the credit should be shared by consul-tant engineers Mike Bowron and Mike Clark, who conducted an exclusive wind-tunnel program in England. The result was a fresh aerodynamic package, including a distinctive engine cover, under-tray and deflectors in front of the sidepods, which bore fruit at Indi-anapolis and especially on the short ovals.

Brayton had a disappointing year, his best finishes a trio of sevenths, while Cheever claimed sixth in a one-off outing at Road America and Gugelmin ran very strongly on his debut at Mid-Ohio. St James showed remark-able application on the ovals, qualifying well at Indianapolis and running strongly at MIS until let down by a mechanical prob-lem. Brabham also drove well in his one-off outing at Surfers Par-adise, and young Frenchman Gre-goire impressed at the wheel of a year-old Buick-powered car, run under the Project Formula ban-ner, at Indianapolis.

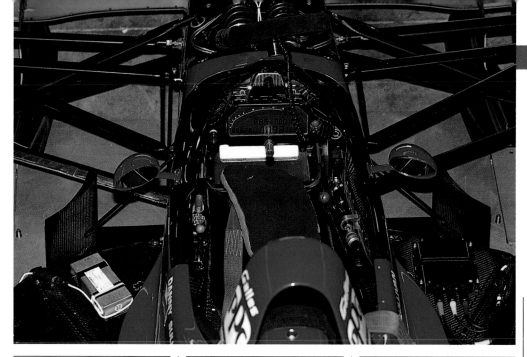

Left: The atmosphere at Galles Racing International was not always sunny, but Danny Sullivan shone sporadically at the wheel of the Molson Lola.

Below: With the encouragement of mentor Mike Kranefuss *(left)* and team owner A.J. Foyt, Robby Gordon matured considerably during an incident-filled season.

Derrick Walker *(below left)* runs a slick operation with limited means. Scott Goodyear's speed confirmed his team's undoubted potential.

Bottom: The advice of veteran engineer Mo Nunn *(left)* helped Arie Luyendyk to pole position at Indy.

Galles Racing International

Base: **Albuquerque, New Mexico**
Drivers:
Al Unser Jr, Danny Sullivan, Adrian Fernandez, Kevin Cogan
Sponsors: **Valvoline, Molson, Conseco**
Chassis: **Lola T93/00**
Engine: **Chevrolet Indy V8/C**
Wins: **2** (*Unser* 1, *Sullivan* 1)
Pole positions: **0**
Points: **150**
Unser **100** (7th), *Sullivan* **43** (12th), *Fernandez* **7** (24th)

In marked contrast to Penske Racing, for example, where Fittipaldi and Tracy worked together and in conjunction with the engineers to extract the maximum potential from their cars, Unser and Sullivan never gelled as a team. Too often they were at odds following on-track incidents.

Also, after shelving the Galmer project which had shown distinct promise in 1992, the team took too long to come to grips with its new Lolas.

Unser, as ever, drove hard in the races and gained in competitiveness as the season progressed, while Sullivan could not muster the motivation to run in mid-pack and complained vehemently he was rarely given a competitive car, especially on the short ovals.

Fernandez impressed the team with his testing skills and entirely positive attitude, while Cogan found the comeback road difficult due to the fact he was still recuperating from injury sustained two years ago at Indy. Cogan wisely stood down after four races and undertook further surgery to remove a large pin from his right thigh. He hopes to return in 1994.

Chip Ganassi Racing Teams

Base: **Indianapolis, Indiana**
Driver: **Arie Luyendyk**
Sponsors: **Target, Scotch Video**
Chassis: **Lola T93/00**
Engine: **Ford/Cosworth XB**
Wins: **0**
Pole positions: **1**
Points: **90** (8th)

Ganassi started the season full of optimism for his team, while new signing Luyendyk was highly motivated following a season on the sidelines. Sadly, the new partnership did not develop as expected until right at the end of the season. Some team members were not entirely in favor of the choice of driver and would have preferred to see young charger Gordon remain on the payroll. Perhaps that conspired against Luyendyk, who was unable to extract the full potential from his equipment on a consistent basis.

On the superspeedway ovals, though, he was superb. Luyendyk qualified on the pole at Indy, gaining valuable kudos for the team, and finished second in the race. He was third at MIS, effectively 'best of the rest' behind the dominant Newman-Haas cars, and also ran strongly in the season finale at Laguna Seca.

Walker Motorsport

Base: **Warrington, Pennsylvania**
Drivers:
Scott Goodyear, Hiro Matsushita, Willy T. Ribbs
Sponsors: **Mackenzie Financial, Panasonic, Service Merchandise**
Chassis: **Lola T93/00 and T92/00**
Engine: **Ford/Cosworth XB**
Wins: **0**
Pole positions: **2** (*Goodyear*)
Points: **102**
Goodyear **86** (9th), *Ribbs* **9** (20th), *Matsushita* **7** (26th)

Derrick Walker's team became stretched after taking on a third car for Ribbs, starting at Indianapolis, even though the '92 chassis was run separately by Steve Erickson and John Miller.

Goodyear, though, continued to make progress despite some mechanical frailty. He performed well with limited backing and came on strong in the later races. Two poles proved testament to the talent of the driver and team, which worked as a cohesive unit. Race engineer Tim Wardrop also made a valuable contribution.

Matsushita never progressed beyond midfield status, while Ribbs, whose commitment and talent is undoubted, showed flashes of fire in his year-old car.

A.J. Foyt Enterprises

Base: **Houston, Texas**
Drivers: **Robby Gordon, A.J. Foyt, John Andretti**
Sponsor: **Copenhagen**
Chassis: **Lola T93/00 and T92/00**
Engine: **Ford/Cosworth XB**
Wins: **0**
Pole positions: **0**
Points: **87**
Gordon **84** (10th), *Andretti* **3** (29th)

Foyt's revitalized team was the surprise of the season. Gordon came into the year with only seven Indy Car starts to his name and a reputation for being fast but fragile – meaning there were many rough edges to be hewn from his ragged driving style.

His learning curve has been steep, and hardly aided by a minimal budget permitting absolutely no testing other than a shakedown run on an infield road course at Texas World Speedway and a brief run at Phoenix after returning from Surfers Paradise. Gordon benefited enormously from the practical knowledge of crew chief John Anderson and unrelated race engineer Ken Anderson. He also gained from the experience of running with Foyt, who surprised even some of his closest friends by announcing his retirement on the morning of first qualifying at Indianapolis.

Also at Indy, Foyt ran the under-employed Andretti in a second car. Andretti responded with a solid drive to tenth place.

Left: The Hall/VDS Racing team looked impressive but, to the consternation of team owners Jim Hall *(bottom left)* and Franz Weis, Teo Fabi's results were mediocre at best.

Kenny Bernstein *(below)* succeeded in attracting the Budweiser sponsorship budget, but he quickly discovered that Indy Car racing is fiercely competitive.

Tony Bettenhausen *(below left)* saw his small team emerge as serious contenders in 1993, although a combination of misfortune and unreliability hampered Stefan Johansson's efforts with the AMAX Penske PC22 *(bottom)*.

Hall/VDS Racing

Base: **Midland, Texas**
Driver: **Teo Fabi**
Sponsor: **Pennzoil**
Chassis: **Lola T93/00**
Engine: **Chevrolet Indy V8/C**
Wins: **0**
Pole positions: **0**
Points: **64** (11th)

For the third successive season, the team owned by Jim Hall and Franz Weis did not live up to expectations. Fabi replaced John Andretti in the driving seat but, frankly, without any noticeable improvement in results. A change in the engineering staff didn't seem to make much difference either. The well-funded Pennzoil car remained a regular top-ten runner, nothing more.

Quite why the team has been unable to come close to duplicating Andretti's fortunate but nonetheless well-earned debut victory at Surfers Paradise in 1991 remains one of modern Indy Car racing's great mysteries. And rest assured, if Hall and his crew ever find the answers, the team will become a force to be reckoned with, as it appears to possess all the ingredients for success.

Bettenhausen Motorsports

Base: **Indianapolis, Indiana**
Drivers: **Stefan Johansson, Tony Bettenhausen, Scott Sharp**
Sponsors:
AMAX Energy & Metals, Rain-X
Chassis: **Penske PC22**
Engine: **Chevrolet Indy V8/C**
Wins: **0**
Pole positions: **0**
Points: **43** Johansson (13th)

For Tony Bettenhausen, the 1993 season was a case of so near and yet so far. Finally, after years of struggling himself with second-rate equipment and a minimal budget, he hired a well-respected and worthy driver in Johansson and reached agreement with long-time mentor Roger Penske to field a couple of new PC22 chassis powered by the latest Chevy/C engines. The addition of gifted and down-to-earth Penske design engineer Tom Brown also was a major boon.

The benefits were there to be seen. Johansson qualified strongly in several races and raced well too – but luck just wasn't on his side. Furthermore, the Penske was a high-maintenance item and Bettenhausen didn't really have the resources to enable him to maximize either its reliability or its full potential.

The team also fielded a second car for Tony B. at Indy, while two-time Trans-Am champion Scott Sharp made a promising open-wheel debut at Laguna Seca.

Budweiser King Racing

Base: **Indianapolis, Indiana**
Drivers:
Roberto Guerrero, Jim Crawford, Al Unser, Eddie Cheever
Sponsor: **Budweiser**
Chassis: **Lola T93/00**
Engine: **Chevrolet Indy V8/C**
Wins: **0**
Pole positions: **0**
Points: **43**
Guerrero **39** (14th), *Cheever* **3** (of 21 – 17th), *Unser* **1** (33rd)

Kenny Bernstein's first full-time foray into the PPG Cup series was fraught with problems. Budweiser chose to ally itself with the drag racing star after receiving proposals from just about every team along pit lane, but the promise of an ambitious three-car program at Indianapolis backfired after Buick announced it would not continue to support development of its V6 engines.

The organization was sorely stretched at Indy – where Guerrero crashed, Crawford had an awful time and 'Big Al' Unser managed to lead for several laps before his engine began to overheat – and the repercussions continued long afterward. In addition, following Bruce Ashmore's switch from Lola to Reynard, Bernstein's race engineer John Travis was recalled to England to concentrate on designing the 1994 Indy car.

Guerrero, who like Luyendyk was back after a year's enforced sabbatical, did not have any kind of technical stability until the arrival of Steve Newey, who worked last year with Rahal and the early part of this season with Vasser. Guerrero showed his capabilities on the short ovals but was fired three races from the end of the season despite scoring a best finish of fourth at New Hampshire. Cheever took over the drive and was unable to turn the team's performance around.

Right: German Christian Danner started three races with Euromotorsport's Lola T92/00-Chevy/A and scored a couple of points at Road America. David Kudrave *(below center)* also drove the car on occasion, and rewarded enthusiastic team owner Antonio Ferrari *(below right)* with eighth place at Phoenix.

Bottom: Brian Till replaced Eddie Cheever at the wheel of Norm Turley's Say NO To Drugs Penske PC21, and lost no time in confirming the promise he had shown in 1992.

Below: Scott Pruett demonstrated that he had lost none of his natural ability in a handful of outings in a two-year-old Lola-Chevy entered by Tim Duke *(bottom)* under the Pro Formance Motorsports banner.

Turley Motorsports

Base:	**Long Beach, California**
Drivers:	**Eddie Cheever, Brian Till**
Sponsors:	**Say NO To Drugs**
Chassis:	**Penske PC21**
Engine:	**Chevrolet Indy V8/B**
Wins:	**0**
Pole positions:	**0**
Points:	**17**

Cheever **10** (of 21 – 17th), *Till* **7** (25th)

Former Long Beach policeman Norm Turley and his enthusiastic band of supporters also raised their profile in 1993. The team acquired two ex-works PC21 chassis from Penske, complete with Chevy/B motors. Cheever came with the package, albeit for only the first four races pending the procurement of additional sponsorship. When none was forthcoming, a parting of the ways was inevitable – although, sadly, it was not an amicable one.

Till, who had showed promise in his freshman season in 1992 with an ex-Truesports chassis, replaced Cheever and despite a small budget posted some very strong showings, especially at Mid-Ohio where he was fifth fastest in practice and ran with the front-runners following an early delay.

Euromotorsport Racing

Base:	**Carmel, Indiana**
Drivers:	**Andrea Montermini, Andrea Chiesa, David Kudrave, Jeff Wood, Davy Jones, Christian Danner**
Sponsors:	**Agip, Andrea Moda**
Chassis:	**Lola T92/00 and T91/00***
Engines:	**Chevrolet Indy V8/A and *Cosworth DFS**
Wins:	**0**
Pole positions:	**0**
Points:	**20**

Montermini **12** (18th), *Kudrave* **6** (27th), *Danner* **2** (31st)

Antonio Ferrari somehow found the budget to be present with two drivers at every race, excluding Indianapolis where he wisely concentrated on running Jones in a solo effort with the ex-Rahal Lola-Chevy/A. He finished a solid 15th, despite an abnormally low rate of attrition. Jones was only three laps behind after 500 miles, which in any other year would have guaranteed at the very least a top-ten result.

Good work, especially by John Weland and Paul Murphy, ensured the same chassis also was used to excellent effect on occasion by Montermini, who qualified sixth in Detroit (where he finished a startling fourth) and seventh in Vancouver, as well as by Danner and, especially on the ovals, by Kudrave.

Wood soldiered on with the outclassed '91 Lola and DFS engine, despite which he showed a decent turn of speed on occasion.

Pro Formance Motorsports

Base:	**Chandler, Arizona**
Driver:	**Scott Pruett**
Sponsors:	**Sprint, Jones Chemicals, Pro Formance Driving Schools**
Chassis:	**Lola T91/00**
Engine:	**Chevrolet Indy V8/A**
Wins:	**0**
Pole positions:	**0**
Points:	**12** (19th)

The newest team on the Indy Car block was established last winter

by Tim Duke, a former racer who has spent recent years running a business involved in new-car launches and ride/drive programs. He expended a great deal of thought on the effort and hired a select group of experienced and talented people including race engineer John Dick and former Galles mechanic Randy Bain to look after a pair of '91 Lolas.

Pruett was entrusted with driving duties in the team's six starts, with John Paul Jr having had to stand down at Mid-Ohio when he discovered it was a physical impossibility to fit his lanky frame into the tight cockpit. (Paul can take solace from the fact subsequent rule changes have mandated larger cockpits for more recent cars.) Pruett served notice again of his talent by earning a pair of seventh-place finishes early in the season.

Dale Coyne *(right)* was joined in his gallant struggle against the odds by Canada's Ross Bentley *(below)*. Mark Smith *(far right)* played his part in a better year for Frank Arciero *(bottom center)*, but Olivier Grouillard *(bottom/middle right)* made little impression.

Dale Coyne Racing

Base: **Plainfield, Illinois**
Drivers:
Robbie Buhl, Ross Bentley, Johnny Unser, Eric Bachelart
Sponsors: **Mi-Jack, CompUSA, Copper & Brass Sales, Agfa, Rain-X, Ruger Firearms, Marmon Group**
Chassis: **Lola T92/00**
Engine: **Chevrolet Indy V8/A** (**Buick V6** at Indy)
Wins: **0**
Pole positions: **0**
Points: **9**
Buhl 8 (21st), **Bentley 1** (32nd)

Widely respected IndyCar Board member Dale Coyne continues his struggle against the odds to establish himself as a bona fide challenger. He has built the team from scratch and has no proven track record. He works hard. He has an equally highly regarded crew chief in Bernie Myers as well as an experienced race engineer in former driver Dave Morgan. Coyne has succeeded in attracting modest sponsorship for the team. As yet, though, he has been unable to afford up-to-date equipment.

Reigning Indy Lights champion Buhl confirmed his promise — and that of the team — by finishing an excellent sixth at Long Beach, humbling many more well-heeled competitors. He just lacks experience and testing miles. Bentley and Johnny (cousin of Al) Unser have made some progress, while the talented Bachelart endured an appalling time at Indy, as did the entire team which sustained heavy losses through crashes which were due primarily to ill fortune.

Arciero Racing Teams

Base: **Anaheim, California** and **Indianapolis, Indiana**
Driver: **Mark Smith**
Sponsor: **Craftsman Tools**
Chassis: **Penske PC21**
Engine: **Chevrolet Indy V8/B**
Wins: **0**
Pole positions: **0**
Points: **8** (22nd)

Veteran car owner Frank Arciero tried hard to re-establish the credibility of his team after several years of running substandard efforts. He bought a pair of year-old cars from Penske and hired the experienced Mark Weida as crew chief. Indy Lights graduate Mark Smith brought backing from Craftsman Tools. The addition of Gordon Coppuck as race engineer also was a great benefit.

Smith showed tremendous poise in qualifying strongly on several occasions, notably at Portland, Cleveland and Road America, only for the car's Achilles Heel, the high-maintenance transverse gearbox, to let him down more often than not. As is so often the case, it was a question of finance, since the team failed in its efforts to locate substantial associate backing.

Indy Regency Racing

Base: **Indianapolis, Indiana**
Driver: **Olivier Grouillard**
Sponsors: **Marlboro, Eurosport**
Chassis: **Lola T92/00**
Engine: **Chevrolet Indy V8/A**
Wins: **0**
Pole positions: **0**
Points: **4** (28th)

Yet another convert from Formula 1, Grouillard was a major disappointment this season. The Frenchman failed to make the field at Indianapolis with his fellow countryman Sal Incandela's ex-John Andretti Lola T92/00 and never really got to grips with the car at all. His best finish was 11th at Cleveland.

Grouillard's troubles provided evidence, if any were needed, that Indy Car racing is no easy environment in which to shine. All the ingredients need to be in place, with a solid budget the primary requisite.

Jeff Andretti *(right)* made a courageous comeback at Indianapolis from the horrific injuries he suffered in last year's race. He was joined in the field for the Indy 500 by three-time World Champion Nelson Piquet *(bottom right)*, another victim of the crash-strewn 1992 event.

Far right: Buddy Lazier tried three chassis/engine combinations during the season, to little avail.

Brazil's Marco Greco had a discouraging season in the Lola T92/00-Chevy/A *(below)* entered by Dennis McCormack *(bottom)*.

Sovereign Racing

Base: **Indianapolis, Indiana**

Driver: **Marco Greco**

Sponsors: **Alfa Laval, Team Losi**

Chassis: **Lola T92/00**

Engine: **Chevrolet Indy V8/A**

Wins: **0**

Pole positions: **0**

Points: **2** (30th)

Ditto the above. Dennis McCormack, running under the second franchise owned by Chip Ganassi, never gave up hope with his ex-Matsushita Lola, but frequent transmission failures thwarted both him and his driver, Greco, who was running at the finish in only five of 13 starts. And even then he was usually many laps behind the leaders.

McCormack attempted to run a second car at Indianapolis for Rocky Moran, but even the hard-trying veteran's best efforts weren't enough to qualify the two-year-old Buick-powered car.

Those Who Tried . . .

Several other teams and drivers appeared from time to time without scoring any PPG Cup points, chief among them Buddy Lazier, who was present for most of the races, either with Hemelgarn Racing or the Leader Cards team. Sadly, their combined enthusiasm just wasn't enough.

The promising youngster attracted some support from *Financial World* magazine, Viper Auto Security and Foodtown, but he had neither the equipment nor the resources to do himself justice; and the few times he was around at the finish coincided with the races at which attrition was low.

Ron Hemelgarn also ran a couple of Buick-powered cars at Indianapolis, where, with USAC approval, the stock-block V6 motors are allowed more manifold boost pressure than at the regular IndyCar-sanctioned events. The under-utilized Didier Theys and midget star Stan Fox both qualified comfortably, albeit with little prospect of achieving much in the race.

Indianapolis also saw Pagan Racing field a couple of year-old Lola-Buicks – actually the cars run so impressively by Guerrero and Crawford in '92. Jeff Andretti, driving for the first time since his horrible crash at Indy a year ago, qualified solidly before being involved in another, thankfully far less damaging, incident. Mark Smith took over the other car after being bumped from the field on the final day but didn't have enough time to get up to speed.

The most ambitious of the Indy-only entrants was John Menard, who commissioned no fewer than four new Menard/Buick-powered Lolas to be built specially for the one race. Veteran Gary Bettenhausen, four-time IMSA champion Geoff Brabham and none other than Nelson Piquet, who, like Andretti, was back after suffering severe injuries a year ago, each had a car. Only Bettenhausen was around at the finish, a distant 18th.

David Mann also entered an older chassis for John Paul Jr but he failed to make it into the race, while Thom Burns entered a '92 Galmer for Dominic Dobson. The same car and driver reappeared later in the season for a few races, entered by a new team, PacWest Racing.

The enthusiastic Gino Gagliano ran his '91 Lola a couple of times under the Nu-Tech banner, firstly with DFS power at Detroit where Dennis Vitolo made a valiant but futile attempt to qualify, and latterly with a Chevy/A engine for Brian Bonner at Cleveland.

Finally, Jeff Sinden and Joe Kennedy, who have looked after John Menard's entries in recent years, hired one of Dick Simon's '92 Lola-Chevy/A cars for the season finale on behalf of former Super Vee/Atlantic racer John C. Brooks. Sadly, despite backing from the TV show, 'Lifestyles of the Rich & Famous', Brooks had tested the car only briefly and, with 34 cars present, never was likely to make the 29-car field.

These, then, were the runners and riders who provided an interesting and entertaining 1993 season. In all, 55 drivers made the show at least once. The average number of starters showed a significant increase, from 24.4 to 27.19, while, as a measure of improved reliability and ever-improving quality, an average of 17.44 cars, or 64.13 percent, finished the races compared to 59.34 percent in 1992.

Racing into the Future

The world of Ford Motorsport is filled with exciting times – past, present and future. Ford's commitment in racing dates back to the early 1900s, when Henry Ford used a victory in his first race to help draw attention to his fledgling car company. Today, Ford Motor Company is the only major manufacturer involved in what most consider the world's four most significant racing series – PPG Indy Car World Series, NASCAR Winston Cup stockcars, the Formula One World Championship, and the World Rally Championship.

In 1992, after a 21 year hiatus, Ford began participating again on the PPG Indy Car World Series circuit, in a joint effort with long-term partner Cosworth Engineering. The Ford-Cosworth XB V8 engine won five races in its first season.

Powering as many as five teams and ten cars in 1993, the Ford-Cosworth XB V8 was victorious at six events, winning the PPG Indy Car World Series Championship with Newman/Haas driver Nigel Mansell. Mansell scored five of those wins, including four on oval tracks, while Mario Andretti captured a sixth win on the oval at Phoenix.

The engine also powered drivers to 12 of 16 pole positions, including poles by Mansell, Andretti, Raul Boesel, Arie Luyendyk and Scott Goodyear. Luyendyk led a 1-2-3 Ford-Cosworth front row sweep at the Indianapolis 500, and Andretti's 234 mph run on the oval at Michigan was the fastest ever in racing history.

"The feelings I have are exactly the same, if not better than when I won the championship last year," said Mansell, the 1992 Formula One World Champion. "And I think I had a lot of things going for me last year.

"Number one, I didn't have a major accident at the second race (Phoenix). And I didn't have to undergo an operation during the course of the year.

"There's no question we had some great backing and some great machinery behind us. The main thing was we wanted to enjoy ourselves. We thought we'd win a few races. We hoped to be competitive. We knew we'd have good weekends and we knew we would have bad weekends. I'd say we just had a bit of luck.

"It makes you feel so proud. The two greatest feelings I've ever had - well, actually five: the birth of my three children, and I was there; and winning the championship in Formula One; and this championship."

Mansell became the only reigning Formula One World Champion to also hold the PPG Cup Champion title.

Ford and Cosworth's efforts have now resulted in 252 Indy Car victories, including 16 Indianapolis 500 wins (six for Ford, 10 for Cosworth). The six wins this year gives Ford 99 Indy Car wins overall.

ADVERTISEMENT FEATURE

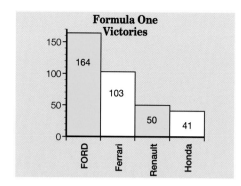

Formula One Victories

FORD 164
Ferrari 103
Renault 50
Honda 41

But Ford and Cosworth also have an excellent racing reputation around the globe as well. Their teamwork has resulted in 12 Formula One World Championships and 164 Formula One Grand Prix victories, more than any other manufacturer.

The Ford engine made a clean sweep of the F1 schedule in 1973, the same year Jackie Stewart took his third World Championship title.

This season, Benetton-Ford drivers Michael Schumacher and Riccardo Patrese, and McLaren-Ford drivers Ayrton Senna, Michael Andretti, and Mika Hakkinen, have led Ford's efforts in the 16-race, worldwide series. Following 14 events, Senna had three victories and Schumacher has one. Ford has powered more drivers into the 1993 Formula One World Championship points standing than any other engine supplier. Ford and Renault are the only manufacturers to have at least one Formula One victory over the past four years.

Schumacher's victory in Portugal, and performances elsewhere, have secured his reputation as one of Formula One's rising stars. "I've been very fortunate to have Ford power during my entire Formula One career. Having the Ford power and reliability package meant that I was able to score several podium finishes early on. Next year we will be battling for the championship," Schumacher stated.

In September of this year, Michael Andretti announced his business decision to drive for Chip Ganassi's Indy Car Team in 1994, giving his F1 seat to Mika Hakkinen for the remaining three F1 events. McLaren's Ron Dennis said, "He (Andretti) owes me three races, which I intend to pick up some time in the next two or three years. He's much loved in our team."

Many current and former Formula One and Indy Car drivers started their careers in the highly competitive Formula Ford series run throughout the world.

1994 FIA Formula One World Championship

20 March (provisional)	Argentina
27 March (provisional)	Brazil
17 April	Pacific (Japan)
1 May	San Marino (Imola)
15 May	Monaco
29 May	Spain
12 June	Canada
3 July	France
10 July	Great Britain
31 July	Germany
14 August	Belgium
11 September	Italy (Monza)
25 September	Portugal
6 November	Japan
13 November	Australia

ADVERTISEMENT FEATURE

1994 World Rally Championship

22/29 January	Monte Carlo
28 February/5 March	Portugal
31 March/4 April	Safari Rally
4/8 May	Tour de Corse
28 May/1 June	Acropolis Rally
29 June/3 July	Rally Argentina
30 July/2 August	Rally New Zealand
25/28 August	1000 Lakes Rally
9/13 October	San Remo Rally
19/23 November	RAC Rally

"Formula Ford was instrumental in developing my career as a racing car driver," said Johnny Herbert, current Lotus-Ford F1 pilot.

Mika Hakkinen, McLaren-Ford driver believes, ". . . Formula Ford was the perfect series to teach me the basics of open wheel racing."

The 1993 British Formula Ford Series champion Russell Ingall now joins the who's who list of previous competitors including Nigel Mansell, Ayrton Senna, Johnny Herbert, Michael Schumacher, Paul Tracy, Emerson Fittipaldi and Mika Hakkinen.

But there is much more to the Ford Motorsport program than just open wheel race cars.

1993 saw the debut of the sleek Escort Cosworth on the World Rally Championship. Throughout their extensive winter testing program the boys at Ford's Boreham Motorsport Centre thought they had a special vehicle. What they didn't realise was just how special the Mobil backed Escort Cosworth would be.

Starting with the first Rally in Monte Carlo and continuing throughout the year the Escort Cosworth was leading the charge. Francois Delecour missed a storybook beginning to the long gruelling season by leading the Monte Carlo Rally until the last few stages, eventually finishing second. Delecour remained the man to beat throughout the season by virtue of his two victories in Portugal and Corsica, second place finishes in Monaco and New Zealand, and third in Australia. Francois' factory team-mate Miki Biasion also had a productive year in his Escort Cosworth, winning the Acropolis Rally and finishing second in the Portuguese and Argentine rallies. Franco Cunico, Ford Italy's entry in the San Remo Rally, showed the power of the Escort Cosworth by capturing his first ever World Rally Championship event ahead of many factory drivers and teams.

Top right.
Russell Ingall became the Class A Champion in the 1993 Open Formula Ford Championship.

Top left.
Francois Delecour the driver who set the pace.

Inset.
Miki Biasion taking the honours on the arduous Acropolis Rally.

Main picture.
Francois Delecour powering to victory in the Portugese Rally.

Almost 20 stock car teams showcase Ford Thunderbirds on the NASCAR Winston Cup racing circuit. Ford has had additional involvement in IMSA road racing's GTS class (formerly GTO) and the SCCA Trans-Am, both with Ford Mustang Cobras; the National Hot Rod Association (NHRA) with the Ford Probe; and a unique, championship program away from the asphalt tracks with the Ford/BFGoodrich Rough Riders, racing trucks on the off-road desert venues and MTEG stadium dirt tracks. Heading up Ford's NASCAR Winston Cup program are drivers Bill Elliott, Mark Martin, Ernie Irvan and Geoff Bodine. Elliott left his family-run race team in 1992 to drive the Budweiser Thunderbird of the famous Junior Johnson team.

He has 39 career victories, all in Ford products, and was the 1988 Winston Cup Champion. He also owns NASCAR's fastest qualifying lap of 212.809 mph, set at Talladega in 1987. Mark Martin, driving the Valvoline Ford Thunderbird for Roush Racing, scored a NASCAR-record four consecutive Winston Cup wins earlier this year, and ranks third in the championship with three races remaining. Irvan, a former Chevrolet Lumina driver, made the switch to a Ford Thunderbird in September, replacing the late Davey Allison, and quickly tallied two victories for Ford and the Robert Yates' team in his first six races.

Bodine began the season driving the Motorcraft Thunderbird for Bud Moore's team, scoring a win at Sears Point in mid-May. With back-to-back wins in October, 1992, Bodine sealed Ford's first NASCAR Manufacturer's Championship.

In Europe the prominent 2-litre saloon series is the British Touring Car Championship and Ford has quickly made its presence felt in this arena. Despite only entering the 1993 Championship in round 8 the aerodynamic Mondeos of Andy Rouse and Paul Radisich amassed seven podium places by the end of the season. Radisich then went on to impress motorsport fans the world over by winning the first ever FIA World Touring Car Challenge. Not only did Paul and his Mondeo capture pole position, but they also led every lap of both Challenge races.

British Touring Car Championship Victories

Manufacturer	Victories
FORD	202
Chevrolet	54
Jaguar	51
Rover	36
BMW	33

ADVERTISEMENT FEATURE

Top left insert ..Bill Elliot's famous Budweiser Thunderbird.

Main left ....No. 6 Valvoline Ford Thunderbird driven by Mark Martin.

Middle left ....New Zealander Paul Radisich finished an outstanding third in the Driver's Championship.

Bottom left ....Drivers Rouse and Radisich celebrate first and second at Silverstone.

Top right..........10 times champion Glidden's NHRA Pro stock Ford Probe.

Second right ....IMSA ChampionTommy Kendall flooring his GTS class Mustang Cobra.

Third right ......Ron Fellows in action in the SCCA Trans-Am.

Bottom right ....Ford's Rangers meeting the challenges of the Rough Rider off road racing programme.

In Pro Stock drag racing, Bob Glidden pilots the rocket-like Motorcraft-Ford Probe down the quarter-mile straightaways of the NHRA circuit. Glidden is the the premier drag racer of all-time, collecting 84 NHRA Pro Stock career wins, two of those in 1993, and almost double his nearest competitor. He won five consecutive Pro-Stock championships from 1985 to '89, with a NHRA record total of 10 for his career. Glidden has at least one victory in each of the last 21 consecutive seasons.

On the IMSA road racing circuit, Roush Racing, with drivers Roddy Gordon, Wally Dallenback Jr, Tommy Kendall, Mark Martin, and Robbie Buhl at the wheel of a Ford Mustang Cobra, began the 1993 season by winning its ninth consecutive Daytona Rolex 24 hour endurance race in the GTS class. Kendall, who rebounded from a serious crash in 1993, went on to win the 1993 IMSA Exxon Supreme GTS Championship, his seventh career racing title and his first for Ford. "They say that when you've had rough times that it makes you appreciate the good times more," Kendall said. "This championship was not an accident. It was a lot of hard work by the Roush team and the guys at Ford Electronics."

In SCCA Trans-Am, Ford was in the hunt for its first title since 1989, with driver Ron Fellows leading the way. Ford won four Trans-Am events this year, three of those victories belonging to Fellows, who finished second in the championship standings.

"Last season we were fourth in the points," Fellows said, "and this year we finished second. Now we just have one more step to go and we'll shoot for that next year."

Ford's Rough Rider off-road racing program had plenty to boast about in their first season – 1990. The Simon brothers, Paul and Dave, head up an eight truck, 1993 effort in the desert. The Simons and their Ford Ranger had won four consecutive Class 7S off-road titles, but switched to the high-tech Class 1/2 series with a new F-150 in '92. John Swift returned to defend his 1992 Class 6 title with his Ford Explorer, and David Ashley returned in his Class 4 Ford F-150.

Ford trucks won a total of seven off-road season championships in 1992, capturing 28 class victories, more than triple its nearest competitor. In 1993, Ford trucks have 29 class victories and have a chance for seven more championships with one event remaining – the rugged Baja 1,000.

"Motorsport is a highly-charged, extremely-competitive sport, attended and watched on television by almost two billion people every year," said Michael Kranefuss, who has been the head of Ford's worldwide motorsport program since 1980 and who will retire on November 1. "It provides Ford with an emotional focus for intense product loyalty and fan support, while competing head-to-head with other auto manufacturers around the globe."

INDY CAR

TOP TEN

1	NIGEL MANSELL
2	PAUL TRACY
3	EMERSON FITTIPALDI
4	RAUL BOESEL
5	SCOTT GOODYEAR
6	ROBBY GORDON
7	BOBBY RAHAL
8	AL UNSER JR
9	STEFAN JOHANSSON
10	MARIO ANDRETTI

Photographs by Michael C. Brown

The Editor's evaluation of the leading Indy Car drivers in the 1993 PPG Cup series

1

Nigel Mansell

Date of birth: August 8, 1953

Residence: Clearwater, Florida

Indy Car starts in 1993: 15

Wins: 5; Poles: 6

No question about who has been the top driver in the 1993 PPG Indy Car World Series. When Mansell arrived from Formula 1, he brought an immense amount of media interest, especially after winning the opening race at Surfers Paradise. Suddenly, Indy Car racing shifted from being a curiosity to a centerpiece.

His debut victory was not unexpected, since he had shown well in preseason testing. It came on the type of circuit on which Mansell was expected to shine, favoring someone who was prepared to take a few risks and court potential disaster with the omnipresent cement walls. Right up Mansell's street, if you'll pardon the pun. He duly etched his name in the history books – not for the last time – by becoming the first driver since Graham Hill in 1966 to win on his Indy Car debut.

Casting aside the pain of Phoenix, where he crashed heavily in practice and failed to start the race, the most impressive aspect of Mansell's season was his mastery of the ovals. His lack of experience left him a little short in a spectacular debut at Indianapolis, but after that he was unbeaten on the ovals.

At Michigan he left veteran teammate Mario Andretti gasping in his wake, while at New Hampshire he outraced the gutsy Paul Tracy. In many ways his win at Nazareth was even more impressive, since there was no caution-flag respite from the constant traffic. It was a fitting manner in which to clinch the title.

Mansell also served to remind of his outright pace by posting some truly superb performances in qualifying, notably at Long Beach, where he was in considerable pain, and Portland.

Mansell clearly enjoyed his racing this season. He was positively buoyant in the pressroom interviews, smiling easily and often. Sure, there was disappointment at Detroit and Toronto, where he departed swiftly and with barely a word, while at Mid-Ohio he had some choice phrases for Tracy following an apparent 50-50 incident on the first lap; but by and large Mansell was a pleasure to be around. Behind the wheel he displayed immense confidence; outside the car he was a paradigm of magnanimity, heaping praise on his crew and, especially, Carl Haas and Paul Newman for offering him the opportunity to join the Indy Car scene. The fact he will be back, having signed for two more years, is good news for everybody.

2

Paul Tracy

Date of birth: December 17, 1968

Residence: Toronto, Ontario, Canada

Indy Car starts in 1993: 16

Wins: 5; Poles: 2

Tracy remains something of an enigma. His speed is undoubted. He has shown that throughout his career, including the 1992 season when he stepped confidently into the seat at Penske left vacant by an injured Rick Mears. But he remains prone to mistakes – a fact which cost him dear this year.

Tracy took full advantage of Nigel Bennett's excellent PC22 design to leave everyone far behind at Phoenix, only to crash less than 40 miles from the end while trying to lap yet another car. He held a two-lap advantage at the time. He should have waited. But hindsight is 20-20.

He atoned with a magnificent victory at Long Beach, earned despite a couple of hiccups along the way. Youthful bravado caught him out at Indianapolis, while at Milwaukee, again clearly in the lead, he was unfortunate, caught blind-sided behind Arie Luyendyk's car when another hit the wall in Turn Two. In Detroit he was looking good in the lead until caught exceeding the speed limit in pit lane. The error cost him a stop-and-go penalty and another likely win.

Portland proved to be the turning point. He wasn't able to match Fittipaldi's pace, curiously, for the only time this year, yet he drove sensibly in difficult conditions and brought the car home safely in third. Then came back-to-back victories at Cleveland and Toronto, along with affirmation of his prodigious talent.

Rick Mears has had a sobering effect on the young Canadian. Having surprised even some of his closest colleagues by announcing his sudden retirement last December, Mears opted to remain with the team as a consultant engineer/coach. He has enjoyed virtually every minute, offering sage advice on setup and assisting with strategy. The influence resulted in a more composed, relaxed Paul Tracy, his naturally spectacular style tempered to produce speed with economy of effort. So smooth did he look at times, especially in qualifying at Vancouver, one would have sworn it was Mears, not Tracy, behind the wheel.

Tracy has arrived. Certainly, mistakes cost him a shot at the PPG Cup title, but perhaps that can be excused for an Indy Car sophomore. Next year, I fancy, he will take some catching.

3

Emerson Fittipaldi

Date of birth: December 12, 1946

Residence: Miami, Florida and São Paulo, Brazil

Indy Car starts in 1993: 16

Wins: 3; Poles: 2

The top two drivers, for me, stood plainly above the rest this year. Fittipaldi finished second in the season standings but perhaps should have done better. The Penske was consistently the best car, and while the Chevrolet Indy V8/C engine did lack top-end power in comparison to the Ford/Cosworth, particularly in qualifying trim, the Chevy was every bit as good on the bottom end and quite capable of mixing it with the Fords on raceday.

Fittipaldi – and/or his team – made a tactical error at Phoenix by deciding not to make a pit stop right after Tracy's crash, even though Fittipaldi knew he had run over a chunk of debris. He held a one-lap lead at the time. A precautionary pit stop would have left him with a sizable advantage, plus peace of mind and the knowledge he had the fastest car left in the race. Instead he crashed due to a puncture. Twenty points were needlessly thrown away.

In Detroit, where he was unfortunate to be penalized at the start, he ran off the road while trying to pass Arie Luyendyk in an impatient maneuver. At the time he was running 11th, only just behind eventual third-place finisher Mario Andretti. At Michigan he ran strongly at the beginning of the race and at the end; but in the middle he was way, way off the pace and finished a distant 13th. On several other occasions he was plain and simply not fast enough to keep pace with Tracy.

The likable Brazilian appears to have lost none of his zeal, but perhaps a little zip has gone. Maybe his increasing business commitments are preying too much on his mind. Be that as it may, his win at Indianapolis was a classic. May there be many more.

4

Raul Boesel

Date of birth: December 4, 1957

Residence: Miami, Florida and Curitiba, Brazil

Indy Car starts in 1993: 16

Wins: 0; Poles: 1

This was the year in which Raul Boesel – and the Dick Simon Racing team – came of age. The fruits of an exclusive wind-tunnel program afforded a distinct advantage, especially on the ovals, and he became a force to be reckoned with on a regular basis. The talents of race engineer Julian Robertson also proved of great benefit, although the Briton departed swiftly once Simon heard news of his impending switch to Reynard. Fortunately, David Cripps was able to take up the slack, despite the additional workload of having to look after at least two other cars.

Boesel was looking good at Indianapolis until being assessed not one but two stop-and-go penalties which eventually restricted him to fourth place. Undeterred, he bounced back to gain the first pole of his Indy Car career at Milwaukee the following weekend and again raced hard until succumbing to pressure from Mansell in the closing stages.

Excellent preparation ensured a reliable car, and Boesel's only mistake came at New Hampshire, where he spun into the wall after losing downforce, ending his streak of 17 point-scoring finishes.

Then again, perhaps he could show a little more aggression. Mid-Ohio was a case in point. He drew alongside Fittipaldi several times without being able to complete the pass, and later in the race was unable to follow Robby Gordon past a noticeably ailing Scott Goodyear. Boesel, though, has signed a three-year contract with Simon and looks set to benefit from the continuity.

5

Scott Goodyear

Date of birth: December 20, 1959

Residence: West Palm Beach, Florida

Indy Car starts in 1993: 16

Wins: 0; Poles: 2

In the first five races of the season, Goodyear qualified only once outside the top two rows of the grid. Yet he finished only twice – tenth in Australia, despite an early spin, and seventh at Indianapolis. He had a disastrous weekend in Detroit, where he was nowhere near the pace, but generally was a solid contender for whom nothing seemed to go right. Finally, toward the end of the season, his fortunes began to turn around. A switch to Penske three-way adjustable shock absorbers and acquisition of the latest aerodynamic tweaks from Lola helped to find a more consistent balance for the car and he was able to show his true mettle. Goodyear's outside pass of Al Unser Jr in Turn One at Mid-Ohio was majestic and his qualifying run at Vancouver provided confirmation he can run as fast as anyone given the right equipment.

Sadly, Derrick Walker's team probably found itself a little too stretched by running three cars, at least until late summer when matters seemed to improve. Mechanical reliability was far from the best, which proved critical in terms of points. Still, the Canadian remains full of confidence and is a forceful racer. I believe the best of Scott Goodyear is still to come.

Robby Gordon

Date of birth: January 2, 1969

Residence: Orange, California

Indy Car starts in 1993: 16

Wins: 0; Poles: 0

Robby Gordon is the embodiment of a raw talent. He is immensely gifted and brave. He has total belief in his own ability. He really is a potential world-beater. But he lacks experience. And it shows.

Last year he burst onto the Indy Car scene with Chip Ganassi's team at the behest of Ford SVO boss Michael Kranefuss. Gordon's previous experience consisted of off-road racing, a successful foray into IMSA sedans, a couple of impressive NASCAR races and two Formula 3000 tests, in one of which he contrived to crash twice and incur the wrath of Jackie Stewart. Gordon had never even started a single open-wheel race. Nevertheless he was fast right away in Ganassi's car, humbling regular driver Eddie Cheever on a couple of occasions.

This year he was picked up by A.J. Foyt, who soon recognized Gordon as a chip off the old block – cocky, confident and quick. He started the season brilliantly, passing Mansell on the opening lap at Surfers Paradise and ultimately finishing third. At Phoenix, following minimal practice, he drove through the field to third place before crashing.

Only toward the end of the season did he learn how to keep the car on the road. His drive at Mid-Ohio suggested a newfound maturity. If he can build on that next year, watch out!

7

Bobby Rahal

Date of birth: January 10, 1953

Residence: Dublin, Ohio

Indy Car starts in 1993: 15

Wins: 0; Poles 0

The primary reason for Rahal's relatively lowly ranking is because perhaps the defending series champion should have achieved more this year with the resources at his disposal. He and partner Carl Hogan have a top-class facility and an excellent staff with a great depth of knowledge. Having taken over the old Truesports shop, they made the decision to try to develop the Don Halliday-designed chassis, renamed a Rahal/Hogan, without seeming to realize the car itself was little more than an update of the '91 car which had been penned around the outdated Judd/True-Power engine.

Little wonder it wasn't up to par with the latest Lolas and Penskes which were built specifically around the latest lightweight, slimline Chevy/C or Ford motors. And rather than go ahead with the original plan to build a new car, the team opted to shelve the project entirely and buy Lolas after failing to qualify at Indianapolis.

Rahal's driving, meanwhile, was as good as ever. He earned a worthy second-place finish at Long Beach with the R/H chassis and came on strong in the later stages of the season after he had finally gotten to grips with the Lola. He rarely made a mistake and was, as usual, consistently fast. Next year with the new Honda engines he will surely return to his rightful position as a championship contender.

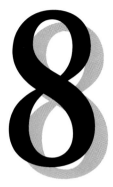

Al Unser Jr

Date of birth: April 19, 1962

Residence: Albuquerque, New Mexico

Indy Car starts in 1993: 16

Wins: 1; Poles 0

This was not a stellar year for the 1990 PPG Cup champion. It started off badly when a water leak sent him spinning into the wall at Phoenix during his very first test with the new Lola. Unser suffered a separated shoulder in the ensuing crash. It was some time before matters improved.

For all the bad things said about the Galmer chassis last season, it did win two races and earn six other podium finishes. Unser finished all 16 races in the points. And only in two races this year has he qualified higher with the Lola than last year in the Galmer.

As ever, he has raced more strongly than he's qualified. Yet a couple of his passes have seemed somewhat desperate – notably at Long Beach where he tried to go around Mansell, of all people, on the outside at Turn Two, where few front-runners even would contemplate passing an accommodating backmarker, and at Mid-Ohio where he attempted a similarly low-percentage maneuver on Fittipaldi in the Esses. Of course, charging is what Unser does best; it's just that on those occasions his tactic didn't work. At least he tried. Certainly there is no doubting he still has the desire, the will to win. He's an Unser, after all. And his victory at Vancouver was well-earned, biding his time and taking advantage of his Galles crew's typically fine pit service. Next year, for sure, will be better.

9

Stefan Johansson

Date of birth: September 8, 1956

Residence: Indianapolis, Indiana and Monte Carlo

Indy Car starts in 1993: 15

Wins: 0; Poles 0

This season has been a case of so near yet so far for the likable Swede. Once some gearbox gremlins had been exorcised from his Penske PC22 early in the year he began to show the form of which he has long been capable. He qualified particularly well on the string of road and temporary courses in midseason, although rarely was luck on his side.

At Long Beach he was sidelined in a needless incident with Mario Andretti even before the green flag. At Detroit he hounded Mansell mercilessly and was aggravated at the manner in which the Formula 1 champion resisted his attempts at a pass; ultimately he was put out of the race again due to an unfortunate wreck. At Cleveland he was penalized for exceeding the speed limit in pit lane, yet his computer system clearly showed the officials had erred. He was fast, too, at Mid-Ohio, only to be put out of contention by a first-lap incident.

Johansson's presence surely has enabled Tony Bettenhausen to elevate his team from being a solid midfield runner to the role of a true contender. Race engineer Tom Brown also has proved a major benefit. Against that, the PC22 has been a high-maintenance piece of equipment and Tony B. has not been blessed with sufficient resources to maintain the level of reliability and competitiveness necessary to win races. Not yet, at least.

10

Mario Andretti

Date of birth: February 28, 1940

Residence: Nazareth, Pennsylvania

Indy Car starts in 1993: 16

Wins: 1; Poles: 1

It must be tough to have a teammate like Nigel Mansell. The Englishman has been on a different plane by comparison to most of his competitors; and let's face it, at 53, Mario is hardly in the flush of youth. Yet maybe working with his son Michael the previous few years helped. Very little fazes the crusty veteran and his motivation remains at a staggeringly high level. He loves to drive. He loves to win. He thinks he can still win. And indeed he did win this year, at Phoenix in April.

Admittedly, he had a little luck on his side. Tracy crashed while holding a three-lap advantage over Mario, and Fittipaldi suffered a similar fate while one lap in the clear. Andretti, though, had qualified a close second and had the legs of almost everybody else. And he didn't make the hint of an error. Chalk up career win number 52.

He ran strongly – again – also at Indianapolis, and by rights should have added another victory in the 500-mile epic to the one he gained way back in 1969. Only a mismatched set of tires toward the end of the race cost him the realization of another dream.

Andretti unearthed another superb effort to claim the pole at MIS at a new world closed-course record of 234.275 mph. On raceday he was out-driven by Mansell, again, yet he still had the legs of everyone else. Maybe next year at Indy . . .

Close, But ...

Several young drivers were on the brink of making my entirely unofficial top ten, prime among them being Jimmy Vasser, Mark Smith and Andrea Montermini. All three should make their mark on the Indy Car scene within the next few years if afforded the right opportunity.

Vasser has done a fine job this season. Running year-old Lolas, firstly one with Chevy/A motivation and later a Ford/Cosworth car, the 27-year-old Californian and his mentor Jim Hayhoe benefited from running under Dick Simon's broad umbrella. Vasser posted several strong performances, despite extremely tight purse strings and losing race engineer Steve Newey to the Budweiser King camp at midseason. In the past Vasser has been a front-runner in Formula Ford and Atlantic. In the future he has the capability to be a leading contender at the highest level.

Smith, 26, has done a fine job in his first season out of Indy Lights, often qualifying well in the ex-works, year-old Penske PC21-Chevy/B run by Mark Weida under the auspices of Frank Arciero Racing. Sadly, some internal conflicts and funding difficulties hindered his progress and Smith was all too often sidelined by mechanical problems.

Montermini made a tremendous impact on the scene even though he competed in only four races with Antonio Ferrari's Lola T92/00-Chevy/A. In the first of those, at Surfers Paradise, the diminutive 29-year-old Italian hit the wall twice inside very few laps. Next time out, in Detroit, he was sensational, qualifying sixth and eventually finishing fourth. Montermini has a contract to test with the Benetton team in Formula 1, but if that fails to lead to anything, he would like nothing more than to set his sights on a career in Indy Car racing.

This trio, along with Robby Gordon and Paul Tracy, will form the basis of Indy Car racing's young guard in the coming years. Robbie Buhl, the 1992 Firestone Indy Lights champion, also is a very capable young driver, as evidenced by an excellent sixth-place finish at Long Beach in Dale Coyne's drastically underfinanced Lola T92/00-Chevy/A. Mike Groff, who won the Indy Lights crown in '89, finally has an opportunity to display his worth, having tested the development Honda engines this year and raced half a dozen times for Rahal/Hogan Racing.

Young Mexican Adrian Fernandez, another Indy Lights graduate, showed promise in several outings with Galles Racing International, as did David Kudrave with Euromotorsport Racing. Buddy Lazier, meanwhile, did not show his true potential during a disastrous '93 season in uncompetitive equipment.

Plenty of other drivers excelled at least on occasion during what has been an enthralling PPG Cup season. Danny Sullivan, for example, capped a largely disappointing year with a hard-earned victory at Detroit. Sure, he was lucky to get into a position to win, but give Sullivan the sniff of a podium finish and he's a tough man to beat. He remains one of the most gifted drivers on the tour.

Arie Luyendyk's finest hour came at Indianapolis, where he won the pole and finished a fighting second. He also claimed third at Michigan and Laguna Seca. Often, though, Luyendyk struggled to match the front-running pace, as did the likes of Teo Fabi, Roberto Guerrero and Scott Brayton.

The 1993 season will be remembered as the year in which Nigel Mansell and Paul Tracy swept to prominence, eclipsing all the old Indy Car favorites. Times, indeed, are a-changing.

Michael C. Brown

JIMMY VASSER

Michael C. Brown

MARK SMITH

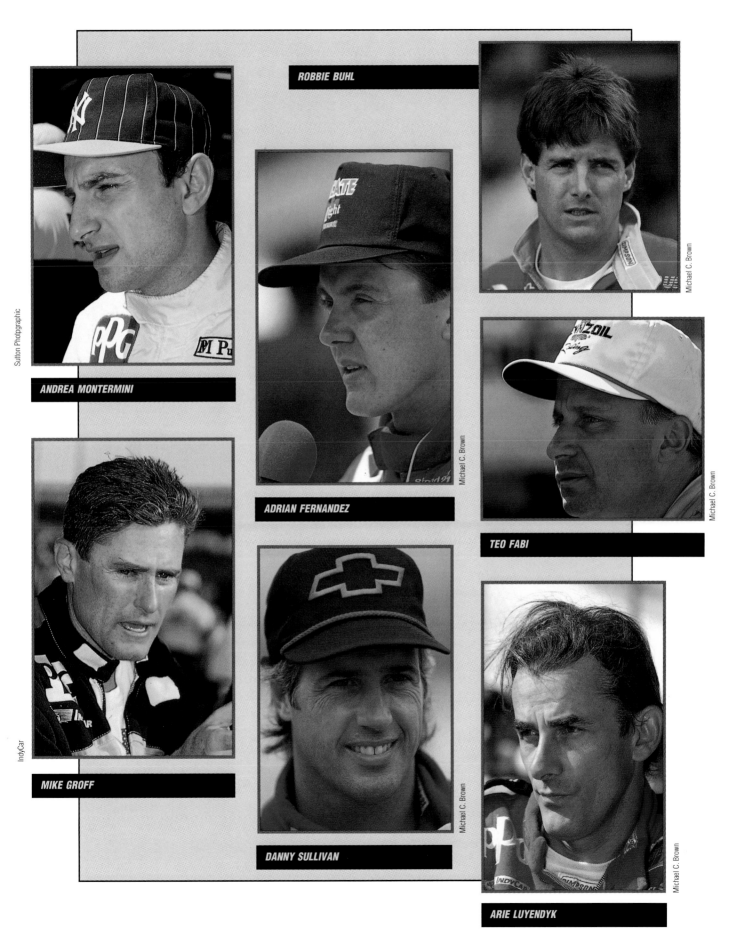

Sutton Photographic

ANDREA MONTERMINI

ROBBIE BUHL

Michael C. Brown

ADRIAN FERNANDEZ

Michael C. Brown

Michael C. Brown

TEO FABI

IndyCar

MIKE GROFF

Michael C. Brown

DANNY SULLIVAN

Michael C. Brown

ARIE LUYENDYK

59

Position	Driver	Nationality	Car	Surfers Paradise	Phoenix	Long Beach	Indianapolis	Milwaukee	Detroit	Portland	Cleveland	Toronto	Michigan	New Hampshire	Road America	Vancouver	Mid-Ohio	Nazareth	Laguna Seca	Points total
1	Nigel Mansell	GB	Kmart/Texaco Havoline Lola T93/00-Ford	P1	WDN	P3	3	1	P15	P2	3	20	*1	P1	2	6	P12	*1	23	191
2	Emerson Fittipaldi	BR	Marlboro Penske PC22-Chevy/C	*2	14	13	1	3	23	P1	2	P2	13	3	5	7	*1	5	P2	183
3	Paul Tracy	CDN	Marlboro Penske PC22-Chevy/C	21	*16	*1	30	20	9	3	P*1	*1	19	*2	P*1	13	25	3	*1	157
4	Bobby Rahal	USA	Miller Genuine Draft R/H 001-Chevy/C	6	22	2	DNQ	—	—	—	—	—	—	—	—	—	—	—	—	133
			Miller Genuine Draft Lola T93/00-Chevy/C	—	—	—	—	4	5	4	28	4	9	7	3	*2	6	6	7	
5	Raul Boesel	BR	Duracell/Mobil 1/Sadia Lola T93/00-Ford	8	2	12	4	P*2	2	7	7	7	4	21	4	9	4	9	11	132
6	Mario Andretti	USA	Kmart/Texaco Havoline Lola T93/00-Ford	4	1	18	*5	18	3	6	5	8	P2	20	15	5	7	13	9	117
7	Al Unser Jr	USA	Valvoline Lola T93/00-Chevy/C	15	4	21	8	5	6	5	19	5	8	8	25	1	8	25	5	100
8	Arie Luyendyk	NL	Target/Scotch Video Lola T93/00-Ford	5	6	11	P2	22	17	10	10	22	3	25	9	25	5	8	3	90
9	Scott Goodyear	CDN	Mackenzie Special Lola T93/00-Ford	10	P20	16	7	23	10	12	20	9	5	19	10	P4	3	2	4	86
10	Robby Gordon	USA	Copenhagen Racing Lola T92/00-Ford	3	18	—								15			23		10	84
			Copenhagen Racing Lola T93/00-Ford	—	—		DSQ	27	10	8	8	6	6	—	5	20	—	2	4	
11	Teo Fabi	I	Pennzoil Special Lola T93/00-Chevy/C	9	5	4	9	9	22	25	8	14	6	16	8	8	24	11	8	64
12	Danny Sullivan	USA	Molson Lola T93/00-Chevy/C	13	23	8	33	16	*1	14	14	3	—	22	26	10	27	20	27	43
13	Stefan Johansson	S	AMAX Energy & Metals Penske PC22-Chevy/C	12	21	DNS	11	25	20	26	4	24	23	14	21	3	26	7	6	43
14	Roberto Guerrero	USA	Budweiser King Lola T93/00-Chevy/C	19	15	5	28	7	26	24	29	10	7	4	23	11	—	—	—	39
15	Scott Brayton	USA	Amway/Northwest Airlines Lola T93/00-Ford	16	25	24	6	6	—	17	18	19	11	6	7	24	9	15	24	36
			Amway/Northwest Airlines Lola T92/00-Ford	—	—	—	—	—	14	—	—	—	—	—	—	—	—	—	—	
16	Jimmy Vasser	USA	Kodalux Processing/STP Lola T92/00-Chevy/A	24	3	22	—	8	16	11	—	—	—	—	—	—	—	—	—	30
			Kodalux Processing/STP Lola T92/00-Ford	—	—	—	13	—	—	—	—	11	—	9	—	18	10	—	21	
17	Eddie Cheever	USA	Say NO To Drugs Penske PC21-Chevy/B	7	24	9	—	—	21	—	—	—	—	—	—	—	—	—	—	21
			Glidden/Menard Special Lola T92/00-Buick	—	—	—	16	—	—	—	—	—	—	—	—	—	—	—	—	
			Menard/Immobiliser Lola T93/00-Ford	—	—	—	—	—	—	—	—	—	—	—	6	—	—	—	—	
			Budweiser King Lola T93/00-Chevy/C	—	—	—	—	—	—	—	—	—	—	—	—	—	28	10	14	
18	Andrea Montermini	I	Andrea Moda/Agip Lola T92/00-Chevy/A	25	—	—	—	4	—	—	27	—	—	—	19	—	—	—	—	12
19	Scott Pruett	USA	Pro Formance/Sprint Lola T91/00-Chevy/A	—	7	7	DNQ	—	25	—	—	26	—	—	—	—	15	—	25	12
20	Willy T. Ribbs	USA	Cosby/Service Merchandise Lola T92/00-Ford	—	—	—	21	11	12	16	27	18	10	15	12	16	11	19	28	9
21	Robbie Buhl	USA	Mi-Jack Lola T92/00-Chevy/A	23	19	6	—	—	28	—	24	—	—	—	—	14	17	16	—	8
			Mi-Jack Lola T92/00-Buick	—	—	—	DNQ	—	—	—	—	—	—	—	—	—	—	—	—	
			Mi-Jack Lola T91/00-Chevy/A	—	—	—	—	17	—	—	—	—	—	—	—	—	—	—	—	
22	Mark Smith	USA	Craftsman Penske PC21-Chevy/B	18	9	10	DNQ	—	27	29	15	23	—	24	22	19	12	17		8
23	Mike Groff	USA	Miller Genuine Draft Rahal/Hogan 001-Chevy/C	—	—	—	—	19	11	9	—	—	—	11	—	—	—	—	—	8
			Miller Genuine Draft Lola T93/00-Chevy/C	—	—	—	—	—	—	—	—	—	—	—	—	18	—	22	—	
24	Adrian Fernandez	MEX	Amway Mexico/Conseco Lola T93/00-Chevy/C	—	—	23	—	21	7	—	—	WDN	—	29	—	—	—	—	12	7
25	Brian Till	USA	Say NO To Drugs Penske PC21-Chevy/B	—	—	—	—	—	22	9	13	—	10	22	—	17	16	29		7
26	Hiro Matsushita	J	Panasonic Special Lola T93/00-Ford	11	10	14	18	13	13	21	12	16	14	13	13	12	13	21	19	7
27	David Kudrave	USA	Andrea Moda/Agip Lola T92/00-Chevy/A	—	8	DNS	—	24	—	23	—	—	12	23	—	23	14	—		6
28	Olivier Grouillard	F	Eurosport/Marlboro Lola T92/00-Chevy/A	—	—	DNQ	12	24	13	11	DNS	17	12	16	26	16	18	20		4
29	John Andretti	USA	Copenhagen Racing Lola T92/00-Ford	—	—	—	10	—	—	—	—	—	—	—	—	—	—	—	—	3
30	Marco Greco	BR	Alfa Laval/Team Losi Lola T92/00-Chevy/A	22	11	25	DNQ	DNQ	19	19	22	21	18	17	28	20	18	23	DNQ	2
31	Christian Danner	D	Andrea Moda/Agip Lola T92/00-Chevy/A	—	—	—	—	—	—	—	25	—	—	—	11	—	—	26		2
32	Ross Bentley	CDN	AGFA/Rain-X Lola T92/00-Chevy/A	17	12	15	—	14	DNQ	15	16	25	16	—	17	17	DNQ	22	DNQ	1
			AGFA/Rain-X Lola T92/00-Buick	—	—	—	DNQ	—	—	—	—	—	—	—	—	—	—	—	—	
33	Al Unser	USA	Budweiser King Lola T93/00-Chevy/C	—	—	—	—	12	—	—	—	—	—	—	—	—	—	—	—	1
34	Bertrand Gachot	F	CAPA Lola T93/00-Ford	—	—	—	—	—	—	—	12	—	—	—	—	—	—	—	—	1
35	Kevin Cogan	USA	Conseco Lola T93/00-Chevy/C	—	—	—	14	—	—	—	27	13	15	—	—	—	—	—	—	
36	Lyn St James	USA	JC Penney/Nike Lola T92/00-Ford	—	13	17	—	—	—	—	—	—	—	—	—	—	—	—	—	
			JC Penney/Nike Lola T93/00-Ford	—	—	—	25	—	—	20	23	—	22	—	—	—	—	—	—	
37	Mauricio Gugelmin	BR	Hollywood Lola T93/00-Ford	—	—	—	—	—	—	—	—	—	—	—	—	—	21	24	13	
38	Buddy Lazier	USA	Foodtown/Pacific/Viper Lola T91/00-Chevy/A	20	17	19	—	—	18	—	21	—	—	—	—	—	—	—	—	
			Viper/Financial World Lola T91/00-Buick	—	—	—	DNQ	15	—	—	—	—	—	DNQ	14	—	20	26	DNQ	
			Leader Cards Lola T92/00-Buick	—	—	—	—	—	—	—	—	—	21	—	—	—	—	—	—	
39	Dominic Dobson	USA	Coors Light/Winning Spirit Galmer G92B-Chevy/A	—	—	—	23	—	—	—	—	—	—	—	—	14	DNS	—	—	
			Skycell Galmer G92B-Chevy/C	—	—	—	—	—	—	—	—	—	—	—	—	—	—	—	18	
40	Gary Brabham	AUS	Split Cycle Lola T92/00-Chevy/A	14	—	—	—	—	—	—	—	—	—	—	—	—	—	—	—	
41	Jeff Wood	USA	Agip/Rubaway/Hawaiian Tropic Lola T91/00-DFS	—	DNQ	20	—	DNQ	DNQ	28	17	28	20	24	27	15	DNQ	DNQ	DNQ	
42	Didier Theys	B	Delta Faucet/Kinko's Lola T92/00-Buick	—	—	—	22	—	—	—	—	—	—	—	—	—	—	—	—	
			Kinko's Lola T92/00-Ford	—	—	—	—	—	—	—	—	—	—	—	—	—	—	—	15	
43	Davy Jones	USA	Andrea Moda/Agip Lola T92/00-Chevy/A	—	—	—	—	15	—	—	—	—	—	—	—	—	—	—	—	
44	Johnny Unser	USA	Ruger Special Lola T92/00-Chevy/A	—	—	—	—	—	—	18	—	17	—	18	—	21	—	—	—	
45	Gary Bettenhausen	USA	Glidden Paint Special Lola T93/00-Menard/Buick	—	—	—	17	—	—	—	—	—	—	—	—	—	—	—	—	
46	Stephan Gregoire	F	Formula Project/Maalox/GSF Lola T92/00-Buick	—	—	—	19	—	—	—	—	—	—	—	—	—	—	—	—	
47	Tony Bettenhausen	USA	AMAX Energy & Metals Penske PC22-Chevy/C	—	—	—	20	—	—	—	—	—	—	—	—	—	—	—	—	
48	Scott Sharp	USA	Rain-X/AMAX Penske PC22-Chevy/C	—	—	—	—	—	—	—	—	—	—	—	—	—	—	22	—	
49	Jim Crawford	GB	Budweiser King Lola T93/00-Chevy/C	—	—	—	24	—	—	—	—	—	—	—	—	—	—	—	—	
50	Geoff Brabham	AUS	Glidden/Menard Special Lola T93/00-Menard/Buick	—	—	—	26	—	—	—	—	—	—	—	—	—	—	—	—	
51	Brian Bonner	USA	Applebee's/Office Depot Lola T91/00-Buick	—	—	—	DNQ	—	—	—	—	—	—	—	—	—	—	—	—	
			Applebee's/Office Depot Lola T91/00-Chevy/A	—	—	—	—	—	—	—	26	—	—	—	—	—	—	—	—	
52	Andrea Chiesa	CH	Agip/Rubaway/Hawaiian Tropic Lola T91/00-DFS	26	—	—	—	—	—	—	—	—	—	—	—	—	—	—	—	
53	Jeff Andretti	USA	Interstate Battery/Gillette 1 Lola T92/00-Buick	—	—	—	29	—	—	—	—	—	—	—	—	—	—	—	—	
54	Stan Fox	USA	Delta Faucet/Jack's Tool Lola T91/00-Buick	—	—	—	31	—	—	—	—	—	—	—	—	—	—	—	—	
55	Nelson Piquet	BR	Arisco/STP Special Lola T93/00-Menard/Buick	—	—	—	32	—	—	—	—	—	—	—	—	—	—	—	—	

* led most laps   P pole position   DNQ did not qualify   DNS did not start   WDN withdrawn   DSQ disqualified

ap RACING

FIT TO WIN

Check the record books.
No other manufacturer of racing brakes
or clutches even comes close.

AP Lockheed and AP Borg & Beck
components have become a byword for
performance - the standard by which
all others are judged.

Ask this years World Formula One
Grand Prix Champion, Formula One
Motorcycle Champion, Indycar Champion
and British Open Rally Champion.

AP Racing, Wheler Road,
Seven Stars Industrial Estate,
Coventry CV3 4LB. Tel: (0203) 639595
International: +44 203 639595
Fax: (0203) 639559

SURFERS PARADISE

Michael C. Brown

In his Formula 1 days, Nigel Mansell never had much luck in Australia. His seven Grand Prix starts Down Under yielded only two finishes: a pair of second places, one for Ferrari in 1990 and the other for Williams-Renault in the rain-shortened race 12 months later. In 1986, while seemingly *en route* to the World Championship, he suffered that infamous tire blow-out. And on his F1 swansong last season Mansell had a controversial collision with Ayrton Senna while disputing the lead.

Maybe it was just South Australia he had a problem with (despite the fact his sister now lives in Adelaide). Because on his first competitive outing in distant Queensland, for the Australian FAI IndyCar Grand Prix, the opening round of the 1993 PPG Indy Car World Series, Mansell scored a fairy-tale victory aboard Newman-Haas Racing's Kmart/Texaco Havoline-backed Lola-Ford/Cosworth XB.

The streets of aptly named Surfers Paradise once again provided an action-packed race for the record-sized crowd, and Mansell clearly was the driver most of them came to see. The 'Pom' did not disappoint. Yet the reigning Formula 1 World Champion had to work hard before placing his name in the history books as only the second driver ever to win on his Indy Car debut. (The other, incidentally, was the late Graham Hill, who triumphed in the 1966 Indianapolis 500.)

'This is just brilliant,' said Mansell. 'It's my first win in Australia, and Australia is almost like a home country for me. It's the closest thing to England and I'm just absolutely thrilled. It was a fantastic race.'

He's right. It was.

1st – MANSELL   **2nd – FITTIPALDI**   **3rd – GORDON**

QUALIFYING

A huge crowd was on hand throughout the weekend, many of them decked out in red, white and blue in support of Mansell. The Englishman responded superbly, claiming the coveted pole position with a time of 1m 38.555s. His best was some two-tenths faster than Al Unser Jr's year-old lap record.

'I'm just delighted,' said Mansell, whose presence also attracted a vast gathering of reporters and television crews from around the world. 'The credit goes to the team. The baseline setup for the car is much the same as they ran last year, so it's really all credit to my crew.'

Emerson Fittipaldi, another former F1 champion and the winner at Surfers in '92, set the second-fastest time in his Marlboro-liveried Penske PC22, powered by the all-new Chevy Indy V8/C engine. The experienced Brazilian was fastest of all on Saturday, failing by just a couple of tenths to beat Mansell's Friday best.

Fittipaldi's young teammate, Paul Tracy, was content with third on the grid, confident he had a good, consistent balance which would serve him well in the race.

Right behind was the amazing Robby Gordon, who hustled A.J. Foyt's year-old Copenhagen Lola-Ford/Cosworth spectacularly on his debut for the team. Gordon's progress was a joy to behold, especially through the fast chicane adjacent to Main Beach, where he alone matched Mansell for speed and bravado. It wasn't especially pretty but it sure was spectacular, both cars catching plenty of 'hang time' due to solid contact with the curbs.

There was, however, one notable difference between the pair. Mansell was consistent, clobbering the curbs with inch-perfect precision each time through, whereas Gordon's inexperience saw him bouncing haphazardly through the chicane in a different

manner each lap. How he refrained from spinning will remain one of the season's great mysteries. Uncouth but effective.

Gordon, indeed, was fastest in both morning sessions. Unfortunately, come final qualifying, he was left stranded in pit lane by a faulty gearbox which prevented him from selecting fifth or sixth gears.

'It's frustrating,' he commented, 'because I know we could've challenged for the pole.'

The most significant improvement from Friday's provisional grid was posted by Arie Luyendyk at the wheel of Chip Ganassi's Target/Scotch Video Lola-Ford. The 1990 Indianapolis 500 winner had all sorts of handling problems the first day but made tremendous progress to move up from 15th overnight to fifth.

Mansell's Newman-Haas teammate, Mario Andretti, shared row three of the grid with Luyendyk, followed by yet another Lola-Ford/Cosworth driven by Scott Goodyear. The Canadian's Mackenzie Financial-backed Walker Motorsport car had been picked by many as one of the pre-season favorites. But Goodyear lost valuable time on Saturday morning with a water leak, then damaged his car when he slid wide on a corner in the closing minutes of qualifying and hit one of the ever-present cement walls.

RACE

An intriguing race was in prospect, with numerous issues remaining unresolved. How, for example, would Mansell cope with a rolling start, the first since his karting days almost 20 years ago? How would Ilmor Engineering's latest Chevrolet Indy V8/C engine fare against the tried-and-tested Ford/Cosworth XBs? How would young Gordon, starting fourth with only seven open-wheel races to his name, react under the new-found pressure?

Some of the answers came early.

65

Robby Gordon drove a storming race in A.J. Foyt's Copenhagen Racing Lola. Despite losing the use of his clutch, the tenacious Gordon hounded Fittipaldi all the way to the flag in their battle for second spot.

Bottom: Mark Smith caught the eye, and not just because of this airborne maneuver at the chicane. The rookie from McMinnville, Oregon, claimed 11th spot in qualifying but a tangle with Cheever in the race destroyed his chances of a points finish.

Mansell, the pole-sitter, was back in fourth place before the end of the opening lap. First of all he found himself running too close to the pace car coming up toward the start. Mansell had to lift off, which allowed Fittipaldi and Tracy to get the jump and power past before the first chicane. Less than a mile later Mansell was demoted also by the impressive Gordon.

'It was a fantastic maneuver,' praised Mansell. 'He was *totally* committed and I knew he was totally committed, so I made room for him. All credit to him.'

Two laps later, Gordon continued his startling progress by passing Tracy for second place when the Penske driver was held up slightly by a slower car leaving the pits.

Tracy dutifully tucked in behind. He was content to run close behind in third place, ahead of Mansell . . . until disaster struck on lap six.

'I was just pacing along and the suspension folded up,' lamented Tracy, who did well to maintain control of the car.

After repairs, Tracy continued some nine laps behind, only to retire later in the race when his engine failed.

Compatriot Goodyear fared little better. He ran in seventh until making an ill-fated attempt to out-brake Luyendyk at the end of

the Esplanade.

'I got a bit of a run on Arie when he missed his shift to fourth gear,' related Goodyear. 'I went to try and pass him on the inside but he blocked me, so then I went to the outside. Unfortunately I went in [to the corner] too deep and did a graceful pirouette.'

Goodyear lost a lap before he could rejoin.

Meanwhile, all eyes were on Mansell. On lap eight he dive-bombed Gordon on the inside under braking at the end of the long back straightaway. Mansell was up into second place. Soon he was nipping at the heels of Fittipaldi. He wanted past.

Mansell made his bid for the lead at the same corner. Once again it was a spectacular move, smoke pouring from his locked-up wheels as Mansell dived for the inside.

Unwittingly, however, Mansell had made the pass under yellow flags. Soon afterward the race stewards responded by waving a black flag to indicate he had been assessed a stop-and-go penalty. But Mansell was lucky. It was time anyway for his first fuel stop.

On lap 19 he pulled into the pits, taking on a full load of

methanol and four fresh tires; and under IndyCar rules he was able to make the stop with no additional delay. He resumed in fourth place but soon regained the lead when the other front-runners also made their first scheduled stops.

The next drama came on lap 30. Mansell, after inching away to an almost five-second lead over Fittipaldi, felt the handling of his car had gone awry. Mansell assumed he had picked up a puncture, having clipped a wall on the exit of one of the chicanes a few laps earlier. So he dived into the pits for immediate service.

The tire in fact was found to be fully inflated but, by the time he rejoined, Mansell was back in fourth place. He then began another stirring recovery drive.

'I was driving as hard as I knew,' he declared. 'I wasn't interested in the fuel [consumption], I was just driving as hard as I could to catch up with the leaders.'

Mansell dispatched teammate Andretti with a typically audacious pass on lap 39, then moved from third place into the lead when both Fittipaldi and Gordon made their second fuel stops, right on schedule, after 44 laps.

Mansell continued to run at a blistering pace, setting a new track record of 1m 39.67s. Fittipaldi, meanwhile, was beseeched by his crew via radio to conserve fuel. He was unable to mount a serious challenge. Neither was Gordon, who had no clutch and lost valuable time being push-started by his crew after his second pit stop.

Mansell, firmly in the lead, was able to run his own conservative pace in the waning laps. He allowed the advantage over Fittipaldi to dwindle from almost half a minute to just 5.113 seconds at the finish. It was enough. The

huge crowd went wild with delight.

Then, just to add to the high drama, Mansell's car suddenly slowed just after the finish line. It was out of fuel.

'I was very, very concerned,' said Mansell after hitching a ride back to the victory podium. 'On the last lap, going into the last chicane, the car started to splutter. I had to drive it in fourth gear through the last few corners, but we just made it to the finish.'

Fittipaldi, behind, just managed to hold off the last-ditch efforts of a determined Gordon.

'It was a great race,' said the Brazilian. 'I could see [Gordon's] nose under my gearbox at the last corner. It was a tense last lap.'

Soon after the race, Fittipaldi learned of a problem with his car's computerized fuel metering system which left almost two gallons of usable fuel in his tank. He was furious. Had he known, he could have placed Mansell under far more pressure, perhaps forcing the Briton to run dry a few hundred yards before the finish line instead of after it . . .

Gordon, too, had harbored hopes of victory. The 24-year-old Californian underlined his prodigious talent by claiming third in only his eighth Indy Car start. He pressured the two Formula 1 champions all the way to the end.

'We had a great car all weekend,' commented Gordon. 'I'm really excited with the new team.'

Behind the consistent Andretti and Luyendyk, defending PPG Cup champion Bobby Rahal persevered to sixth despite a lack of straightline speed in his Miller Genuine Draft R/H 001 (*née* Truesports) chassis. Eddie Cheever also drove well in his year-old Say NO to Drugs Penske-Chevy/B, losing out to Rahal only during his second pit stop.

SNIPPETS

IndyCar

• Buddy Lazier's under-funded team arrived in Australia without a spare nose for its '91 Lola. None was available either, which led to a mad scramble on Saturday after a locking rear brake in practice sent him into the wall. The only suitable replacement was found on a show car in Las Vegas. It was hurriedly driven to Los Angeles, arriving just in time to catch the (thankfully delayed) overnight Qantas flight to Sydney. It was then ferried to Coolangatta, picked up by a police escort and fitted to the car just in time for the race morning warmup. Lazier *(above left)*, though, was nowhere to be found. He was in the hotel, blissfully assuming the car wouldn't be ready until the race! When Buddy did arrive, in time for a few laps, he promptly set 11th-best time of the session. The promise was fulfilled in the race when he rose from 25th on the grid to 11th before being sidelined by a bent suspension pushrod.

• Robby Gordon phoned his father back in California on Saturday evening with the good news from qualifying: 'Hey, Dad, I'm fourth on the grid!' To which his father replied: 'Who's this?'

• Stefan Johansson was an unrepresentative 18th on the grid in Tony Bettenhausen's new AMAX Penske PC22. The Swede was hampered throughout practice and qualifying by gear-selection problems with the new sequential gearbox. Due to an apparent oversight the team didn't get the new modifications which had been fitted to the 'works' cars following similar problems in testing. Johansson's car, incidentally, was the same one used for most of the pre-season testing by Fittipaldi and Tracy.

• Bobby Rahal struggled all weekend with his R/H 001 chassis, a mildly updated version of last year's Truesports 92C, which was itself an update of the Judd-engined 91C. A severe lack of testing time also hampered his progress. While pole-winner Mansell clipped a couple of tenths from the old track record, Rahal was more than a second slower than Scott Pruett managed last year in the same car.

Michael C. Brown

• Formula 3000 graduate Andrea Montermini *(left)* showed a good turn of speed on his Indy Car debut, although the young Italian had a few mechanical problems with Antonio Ferrari's ex-Bobby Rahal Lola T92/00-Chevy/A, which cost valuable track time. He also had a couple of minor skirmishes with the wall due to his inexperience.

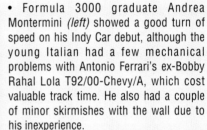

AUSTRALIAN FAI INDY CAR GRAND PRIX, SURFERS PARADISE STREET CIRCUIT, QUEENSLAND, AUSTRALIA • 21 March, 65 laps – 181.675 miles

Place	Driver	No.	Car	Q Speed (mph)	Q Time	Q Pos.	Laps	Time/Retirement	Ave. speed	Pts
1	**Nigel Mansell**	5	*Kmart/Texaco Havoline* Lola T93/00-Ford	102.095	1m 38.555s	1	65	1h 52m 02.886s	97.284 mph	21
2	**Emerson Fittipaldi**	4	*Marlboro* Penske PC22-Chevy/C	101.758	1m 38.882s	2	65	1h 52m 07.999s	97.210	17
3	**Robby Gordon**	14	*Copenhagen Racing* Lola T92/00-Ford	101.192	1m 39.435s	4	65	1h 52m 08.476s	97.203	14
4	**Mario Andretti**	6	*Kmart/Texaco Havoline* Lola T93/00-Ford	100.884	1m 39.739s	6	65	1h 52m 17.533s	97.073	12
5	**Arie Luyendyk**	10	*Target/Scotch Video* Lola T93/00-Ford	100.988	1m 39.635s	5	65	1h 52m 50.106s	96.606	10
6	**Bobby Rahal**	1	*Miller Genuine Draft* Rahal/Hogan 001-Chevy/C	99.530	1m 41.096s	13	64	Running		8
7	**Eddie Cheever**	69	*Say NO To Drugs* Penske PC21-Chevy/B	98.794	1m 41.848s	16	64	Running		6
8	**Raul Boesel**	9	*Duracell/Mobil 1/Sadia* Lola T93/00-Ford	100.131	1m 40.488s	8	64	Running		5
9	**Teo Fabi**	8	*Pennzoil Special* Lola T93/00-Chevy/C	99.559	1m 41.066s	12	64	Running		4
10	**Scott Goodyear**	2	*Mackenzie Special* Lola T93/00-Ford	100.492	1m 40.127s	7	63	Running		3
11	**Hiro Matsushita**	15	*Panasonic Special* Lola T93/00-Ford	94.619	1m 46.342s	24	63	Running		2
12	**Stefan Johansson**	16	*AMAX Energy & Metals* Penske PC22-Chevy/C	96.835	1m 43.908s	18	63	Running		1
13	Danny Sullivan	7	*Molson* Lola T93/00-Chevy/C	95.867	1m 44.958s	21	62	Running		
14	Gary Brabham	90	*Split Cycle* Lola T92/00-Chevy/A	96.425	1m 44.351s	20	62	Running		
15	Al Unser Jr	3	*Valvoline* Lola T93/00-Chevy/C	99.447	1m 41.180s	13	62	Running		
16	Scott Brayton	22	*Amway/Northwest Airlines* Lola T92/00-Ford	99.643	1m 40.980s	10	61	Running		
17	Ross Bentley	39	*AGFA/Rain-X* Lola T92/00-Chevy/A	95.635	1m 45.213s	22	56	Running		
18	Mark Smith	25	*Craftsman* Penske PC21-Chevy/B	99.632	1m 40.992s	11	50	Running		
19	Roberto Guerrero	40	*Budweiser King* Lola T93/00-Chevy/C	99.151	1m 41.481s	15	49	Gearbox		
20	Buddy Lazier	20	*Foodtown/Pacific* Lola T91/00-Chevy/A	94.063	1m 46.970s	25	35	Suspension		
21	Paul Tracy	12	*Marlboro* Penske PC22-Chevy/C	101.461	1m 39.171s	3	30	Electrical		
22	Marco Greco	30	*Alfa Laval/Team Losi* Lola T92/00-Chevy/A	93.108	1m 48.068s	26	18	Accident		
23	Robbie Buhl	19	*Mi-Jack* Lola T92/00-Chevy/A	97.396	1m 43.311s	17	15	Gearbox		
24	Jimmy Vasser	18	*Kodalux Processing/STP* Lola T92/00-Chevy/A	99.976	1m 40.645s	9	12	Accident		
25	Andrea Montermini	50	*Andrea Moda/Agip* Lola T92/00-Chevy/A	94.724	1m 46.224s	23	9	Fuel pressure		
26	Andrea Chiesa	42	*Agip/Rubaway/Hawaiian Tropic* Lola T91/00-DFS	96.764	1m 43.985s	19	2	Electrical		

Caution flags: No full-course yellow flags.

Lap leaders: Emerson Fittipaldi, 1-15 (15 laps); Nigel Mansell, 16-18 (3 laps); Emerson Fittipaldi, 19-21 (3 laps); Nigel Mansell, 22-29 (8 laps); Emerson Fittipaldi, 30-44 (15 laps); Nigel Mansell, 45-65 (21 laps). **Totals:** Emerson Fittipaldi, 33 laps; Nigel Mansell, 32 laps.

Championship positions: 1 Mansell, 21 pts; **2** Fittipaldi, 17; **3** Gordon, 14; **4** Mario Andretti, 12; **5** Luyendyk, 10; **6** Rahal, 8; **7** Cheever, 6; **8** Boesel, 5; **9** Fabi, 4; **10** Goodyear, 3; **11** Matsushita, 2; **12** Johansson, 1.

PHOEN

Photos: Michael C. Brown

The Valvoline 200 at Phoenix International Raceway provided a perfect example of the unpredictability of Indy Car racing.

A little over halfway through the 200-lap, 200-mile contest, Marlboro Racing Team Penske's young charger Paul Tracy already was two laps clear of his nearest pursuer, veteran teammate Emerson Fittipaldi. The rest of the field was at least three laps behind. The two Chevrolet Indy V8/C-powered Penske PC22s were in a league of their own.

But how quickly things can change. On lap 162, Tracy's quest for victory came to a crunching halt. A moment's hesitation while lapping a slower car sent him spinning into the wall.

Fittipaldi duly inherited the lead . . . only to crash almost immediately after the restart due to a punctured tire. The Penske team was stunned. Within the space of a dozen laps, a likely blitzkrieg triumph had been transformed into ignominious failure.

And so along came Mario Andretti, who qualified a strong second in Newman-Haas Racing's Kmart/Texaco Havoline Lola T93/00-Ford/Cosworth XB but never did match the pace of the leaders on raceday. It didn't matter. Quite suddenly, the race came to him. And the wily veteran, 53 years young and without a victory since July 1988, certainly wasn't about to throw this one away!

QUALIFYING

In the absence of Surfers Paradise winner Nigel Mansell, who rendered himself *hors de combat* with a frightening crash during practice, Scott Goodyear claimed his first-ever Indy Car pole.

The 33-year-old from Toronto had set the pace in pre-season testing and was delighted to prove it was no fluke by circulating Walker Motorsport's Mackenzie Financial-sponsored Lola-Ford/Cosworth XB at a new track record of 20.833 seconds, for an average of 172.804 mph. The old mark, incidentally, stood to Michael Andretti at 20.952 seconds (171.825 mph).

Goodyear's effort rewarded former Penske and Porsche team manager Derrick Walker with his first pole since establishing his own team two years ago.

'The weather conditions changed a lot from when we tested here in the wintertime, which always happens,' declared Walker, 'but the consistency stayed with us. Psychologically, it's a good place to be – on the front row.'

Andretti, left alone to carry the standard for Newman-Haas Racing, rose to the occasion by setting the second-fastest time, despite having struggled with a handling imbalance in practice. Ultimately he was disappointed not to earn the ninth Phoenix pole of his distinguished career.

'We weren't fast enough. Close but no cigar,' he commented after struggling to find a workable balance during earlier practice. 'But considering where I was this morning, I'm happy.'

Fittipaldi also bounced back from adversity, qualifying third after being obliged by a split oil tank early in practice to switch across to his spare Marlboro Penske PC22-Chevy/C.

Tracy started two places farther back, split from his teammate by Roberto Guerrero in the Budweiser King Lola T93/00-Chevy/C owned by drag racing star Kenny Bernstein. Guerrero was delighted with the handling of his car but not quite so happy with the fact his engine was slightly down on boost pressure.

1st – MARIO ANDRETTI

2nd – BOESEL

3rd – VASSER

Left: Two wins out of two for Newman-Haas Racing, with Mario Andretti taking the honors this time round.

Inset below: The Marlboro Penskes of Fittipaldi and Tracy run just ahead of the Budweiser King car of Roberto Guerrero in the opening laps. Chasing are Boesel, Rahal, Fabi and Luyendyk.

When in a position of total dominance, both Penskes crashed out of the lead. Fittipaldi's car *(inset left)* hit the wall after a puncture.

RACE

There was widespread disappointment when it became apparent Mansell would not be starting. Even so, a large crowd gathered in glorious weather for the start.

Andretti brought his vast experience on the ovals to bear at the green flag as he moved instantly ahead of pole-winner Goodyear. Behind them at the end of lap one came a high-speed train comprising Fittipaldi, Guerrero, Tracy, Raul Boesel (Duracell/ Mobil 1/Sadia Lola-Ford/Cosworth) and the rest.

Tracy was content to bide his time through the early laps. Then he began to make his move, whistling past Guerrero on lap five. Three laps later he demoted Goodyear, who had himself been bundled down to third place by Fittipaldi.

On lap 11, Tracy belied his relative lack of experience by neatly dispatching his senior colleague Fittipaldi in Turn One, then driving calmly around the outside of both Andretti and a backmarker in Turn Four. It was an audacious move, the hallmark of a champion.

Plainly, no one this day could hold a candle to Tracy. And when Goodyear's fine run was ended by transmission failure after 104 laps, Tracy inherited a two-lap advantage. Sadly, it was not to last.

Soon after making his second scheduled pit stop, Tracy abruptly lost control in Turn One while attempting to pass Jimmy Vasser's ex-Rahal Kodalux Processing/STP Lola-Chevy/A, which was running sixth.

Tracy emerged, shaken but not stirred, his magnificent run at an end. His immense promise remained unfulfilled.

There was speculation during the ensuing caution period that Fittipaldi, the new race leader, might have picked up a puncture after running over a piece of debris from his teammate's crash.

'We talked about bringing him in [to the pits for a change of tires] but we didn't want to lose our [one-lap] advantage over Mario,' said team manager Chuck Sprague. 'We decided not to.'

It was a bad call. Right after the restart on lap 173, Fittipaldi's car suddenly snapped out of control as the Brazilian sped into Turn Three. The right-rear tire had been punctured. Exit the second member of the hitherto dominant Penske team.

An excellent run by Robby Gordon also ended with solid contact against the wall. Fresh from a brilliant third-place finish in Australia, Gordon endured a torrid

It had been a long wait for Mario Andretti *(right)*, whose last Indy Car win was back in 1988 at Cleveland.

Far right: Raul Boesel looks pleased with his second place – and the competitiveness of the Duracell/Mobil 1/Sadia Lola-Ford.

Michael C. Brown

time in practice. He qualified a lowly 20th in his year-old Copenhagen Lola-Ford/Cosworth after two separate engine problems permitted him precious little track time. Then, in the race morning warmup, the Californian spun into the wall after making contact with another car at the pit exit.

'It was my fault,' admitted Gordon honestly.

The car was repaired just in time for the race, whereupon Gordon repaid his crew's efforts with a superb charge. He had risen as high as third before crashing in Turn One on lap 135. Team owner A.J. Foyt was disappointed but

nonetheless impressed.

'I think he did a great job,' said the most successful driver in Indy Car history. 'The race was going terrific. That's racing. But I'm proud of him.'

Former Phoenix winner Guerrero also ran strongly in third place until forced out by a wheel bearing failure.

The series of misfortunes had taken its toll on the front-running contenders. All except Andretti. Quite suddenly the veteran found himself in the lead, and he duly reeled off the remaining laps to score a hugely popular win.

'It's a lucky day, no question

about it,' admitted Andretti after claiming the 100th major victory of his professional career, his 52nd in an Indy car. 'I thank the man upstairs, but I'll take it because I've had races taken away from me while I've been leading. It's a very special day.'

Boesel parlayed a consistent run into a career-best-equaling second for himself and Dick Simon Racing, while teammate Vasser earned his first visit to the victory podium.

'We knew if we ran all day we'd finish in the top ten,' said Vasser, 'but to finish third is a bonus for us. This is a dream for me. To be

on the podium is just fantastic.'

Al Unser Jr persevered to fourth in an ill-handling Valvoline Lola-Chevy/C, ahead of Teo Fabi's similar Pennzoil-backed car. Next came Arie Luyendyk (Target/Scotch Video Lola-Ford) and Scott Pruett, who drove sensibly and without major drama in the two-year-old Lola-Chevy/A run by a brand-new locally based team, Pro Formance Motorsports.

Rookie David Kudrave also performed well to place eighth in his '92 Lola-Chevy/A, just holding off the Craftsman Penske-Chevy/B of fellow Indy Lights graduate Mark Smith through the closing laps.

Learning the hard way

Nigel Mansell arrived at PIR with a fresh outlook on life. He was all set for his first Indy Car race on American soil and his debut appearance, save for a couple of test sessions, on an oval track. He came, too, as the PPG Cup points leader following his victory in Surfers Paradise.

Mansell admitted he had much to learn about ovals, although you wouldn't have thought so after a glance down the official EDS timing sheet following first practice on Saturday. For there atop the listing was Mansell's car No. 5. He had recorded a best of 20.760 seconds, an average speed of 173.414 mph, some two-tenths underneath Michael Andretti's record.

The entire Indy Car contingent was stunned. Less than five minutes into the second session, however, Mansell also was stunned – quite literally – following a heavy crash in Turn One. Mansell already had turned in a quick lap at 20.804s, which was to remain fastest of the session, when without warning his car snapped sideways. Even Mansell's phenomenal reflexes were not enough to prevent his Lola from looping into a lazy spin and then slamming backward, with brutal force, into the wall.

'The back end went and that was it,' said Mansell. 'I knew I was going to go in. I just ducked down and hung on. I tried not to think about it.'

Mansell, knocked unconscious by the impact, came to in the helicopter *en route* to a Phoenix hospital. He was treated for a concussion, kept overnight for observation, then released. By the time the race started he was back at home in Florida.

Michael C. Brown

Michael C. Brown

• For the first time, official Indy Car practice began on Saturday morning instead of the usual Friday. The intended cost-cutting measure did not seem to work, however, nor was it popular with either the teams or drivers, since the majority instead spent Thursday shaking down their cars at nearby Firebird Raceway.

Michael C. Brown

• After posting his best Indy Car performance to date, Jimmy Vasser *(above)* was full of praise for race engineer Steve Newey, who last year worked with PPG Cup champion Bobby Rahal. 'The car's got a really good setup,' noted the Toyota Atlantic graduate. 'It feels very stable. Steve and Bobby did a lot of work last year and maybe I'm the beneficiary of that. It certainly makes my job a bit easier.'

VALVOLINE 200, PHOENIX INTERNATIONAL RACEWAY, PHOENIX, ARIZONA • 4 April, 200 laps – 200.000 miles

Place	Driver	No.	Car	Q Speed (mph)	Q Time	Q Pos.	Laps	Time/Retirement	Ave. speed	Pts
1	**Mario Andretti**	6	*Kmart/Texaco Havoline* Lola T93/00-Ford	172.294	20.895s	2	200	1h 36m 53.630s	123.847 mph	20
2	**Raul Boesel**	9	*Duracell/Mobil 1/Sadia* Lola T93/00-Ford	170.777	21.080s	6	199	Running		16
3	**Jimmy Vasser**	18	*Kodalux Processing/STP* Lola T92/00-Chevy/A	167.582	21.482s	9	197	Running		14
4	**Al Unser Jr**	3	*Valvoline* Lola T93/00-Chevy/C	165.442	21.760s	13	197	Running		12
5	**Teo Fabi**	8	*Pennzoil Special* Lola T93/00-Chevy/C	168.872	21.318s	8	196	Running		10
6	**Arie Luyendyk**	10	*Target/Scotch Video* Lola T93/00-Ford	167.039	21.552s	10	195	Running		8
7	**Scott Pruett**	45	*Tobacco-Free America* Lola T91/00-Chevy/A	160.485	22.432s	15	194	Running		6
8	**David Kudrave**	50	*Andrea Moda/Agip* Lola T92/00-Chevy/A	154.614	23.284s	22	193	Running		5
9	**Mark Smith**	25	*Craftsman* Penske PC21-Chevy/B	166.409	21.633s	11	192	Running		4
10	**Hiro Matsushita**	15	*Panasonic Special* Lola T93/00-Ford	159.755	22.535s	17	187	Running		3
11	**Marco Greco**	30	*Alfa Laval/Team Losi* Lola T92/00-Chevy/A	149.342	24.106s	24	183	Running		2
12	**Ross Bentley**	39	*AGFA/Rain-X* Lola T92/00-Chevy/A	146.968	24.495s	25	183	Running		1
13	Lyn St James	90	*JC Penney/Nike* Lola T92/00-Ford	155.549	23.144s	21	179	Running		
14	Emerson Fittipaldi	4	*Marlboro* Penske PC22-Chevy/C	172.093	20.919s	3	171	Accident		
15	Roberto Guerrero	40	*Budweiser King* Lola T93/00-Chevy/C	171.647	20.973s	4	162	Wheel bearing		
16	Paul Tracy	12	*Marlboro* Penske PC22-Chevy/C	171.595	20.980s	5	161	Accident		1
17	Buddy Lazier	20	*Foodtown/Pacific* Lola T91/00-Chevy/A	158.944	22.650s	18	141	Header		
18	Robby Gordon	14	*Copenhagen Racing* Lola T92/00-Ford	157.019	22.927s	20	134	Accident		
19	Robbie Buhl	19	*Mi-Jack* Lola T92/00-Chevy/A	154.496	23.302s	23	116	Header		
20	Scott Goodyear	2	*Mackenzie Special* Lola T93/00-Ford	172.804	20.833s	1	104	Gearbox		1
21	Stefan Johansson	16	*AMAX Energy & Metals* Penske PC22-Chevy/C	157.848	22.807s	19	87	Gearbox		
22	Bobby Rahal	1	*Miller Genuine Draft* Rahal/Hogan 001-Chevy/C	169.711	21.212s	7	63	Handling		
23	Danny Sullivan	7	*Molson* Lola T93/00-Chevy/C	164.969	21.822s	14	41	Throttle		
24	Eddie Cheever	69	*Say NO To Drugs* Penske PC21-Chevy/B	160.304	22.457s	16	38	Vibration		
25	Scott Brayton	22	*Amway/Northwest Airlines* Lola T92/00-Ford	166.223	21.658s	12	34	Electrical		

Caution flags: Laps 95-100, tow car/Johansson; laps134-144, accident/Gordon; laps 161-170, accident/Tracy; laps 171-182, accident/Fittipaldi.

Lap leaders: Mario Andretti, 1-10 (10 laps); Paul Tracy, 11-161 (151 laps); Emerson Fittipaldi, 162-171 (10 laps); Mario Andretti, 172-200 (29 laps). **Totals:** Paul Tracy, 151 laps; Mario Andretti, 39 laps; Emerson Fittipaldi, 10 laps.

Championship positions: 1 Mario Andretti, 32 pts; **2** Mansell and Boesel, 21; **4** Luyendyk, 18; **5** Fittipaldi, 17; **6** Gordon, Vasser and Fabi, 14; **9** Al Unser Jr, 12; **10** Rahal, 8; **11** Cheever and Pruett, 6; **13** Matsushita and Kudrave, 5; **15** Goodyear and Smith, 4; **17** Greco, 2; **18** Johansson, Bentley and Tracy, 1.

LONG BEACH

Paul Tracy truly came of age in the Toyota Grand Prix of Long Beach. The 24-year-old had displayed his prodigious talent during most of his previous 17 Indy Car starts, only to have a variety of problems prevent him from making that all-important trip to Victory Lane.

Two weeks earlier, for example, a simple error of judgment cost him his first win after what until then had been a textbook performance in Phoenix. His day in Long Beach certainly wasn't without its dramas either, yet Tracy was rewarded for his persistence and pace with a fine victory at the wheel of his Marlboro-backed Penske PC22-Chevy/C.

'It hasn't really sunk in yet,' said Tracy after scoring his first win since claiming the Indy Lights Championship title in 1990. 'I knew the team was capable, I knew the car was capable, and inside I knew I was capable; but a few things had slipped away from me, I had made a few mistakes, and I must admit I was beginning to get a bit down-hearted. Now that's all behind me. I've just got to build on that for the future.'

Pole-winner Nigel Mansell was the only other driver to lead during the race, despite Tracy making two extra stops for replacement tires. Mansell finally finished an exhausted third in his Kmart/Texaco Havoline Lola-Ford/Cosworth XB, hampered by a back injury and the loss of the critical second gear. Defending PPG Cup champion Bobby Rahal brought his recalcitrant Miller Genuine Draft R/H 001 (*née* Truesports) chassis home to a best-ever second-place finish.

1st – TRACY

2nd – RAHAL

3rd – MANSELL

Sponsors' delight. Paul Tracy scored an emphatic win for Marlboro Penske at Long Beach in front of an 85,000-strong crowd.

QUALIFYING

The track had undergone several changes since Mansell last competed in Long Beach back in 1983 when the race was a round of the Formula 1 World Championship. He had the further handicap of suffering considerable pain and discomfort in his lower back, a legacy of his dramatic crash two weeks earlier in Phoenix. Despite those facts, Mansell was very much the man to beat. He set

fastest time in all four sessions.

'I've got a lot of poles in my career,' said Mansell after maintaining his 100 percent record in Indy Car competition, 'but this one is probably the best of my life. That's how much importance I put on it. This was a very special day for me.'

Mansell did not complete many laps, anxious to maintain his limited reserves of strength for the race.

'It was tough out there,' he continued. 'I'm just eking out my energy.

Michael C. Brown

Michael C. Brown

Left: **Reigning Indy Lights champion Robbie Buhl rewarded sponsor Mi-Jack and entrant Dale Coyne by taking their '92 Lola-Chevy/A to sixth place at the finish.**

Injured or not, Nigel Mansell took no prisoners defending his third position at the Toyota Grand Prix of Long Beach. *Right:* **Al Unser Jr tries to pass on the inside, and** *(below right)* **is then forced wide on the outside at Turn One. The Valvoline Lola ended up in the wall and 'Little Al' was left to fume at Mansell's tactics.**

I'm trying to manage it and save some in reserve for Sunday.'

Tracy also wasn't operating at optimum capacity. He was limping heavily, nursing a sore ankle and rapped knuckles, ostensibly the result of falling off his mountain bike in training. (Perhaps it was just a coincidence that close friend and frequent karting companion Mark Smith also was hobbling after a crash at nearby Riverside's Adams kart track earlier in the week.) Nevertheless, Tracy maintained his strong form by annexing the other front-row grid position.

Veteran Marlboro Racing Team Penske teammate Emerson Fittipaldi was relegated to row two, while Stefan Johansson also proved the effectiveness of the Penske chassis by setting fifth-fastest time in Tony Bettenhausen's AMAX-sponsored PC22.

Scott Goodyear, so impressive in Phoenix, again ran strongly to split the Penskes, fourth in his Mackenzie Financial Lola-Ford/Cosworth.

Farther down the 28-car field, Eddie Cheever was fastest of those running year-old equipment. Fired by Chip Ganassi at the end of the '92 season, Cheever instead hooked up with locally based team owner Norm Turley to run a Chevy/B-powered Penske PC21. Cheever celebrated the arrival of a new sponsor, Quorum International, by posting tenth-fastest time, well within a second of Mansell's pole-winning effort.

Indy Car debutant Adrian Fernandez showed promise in 17th with a Galles Racing International-run, Amway Mexico-backed Lola-Chevy/C, qualifying ahead of Indy Car veterans Roberto Guerrero (Budweiser King Lola-Chevy/C) and Arie Luyendyk (Target/Scotch Video Lola-Ford).

RACE

Perfect California weather and a huge crowd provided a colorful setting for promoter Chris Pook's showcase Indy Car street race. Most of the attention once again was focused on Mansell, of course, but many people were tipping Tracy for honors – assuming he could stay away from the omnipresent cement walls.

'My job is just to go out and score some [PPG Cup championship] points,' said Tracy before the start. 'We've been strong the first two races but we've come away with nothing.'

Tracy, however, is not one to err on the side of caution. He pounced right away at the start, jumping ahead of pole-sitter Mansell and winning the drag race along Shoreline Drive.

'I'm too kind at the start,' quipped the reigning Formula 1 World Champion. 'Seriously, it's all credit to Paul. He judged it perfectly. The Penskes have a strong engine and I think he gunned it a little bit before I did.'

Mansell had no option but to tuck into second place, while Goodyear followed fellow Canadian Tracy down the outside line to depose Fittipaldi for third. Next came the second Kmart/Texaco Havoline Lola of Mario Andretti, who already had incurred the wrath of fifth-fastest qualifier Johansson. The Swede had been full of optimism prior to the race, but failed even to take the green flag due to contact with Andretti as the pair exited the hairpin on the pace lap. Poor Johansson reckoned he had been shoved into the wall. He was distinctly unimpressed.

The entire field was obliged to complete the first four laps under caution while Johansson's damaged car was removed, whereupon

Tracy immediately rocketed away into the lead. Within two laps he had stretched his advantage over Mansell to an amazing 5.22 seconds.

Teammate Fittipaldi, however, was in trouble. His Chevy/C engine was drastically down on boost. Curiously, his team decided against making an early stop, so Fittipaldi slipped quickly down the order. He went a lap down as well after only 17 laps.

Finally, after repairs were made, he was able to circulate almost as quickly as the leaders, although by then all hopes of victory were long gone. He finished a frustrated 13th, three laps down and just out of the points.

There were no such problems for Tracy, who pulled out a ten-second lead over Mansell in the first 35 laps. The youngster was negotiating traffic like a seasoned veteran rather than one whose Indy Car debut came only two years ago on the same Long Beach circuit. But then on lap 37 he picked up a puncture after apparently running over a piece of debris.

'I felt a slight vibration and then the tire came off the rim,' related Tracy, who was able to limp back to the pits for a fresh left-rear. He rejoined the race in seventh place.

The pit stop wasn't too costly, however, since it was almost time in any case for the first round of scheduled fuel stops.

Mansell led, to the delight of the crowd, until making his own stop on lap 43. By the time the other leaders had taken service, Tracy had regained the upper hand, closely pursued by Goodyear. Mansell and a charging Al Unser Jr also were chasing hard.

Unser had struggled in the first two races, due primarily to an almost total lack of test time with

Rick Galles' Valvoline-backed Lola-Chevy/C; but he made steady progress throughout the weekend and set fastest lap in the final warmup on race morning. Now, with the leaders in his sight and on a track at which he habitually shines, Unser began to place Mansell under pressure.

Their battle, initially for third place, gained greater significance on lap 53 when second-placed Goodyear was called into the pits for a stop-and-go penalty. He had exceeded the mandatory 70 mph speed limit in pit lane on his first stop.

Two laps later, Unser made an ill-fated bid to pass Mansell in the tight Turn One/Two right-left complex. Afterward Unser claimed Mansell deliberately took him out.

'I set up Nigel on the exit of Turn One and was ready to pass him on the exit of Turn Two,' related the 1990 PPG Cup champion. 'I've never seen anyone block me as bad as Nigel blocked me today. He parked me against the wall.'

Needless to say, Mansell's version of the incident was somewhat at variance with Unser's.

'I didn't see what happened,' said Mansell. 'I felt it. It's very narrow at that point on the track and it's very, very difficult to pass. I think he tried to do what we call a shit-or-bust maneuver . . . and, well, something went bust, didn't it?'

In any case Unser's crash brought out the second full-course caution of the afternoon. Then, soon after the race resumed, Tracy picked up another puncture following contact as he tried to put a lap on Danny Sullivan's eighth-placed Molson Lola-Chevy/C.

Again Tracy was able to duck immediately into the pit. This time he rejoined in sixth position, and with a full tank of fuel.

Mansell regained the lead as a result of Tracy's misfortune, while Roberto Guerrero moved up to second after a consistent run in his Lola-Chevy/C. Andretti ran

third, pursued by Raul Boesel, who also had moved up well in Dick Simon's Duracell/Mobil 1/Sadia Lola-Ford/Cosworth, and Goodyear, who, to his intense annoyance, had been assessed a second stop-and-go penalty.

The order remained unchanged until lap 73, when the caution flags flew again due to a contretemps at the tight Turn Eight hairpin between Eddie Cheever and Robby Gordon (Copenhagen Lola-Ford). The pair already had made contact earlier in the race. Both were later admonished for their actions.

Most of the leaders were able to take advantage of the interruption to make their final stop for fuel. Once again the order was shuffled, with Andretti muscling ahead of Mansell as the Newman-Haas pair accelerated spectacularly out of their pit stalls. Both, however, resumed behind Tracy, who, having stopped just a dozen laps earlier, already had enough fuel on board to go the distance.

Tracy led confidently when the green flags waved again on lap 78,

tailed by Andretti and Mansell. Next up were Boesel, Guerrero, a consistent Rahal and Goodyear.

From there on, Tracy judged his race perfectly. There was not the slightest hint of a slip. He pulled out an appreciable advantage, then set a conservative pace as others ran either into mechanical trouble or the unforgiving concrete walls.

Andretti, the erstwhile PPG Cup points leader, ran out of luck when his engine abruptly failed with just ten laps to go. He was running solidly in second place at the time. Boesel's hopes of another podium finish evaporated just over two laps from the end due to an electrical short-circuit. Goodyear also fell by the wayside on lap 99 after clipping the wall at the exit of the hairpin and breaking his car's suspension.

So Rahal, who had gradually picked up his pace, moved gratefully into second place, posting by far the best result to date for his Don Halliday-designed chassis.

Mansell, *sans* second gear, was delighted to finish third given his physical and mechanical problems.

Teo Fabi, who had run a lonely eighth with ten laps to go, inherited fourth in Hall/VDS Racing's Pennzoil Lola-Chevy/C, while the ever-unlucky Guerrero slipped to fifth, one lap down, when his engine began misfiring with just a few laps remaining.

Next was a delighted Robbie Buhl, who drove splendidly in

Dale Coyne Racing's year-old Mi-Jack Lola-Chevy/A. Buhl, the reigning Firestone Indy Lights champion, had moved up spiritedly from his 23rd starting position to record a first-ever top-six finish for the enthusiastic but perennially under-financed team.

When the dust had settled after an absolutely enthralling event,

Tracy emerged with a well-deserved maiden victory for himself, the new Chevrolet/C engine and the latest Nigel Bennett-designed Penske chassis. It was also team owner Roger Penske's first-ever victory in Long Beach and the perfect morale-booster for his team as the hype began to build up for Indianapolis.

Above: Wild celebrations from the Marlboro Racing Team Penske pit crew at the finish as Paul Tracy scores his first Indy Car victory.

Below: Bobby Rahal qualified 11th in the troubled Ragal/Hogan 001 (*née* Truesports) chassis. But come the race luck was on the side of the defending champion, who finished in a strong second place.

SNIPPETS

• Willy T. Ribbs announced over the weekend he would return to the PPG Cup series having inked a deal with team owner Derrick Walker, long-time mentor and internationally famous actor/comedian Bill Cosby and new sponsor Service Merchandise. 'This is not just the proudest moment of my career, it's the proudest moment of my life,' declared Ribbs.

• Nigel Mansell was a hit on the track and off. As part of his sponsorship commitments, Mansell drew an estimated 600 people to an autograph session at a nearby Kmart department store. 'I've never had a store visit like this in my life,' said Kmart's Darlene Park. 'Nigel was great. He was so accommodating. But it was quite scary, to tell you the truth. We had three local police officers and two hired security guards and we still had trouble getting him out of the store.' Meanwhile at a charity auction before the race, one of Mansell's helmets easily broke all records when it sold for $11,700.

• John Andretti, replaced last fall at Hall/VDS Racing by Italian Teo Fabi, was present in the hope of resurrecting his Indy Car career. In the meantime he had been pursuing a variety of avenues aimed at broadening his career opportunities. The following weekend, Andretti made his debut in an NHRA Top Fuel dragster, qualifying at a superb 4.99 seconds, with an elapsed time of 298 mph, and then defeating reigning champion Joe Amato in the first round of Eliminations.

• Several drivers experienced the wrath of IndyCar chief steward Wally Dallenbach following a series of incidents during the race. The most serious offender was young Robby Gordon *(right)*, who was disqualified from his 21st-place finish, fined $5000 and placed on one year's probation for unsportsmanlike conduct and unsportsmanlike driving following two on-track incidents with Eddie Cheever.

TOYOTA GRAND PRIX OF LONG BEACH, LONG BEACH STREET CIRCUIT, LONG BEACH, CALIFORNIA • 18 April, 105 laps – 166.950 miles

Place	Driver	No.	Car	Q Speed (mph)	Q Time	Q Pos.	Laps	Time/Retirement	Ave. speed	Pts
1	**Paul Tracy**	12	*Marlboro* Penske PC22-Chevy/C	107.705	53.145s	2	105	1h 47m 36.418	93.089 mph	21
2	**Bobby Rahal**	1	*Miller Genuine Draft* Rahal/Hogan 001-Chevy/C	106.453	53.770s	11	105	1h 47m 49.076	92.907	16
3	**Nigel Mansell**	5	*Kmart/Texaco Havoline* Lola T93/00-Ford	108.198	52.903s	1	105	1h 47m 55.883s	92.809	15
4	**Teo Fabi**	8	*Pennzoil Special* Lola T93/00-Chevy/C	106.875	53.558s	7	105	1h 48m 29.331s	92.332	12
5	**Roberto Guerrero**	40	*Budweiser King* Lola T93/00-Chevy/C	105.040	54.494s	18	104	Running		10
6	**Robbie Buhl**	19	*Mi-Jack* Lola T92/00-Chevy/A	103.402	55.357s	23	104	Running		8
7	**Scott Pruett**	45	*Tobacco-Free America* Lola T91/00-Chevy/A	105.845	54.079s	15	103	Running		6
8	**Danny Sullivan**	7	*Molson* Lola T93/00-Chevy/C	105.151	53.923s	12	103	Running		5
9	**Eddie Cheever**	99	*Say NO To Drugs* Penske PC21-Chevy/B	106.464	53.765s	10	103	Running		4
10	**Mark Smith**	25	*Craftsman* Penske PC21-Chevy/B	105.989	54.006s	14	103	Running		3
11	**Arie Luyendyk**	10	*Target/Scotch Video* Lola T93/00-Ford	104.981	54.524s	19	103	Running		2
12	**Raul Boesel**	9	*Duracell/Mobil 1/Sadia* Lola T93/00-Ford	106.493	53.750s	9	102	Electrical		1
13	Emerson Fittipaldi	4	*Marlboro* Penske PC22-Chevy/C	107.548	53.223s	3	102	Running		
14	Hiro Matsushita	15	*Panasonic Special* Lola T93/00-Ford	104.971	54.530s	20	102	Running		
15	Ross Bentley	39	*AGFA/Rain-X* Lola T92/00-Chevy/A	102.641	55.822s	26	101	Running		
16	Scott Goodyear	2	*Mackenzie Special* Lola T93/00-Ford	107.529	53.232s	4	98	Accident		
17	Lyn St James	90	*JC Penney/Nike* Lola T92/00-Ford	99.345	57.618s	27	98	Running		
18	Mario Andretti	6	*Kmart/Texaco Havoline* Lola T93/00-Ford	107.238	53.376s	6	94	Electrical		
19	Buddy Lazier	20	*Viper/Applebee's* Lola T91/00-Chevy/A	103.069	55.536s	24	90	Running		
20	Jeff Wood	42	*Agip/Rubaway/Hawaiian Tropic* Lola T91/00-DFS	99.032	57.799s	28	88	Running		
21	Al Unser Jr	3	*Valvoline* Lola T93/00-Chevy/C	106.505	53.744s	8	53	Accident		
22	Jimmy Vasser	18	*Kodalux Processing/STP* Lola T92/00-Chevy/A	104.902	54.565s	21	36	Engine		
23	Adrian Fernandez	11	*Tecate/Amway Mexico* Lola T93/00-Chevy/C	105.318	54.350s	17	21	Engine		
24	Scott Brayton	22	*Amway/Northwest Airlines* Lola T93/00-Ford	105.474	54.269s	16	20	Gearbox		
25	Marco Greco	30	*Alfa Laval/Team Losi* Lola T92/00-Chevy/A	102.629	55.774s	25	19	Gearbox		
DNS	Stefan Johansson	16	*AMAX Energy & Metals* Penske PC22-Chevy/C	107.247	53.372s	5		Crashed before start		
DNS	David Kudrave	50	*Andrea Moda/Agip* Lola T92/00-Chevy/A	104.094	54.989s	22		Crashed in warmup		
DSQ	Robby Gordon	14	*Copenhagen Racing* Lola T93/00-Ford	106.027	53.986s	13	63	Accident		

Caution flags: Laps 0-3, accident/Johansson; laps 55-58, accident/Unser; laps 72-76, accident/Cheever and Gordon.

Lap leaders: Nigel Mansell, 1-4 (4 laps); Paul Tracy, 5-35 (31 laps); Nigel Mansell, 36-42 (7 laps); Paul Tracy, 43-60 (18 laps); Nigel Mansell, 61-73 (13 laps); Paul Tracy, 74-105 (32 laps). **Totals:** Paul Tracy, 81 laps; Nigel Mansell, 24 laps.

Championship positions: 1 Mansell, 36 pts; **2** Mario Andretti, 32; **3** Fabi, 26; **4** Rahal, 24; **5** Tracy, 22; **6** Boesel, 22; **7** Luyendyk, 20; **8** Fittipaldi, 17; **9** Vasser, 14; **10** Gordon, 14; **11** Al Unser Jr, 12; **12** Pruett, 12; **13** Guerrero, 10; **14** Cheever, 10; **15** Buhl, 8; **16** Smith, 7; **17** Sullivan, 5; **18** Kudrave, 5; **19** Matsushita, 5; **20** Goodyear, 4; **21** Greco, 2; **22** Bentley, 1; **23** Johansson, 1.

INDY 500

Mario Andretti led more than twice as many laps as anyone else in the 77th running of the fabled Indianapolis 500 with Newman-Haas Racing's Kmart/Texaco Havoline Lola T93/00-Ford/Cosworth XB.

Now 53 years old but having maintained as much desire to win as most drivers half his age, Andretti was seeking to end a long sequence of disappointments in the world's most prestigious single motor racing event. Things were looking good for Andretti, who has led the race so many times and yet won it only once, way back in 1969. Once again, though, he was to fall short.

As a reminder of why the race is billed as 'The Greatest Spectacle in Racing', five different leaders emerged in a thrilling final phase to what had been a superb race. A record ten drivers finished on the lead lap after 200 laps, 500 miles.

Finally, it was Emerson Fittipaldi *(below)* who emerged to claim an emotional victory for Marlboro Racing Team Penske on the 25th anniversary of team owner Roger Penske's first appearance at the Indianapolis Motor Speedway.

'The whole team did a beautiful job,' praised the Brazilian, who also won the race in 1989. 'You need the best team to win and we had the best team. Everything worked like a Swiss watch. This was the best race of my life, no question.'

Fittipaldi had languished in the midst of the lead group for much of the race. And contentedly so. He was delighted with the way his Penske-Chevrolet/C was performing and was anxious not to abuse his equipment. The team made not so much as a single change to the PC22's setup all afternoon. Fittipaldi merely paced himself, moved up into contention when necessary, and was perfectly poised to take the lead for the first time with just 16 laps remaining. It was a textbook victory.

Pole-winner Arie Luyendyk had nothing to offer Fittipaldi in the waning stages with Chip Ganassi's Target/Scotch Video Lola-Ford/Cosworth, while a brilliant drive by Indy rookie Nigel Mansell netted third place for Newman-Haas Racing. Teammate Andretti wound up a disappointed fifth after complaining of a slight handling imbalance on his final set of tires.

Photos: Michael C. Brown

1st – FITTIPALDI   **2nd – LUYENDYK**   **3rd – MANSELL**

The most coveted prize in Indy Car racing. Immortal faces gaze from the magnificent Borg Warner trophy, awarded to the winner of the Indianapolis 500-mile race.

The 'Month of May' sees Indianapolis take center stage. It is the prestige event in Indy Car racing, and faces new and old are in demand from the news-hungry press to fill endless column inches during the drawn-out weeks of qualifying.

Amongst those making the news this year were *(top left)* Stephan Gregoire, who was the fastest rookie, qualifying 15th, and vastly experienced champion Bobby Rahal *(top right)*, who failed to qualify his troublesome Rahal/Hogan machine. Nelson Piquet *(above)* made a brave return to the Brickyard after last year's horrendous accident. A.J. Foyt officially announced his retirement from driving, but put in a few farewell laps to mark the occasion for the crowd.

QUALIFYING

An exciting four days of Time Trials, run as per tradition over two consecutive weekends, saw Arie Luyendyk assure himself of the coveted pole position with a four-lap average of 223.967 mph. Yet two of the biggest stories concerned not so much who did make the 33-car field as who did not.

Bobby Rahal, the defending PPG Indy Car World Series champion, was bumped from the field during a dramatic final hour on the final day, and his last-ditch attempt just before the track closed at 6 p.m. wasn't fast enough to get the Miller Genuine Draft Rahal/Hogan into the race.

The other center of attention was, as ever, A.J. Foyt. The four-time Indy 500 winner squeezed his portly, 58-year-old frame into one of his Copenhagen Lola-Fords during the first week of practice and was soon lapping competitively at better than 221 mph. Then, just minutes prior to the start of qualifying on the first Saturday, and not long after his protégé Robby Gordon had crashed in Turn One, Foyt suddenly – and emotionally – announced his retirement.

On the final weekend, Foyt invited his own godson, the previously unemployed John Andretti, to drive one of his 1992 Lola-Ford/Cosworths. Andretti responded by posting the best time of the weekend at 221.746 mph. His speed was sixth fastest overall, although the quirky qualifying rules at Indy meant he would have to start the race from the outside of row eight.

Competition even to get onto the grid was fierce. First-day qualifier Kevin Cogan (Conseco Lola-Chevy/C) was the slowest of all at 217.230 mph. A total of 11 drivers were unable to make the grade, with former Grand Prix driver Eddie Cheever, who started on the front row last year, almost joining the list of non-qualifiers.

Cheever was 'bumped' from the field on Day Three and was unable to coax enough speed from his backup car, another year-old Penske PC21-Chevy/B. Instead, he arranged a deal to take over a Buick-powered '92 Lola from Team Menard. Despite a bare minimum of practice, Cheever ventured out with less than 45 minutes remaining and posted a time fast enough to squeeze out Rahal.

Only five of the 11 'rookie' (first-year) candidates made the show. The most publicized, of course, were former F1 World Champions Nelson Piquet (Arisco Lola-Buick), who overcame the terrible injuries he suffered a year earlier and another non-damaging incident early in practice, and Nigel Mansell. Both qualified comfortably.

Mansell was most impressive. He missed the first few days of practice while recovering from back surgery (a legacy of his crash at Phoenix in April) but immediately bounced into contention by setting fourth-fastest time, 222.855 mph, on his very first day at the track.

Mansell's qualifying run, however, was slightly disappointing. His average of 220.255 mph was good enough only for row three, sandwiched between the Marlboro Penske pair of talented youngster Paul Tracy and veteran Emerson Fittipaldi.

The mantle of fastest rookie fell to unheralded Frenchman Stephan Gregoire, who recorded a fine 220.851 mph run in a year-old Lola-Buick entered by Formula Project.

No one, though, could match Luyendyk. The 39-year-old Dutchman set the stage for his first-ever Indy Car pole by establishing the fastest lap during the previous week of practice at 226.182 mph. After complaining of a speed-sapping 'push' (read understeer) which caused him to abort his first qualifying attempt, a few subtle changes to his car's setup were enough to make the difference.

'When I went out [for the qualifying run], I wasn't really that confident,' said Luyendyk, who earlier in the day had waved off an attempt after completing one lap at a disappointing average of 215.254 mph. 'I wasn't thinking, in the back of my mind, that I was going to put it on the pole, I was thinking about being in the first two or three rows [of the grid].'

Luyendyk claimed the $100,000 PPG Pole Award for his effort, as well as capturing Ford's first pole at Indy since Al Unser achieved the feat in 1970.

RACE

As ever at Indianapolis, a vast crowd was on hand for the traditional 11 a.m. start. The morning was a pleasant one, the sky a hazy blue, although weather forecasters had predicted a distinct possibility of afternoon thunderstorms. Thankfully, they did not materialize until well after the race was over.

Once the parades had been concluded and the bands had struck their final chords, Nick Fornoro, who retired at the end of the 1992 season after 14 years as the official starter of CART Indy Car events, fulfilled one of his lifetime ambitions as he joined USAC Chief Starter Duane Sweeney on the starter's gantry and joyously waved the green flag to get the serious business under way. Fornoro was the first Honorary Starter to be employed in the fabled history of the Indianapolis 500.

Luyendyk paced the field in a somewhat ragged formation, but the start was clean. Raul Boesel moved his Duracell/Mobil 1/Sadia Lola-Ford/Cosworth smartly across from the outside of the front row to take the lead from Luyendyk and fellow front-row qualifier Mario Andretti. In spite of some pessimistic predictions to the contrary, the entire field made it around the first lap without undue incident.

Al Unser Jr nosed his Valvoline Lola-Chevy/C ahead of nemesis Scott Goodyear's Mackenzie Financial Lola-Ford/Cosworth for fourth, followed by a trio of Penske-Chevy/Cs led by impressive rookie Stefan Johansson in Tony Bettenhausen's AMAX-sponsored PC22. Behind the two factory cars of Fittipaldi and Canadian teammate Paul Tracy came Mansell, who was content to maintain a watching brief.

'Going down into the first corner behind eight or nine cars, there's no air [to give the car downforce] and then the [methanol] fumes make your eyes water,' declared Mansell. 'It was a very impressive sight and I had to remind myself I was driving as opposed to watching.'

Out in front, Boesel took off in confident style. He had been delighted with Dick Simon's car all month long and was in a forthright mood. Within eight laps Boesel had pulled out an advantage of over five seconds, lapping at better than 214 mph.

Luyendyk and Andretti circulated close together in second and third places, with veteran Andretti taking over the position on lap 12. A little farther back, Fittipaldi was beginning to make his presence felt. By lap 15 he had moved up into a challenging fifth place. The Brazilian's car was handling entirely to his liking.

The pace soon was slowed, however, when the caution lights flashed on for the first time on lap 16. Jim Crawford, running toward the back of the pack with one of drag racing star Kenny Bernstein's trio of Budweiser King Lola-Chevrolets, had spun in Turn Two. The Scotsman, miraculously, avoided contact with anything solid.

The full-course caution heralded the first round of pit stops, although several runners elected to roll the dice. Instead of taking service, they decided to stay out on the track, preferring to make up valuable track position and hope there would be another caution before they, too, needed to

Putting the emphasis on skill – and safety

Talk throughout practice and qualifying at Indianapolis was centered upon the changes to the track which had been implemented since last year. Speedway officials, in an attempt to slow the cars, had installed a new grass verge on the inside of each of the four turns. The modifications effectively narrowed the race track and forced drivers to use the 'traditional' line around the corners instead of allowing them to cut deep inside the boundary white line and onto the old asphalt 'apron'.

The changes were not universally popular. Some drivers complained that the narrower racing 'groove' heightened the possibility of an accident and that the grass eliminated a potential 'escape route' in case of emergency avoidance. Others claimed the alterations placed even more of a premium on chassis setup.

The majority, however, were in favor. Car setup has always been a critical factor in determining lap speeds. Incidents which occurred during practice and the race were notably less catastrophic than in recent years, due primarily to the fact the impacts with the walls tended to be at far less acute angles.

In 1992, Nelson Piquet and Jeff Andretti received extensive leg and feet injuries after virtual head-on impacts, while Jovy Marcelo lost his life. Hiro Matsushita, Pancho Carter, Jim Crawford, Mario Andretti and Jimmy Vasser all suffered broken bones. A total of 14 drivers were taken to Methodist Hospital during the month, including eight on raceday.

This year only two drivers visited Methodist. Robbie Buhl (Mi-Jack Lola-Buick) was treated for a concussion after a crash in Turn Two and Canadian Ross Bentley (AGFA/Rain-X Lola-Buick) received attention to burns after his car caught fire due to a fuel leak.

The drastically shorter injury list was attributable both to the track changes and some modifications to the rules which demand stronger chassis, with particular attention to the area around the driver's feet.

Speeds, too, were much reduced, with the fastest lap of the race turned by winner Fittipaldi at 214.807 mph just two laps from the end. Last year Michael Andretti posted the fastest lap at 229.118 mph, some seven mph faster than the previous record.

The consensus was that the alterations certainly didn't improve the prospect for overtaking but that they placed a greater emphasis on driver skill. In the past, assuming the car was properly set up, it was no problem to take all four corners 'flat'. Not so this year. Talent and commitment were the primary factors. And isn't that what motor racing is all about?

Michael C. Brown

Michael C. Brown

take on fuel and fresh tires.

Kevin Cogan, starting his first race since suffering a badly broken right arm and leg in a crash at Indy two years ago, was among those not to stop. Cogan took over the lead with Galles Racing International's Lola-Chevy/C. It was the first time one of Rick Galles' cars had led a lap of PPG Cup competition this year.

A few laps after the restart, Al Unser, seeking to become the first-ever five-time Indy 500 winner, took over the running with another of Bernstein's Budweiser Lola-Chevy/Cs.

The gamble by Unser, Cogan and a few others looked to have paid off when the caution flags came out again on lap 30. Danny Sullivan, the 1985 Indy 500 champion, had crashed in Turn Three due to an apparent suspension failure on his Molson Lola. Sullivan emerged unscathed after a heavy impact.

Mario Andretti took his turn at the front of the field when Unser was obliged to stop, only for Luyendyk to motor past him just before one-quarter distance. Already there had been six different leaders, with French rookie Stephan Gregoire credited with leading one lap under an earlier caution period.

John Andretti (Lola T92/00-Ford/Cosworth) and Copenhagen Racing/Foyt teammate Robby Gordon, another rookie, also took turns in front as the race progressed toward halfway, as did Mansell, who certainly wasn't driving as if this was his very first start on an oval.

Mansell's teammate, Mario Andretti, looked solidly in charge of proceedings at the 100-lap mark, followed by the elder Unser. If ever there was an example of the benefit of experience, this was it. Between them, Andretti and Unser could boast 53 previous starts in this once-a-year extravaganza.

Unser's own son also was well in contention, running third as he

sought to become the first man to win back-to-back Indy 500s since 'Big Al' himself achieved the feat in 1970 and '71. Luyendyk ran fourth at 250 miles, followed by a consistent Scott Brayton (Amway Lola-Ford/Cosworth) and Mansell, who had lost some time by overshooting his pit during a scheduled stop.

'Hey, I'm a rookie,' noted Mansell self-mockingly. 'I missed my pit. I drove straight past it.'

Goodyear, John Andretti, Roberto Guerrero (in Bernstein's third Budweiser Lola-Chevy/C) and Fittipaldi rounded out the top ten, the Brazilian also having lost ground when he erroneously stopped at the wrong pit stall! Fittipaldi was duly waved on his way.

Boesel had slipped down to 13th, a lap down, after being assessed a stop-and-go penalty for overtaking Mario Andretti on his way out of the pits.

At this stage in the race as many as ten drivers held legitimate hopes of victory in what was turning out to be a thoroughly absorbing event.

Mario Andretti wasn't content with that. Still looking for that elusive second success, Andretti took charge as the race progressed toward the 300-mile mark. By lap 120, Andretti had stretched his lead to a full 23 seconds over Unser Jr. He in turn was being pressured by Mansell, who had impressively caught and passed Luyendyk, an acknowledged oval expert.

Lapping in tandem, Unser Jr and Mansell clipped a second per lap from Andretti's cushion over the next seven laps.

Next time around the yellow flags were waving as the result of Mario's son, Jeff, having collided with Guerrero in Turn Three. Both cars hit the wall but neither driver was hurt.

The leaders in any case were due for their next scheduled pit stops. Unser Jr stopped on the lap before the caution lights flashed on, while Andretti was making

his way onto pit lane at that very moment.

Uniquely, however, the rules at Indianapolis call for the pits to be 'closed' when the yellow appears. Stops are permitted only after the cars have bunched up behind the pace car.

Andretti's crew thought he had 'beaten' the light. The officials decreed otherwise. A stop-and-go it would be, although curiously Andretti was allowed to serve his penalty under the yellow instead of the usual green. He was fortunate to lose only one position.

Unser Jr took advantage of his earlier stop to lead at the restart. Andretti chased after him and soon began looking for a way past. His opportunity came on lap 152. Unser's father also continued to run well, although he then started to fall away as his engine began to overheat.

Instead it was Fittipaldi who took up the challenge, followed by Mansell and the persistent Brayton. Boesel, too, was on a charge, having regained the lead lap.

On lap 174, following another caution when Gordon's gearbox expired, Mansell pulled off the maneuver of the race. The Englishman had been running third in line as the green flag waved, but instantly surged past both Andretti and Fittipaldi.

Mansell, first oval race or no, was looking good for victory.

Then came another caution after a good run by Lyn St James ended when her 15th-placed JC Penney/Nike Lola-Ford/Cosworth ground to a halt at the pit entrance. This time on the restart, Mansell's lack of experience on the ovals showed. He was caught napping as both Fittipaldi and Luyendyk roared past.

Fittipaldi was in the lead – for the first time. And, boy, did he make it count. The Brazilian rose to the occasion magnificently, turning his fastest laps of the race at better than 211 mph.

There was one final caution after Mansell, pushing as hard as

Nigel Mansell was again sensational on an oval track. But for a late yellow flag he could well have been the victor, but third place was a superb achievement nonetheless.

he knew how, sideswiped the wall on the exit of Turn Two. He was lucky. There was no damage. Just a telltale black mark on the retaining wall and a corresponding white stripe on his right-side tires.

Fittipaldi did not allow the interruption to disturb his concentration. When the green flag was waved one last time, just five laps remained. It was all or nothing.

Fittipaldi was ready. This time the pace was even faster, as he circulated at better than 214 mph. Neither Luyendyk nor anyone else could offer a serious challenge in the closing miles.

'We did it! We did it!' enthused an ecstatic Fittipaldi. 'Roger Penske and all the team, they did a beautiful job.'

Luyendyk had to be content with second, struggling to overcome a loose-handling car in the latter stages, while Mansell survived his close scrape to finish third.

'The team did a fantastic job, and what mistakes were made today were made by me,' he concluded honestly. 'But I'm happy. I don't mind being beaten because I've been beaten by Emerson and Arie. They deserved to be first and second.'

An inspired Boesel battled brilliantly to fourth place despite two stop-and-go penalties, which he felt cost him a legitimate shot at his first Indy Car victory.

'I've no idea why I had two penalties,' said an irate Boesel. 'In my mind I won this race.'

Boesel was followed by Mario Andretti, whose car, like Unser Jr's, developed a handling imbalance in the closing laps. Next came Brayton and Goodyear. Unser Jr, Teo Fabi (Hall/VDS Racing's Pennzoil Lola-Chevy/C) and John Andretti also were on the lead lap at the finish.

INDIANAPOLIS 500, INDIANAPOLIS MOTOR SPEEDWAY, SPEEDWAY, INDIANAPOLIS, INDIANA • 30 May, 200 laps – 500.000 miles

Place	Driver	No.	Car	Q Speed (mph)	Q Time	Q Pos.	Laps	Time/Retirement	Ave. speed	Pts
1	Emerson Fittipaldi	4	*Marlboro* Penske PC22-Chevy/C	220.150	2m 43.525s	9	200	3h 10m 49.860s	157.207 mph	20
2	Arie Luyendyk	10	*Target/Scotch Video* Lola T93/00-Ford	223.967	2m 40.738s	1	200	3h 10m 52.722s	157.168	17
3	Nigel Mansell	5	*Kmart/Texaco Havoline* Lola T93/00-Ford	220.255	2m 43.447s	8	200	3h 10m 54.608s	157.149	14
4	Raul Boesel	9	*Duracell/Mobil 1/Sadia* Lola T93/00-Ford	222.379	2m 41.886s	3	200	3h 10m 54.977s	157.142	12
5	Mario Andretti	6	*Kmart/Texaco Havoline* Lola T93/00-Ford	223.414	2m 41.136s	2	200	3h 10m 55.264s	157.133	11
6	Scott Brayton	22	*Amway/Jonathan Byrd's* Lola T93/00-Ford	219.637	2m 43.907s	11	200	3h 10m 57.743s	157.117	8
7	Scott Goodyear	2	*Mackenzie Special* Lola T93/00-Ford	222.344	2m 41.911s	4	200	3h 10m 58.083s	157.099	6
8	Al Unser Jr	3	*Valvoline* Lola T93/00-Chevy/C	221.773	2m 42.328s	5	200	3h 10m 59.858s	157.070	5
9	Teo Fabi	8	*Pennzoil Special* Lola T93/00-Chevy/C	220.514	2m 43.255s	17	200	3h 11m 06.557s	156.968	4
10	John Andretti	84	*Copenhagen Racing* Lola T92/00-Ford	221.746	2m 42.348s	24	200	3h 11m 06.898s	156.964	3
11	Stefan Johansson	16	*AMAX Energy & Metals* Penske PC22-Chevy/C	220.824	2m 43.026s	6	199	Running		2
12	Al Unser	80	*Budweiser King* Lola T93/00-Chevy/C	217.453	2m 45.553s	23	199	Running		1
13	Jimmy Vasser	18	*Kodalux Processing/STP* Lola T92/00-Ford	218.967	2m 44.408s	19	198	Running		
14	Kevin Cogan	11	*Conseco Special* Lola T93/00-Chevy/C	217.230	2m 45.723s	14	198	Running		
15	Davy Jones	50	*Andrea Moda/Agip* Lola T92/00-Chevy/A	218.416	2m 44.823s	28	197	Running		
16	Eddie Cheever	59	*Glidden/Menard Special* Lola T92/00-Buick	217.599	2m 45.442s	33	197	Running		
17	Gary Bettenhausen	51	*Glidden Paint Special* Lola T93/00-Menard/Buick	220.380	2m 43.354s	18	197	Running		
18	Hiro Matsushita	15	*Panasonic Special* Lola T93/00-Ford	219.949	2m 43.674s	26	197	Running		
19	Stephan Gregoire	36	*Formula Project/Maalox/GSF* Lola T92/00-Buick	220.851	2m 43.006s	15	195	Running		
20	Tony Bettenhausen	76	*AMAX Energy & Metals* Penske PC22-Chevy/C	218.034	2m 45.112s	22	195	Running		
21	Willy T. Ribbs	75	*Cosby/Service Merchandise* Lola T92/00-Ford	217.711	2m 45.357s	30	194	Running		
22	Didier Theys	92	*Delta Faucet/Kinko's* Lola T92/00-Buick	217.752	2m 45.326s	32	193	Running		
23	Dominic Dobson	66	*Coors Light/Indy Parks* Galmer G92B-Chevy/A	218.776	2m 44.552s	27	193	Running		
24	Jim Crawford	60	*Budweiser King* Lola T93/00-Chevy/C	217.612	2m 45.432s	31	192	Running		
25	Lyn St James	90	*JC Penney/Nike* Lola T93/00-Ford	218.042	2m 45.106s	21	176	Engine		
26	Geoff Brabham	27	*Glidden/Menard Special* Lola T93/00-Menard/Buick	217.800	2m 45.289s	29	174	Engine		
27	Robby Gordon	41	*Copenhagen Racing* Lola T93/00-Ford	220.085	2m 43.573s	25	165	Engine		
28	Roberto Guerrero	40	*Budweiser King* Lola T93/00-Chevy/C	219.645	2m 43.901s	10	125	Accident		
29	Jeff Andretti	21	*Interstate Battery/Gillette 1* Lola T92/00-Buick	220.572	2m 43.212s	16	124	Accident		
30	Paul Tracy	12	*Marlboro* Penske PC22-Chevy/C	220.298	2m 43.415s	7	94	Accident		
31	Stan Fox	91	*Delta Faucet/Jack's Tool* Lola T91/00-Buick	218.765	2m 44.560s	20	64	Engine		
32	Nelson Piquet	77	*Arisco/STP Special* Lola T93/00-Menard/Buick	217.949	2m 45.176s	13	38	Engine		
33	Danny Sullivan	7	*Molson* Lola T93/00-Chevy/C	219.428	2m 44.063s	12	29	Accident		

Caution flags: Laps 16-20, spin/Crawford; laps 31-37, accident/Sullivan; laps 89-93, debris on track; laps 95-103, accident/Tracy; laps 128-138, accident/Jeff Andretti and Guerrero; laps 169-174, Gordon/stalled; laps 183-185, St James/stalled; laps 193-195, accident/Mansell.

Lap leaders: Raul Boesel, 1-17 (17 laps); Stephan Gregoire, 18 (1 lap); Kevin Cogan, 19-22 (4 laps); Al Unser, 23-31 (9 laps); Mario Andretti, 32-46 (15 laps); Arie Luyendyk, 47-57 (11 laps); Al Unser, 58-63 (6 laps); John Andretti, 64-65 (2 laps); Robby Gordon, 66-67 (2 laps); Scott Goodyear, 68-69 (2 laps); Nigel Mansell, 70-91 (22 laps); Mario Andretti, 92-128 (37 laps); Nigel Mansell, 129-130 (2 laps); Arie Luyendyk, 131-132 (2 laps); Mario Andretti, 133 (1 lap); Arie Luyendyk, 134 (1 lap); Al Unser Jr, 135-151 (17 laps); Mario Andretti, 152-168 (17 laps); Scott Goodyear, 169-171 (3 laps); Mario Andretti, 172 (1 lap); Raul Boesel, 173 (1 lap); Mario Andretti, 174 (1 lap); Nigel Mansell, 175-184 (10 laps); Emerson Fittipaldi, 185-200 (16 laps). ***Totals:*** Mario Andretti, 72 laps; Nigel Mansell, 34 laps; Raul Boesel, 18 laps; Al Unser Jr, 17 laps; Emerson Fittipaldi, 16 laps; Al Unser, 15 laps; Arie Luyendyk, 14 laps; Scott Goodyear, 5 laps; Kevin Cogan, 4 laps; John Andretti, 2 laps; Robby Gordon, 2 laps; Stephan Gregoire, 1 lap.

Championship positions: **1** Mansell, 50 pts; **2** Mario Andretti, 43; **3** Fittipaldi, 37; **4** Luyendyk, 37; **5** Boesel, 34; **6** Fabi, 30; **7** Rahal, 24; **8** Tracy, 22; **9** Al Unser Jr, 17; **10** Vasser, 14; **11** Gordon, 14; **12** Pruett, 12; **13** Guerrero, 10; **14** Cheever, 10; **15** Goodyear, 10; **16** Brayton, 8; **17** Buhl, 8; **18** Smith, 7; **19** Sullivan, 5; **20** Kudrave, 5; **21** Matsushita, 5; **22** John Andretti, 3; **23** Johansson, 3; **24** Greco, 2; **25** Bentley, 1; **26** Al Unser, 1.

SNIPPETS

• The Marmon Group of companies, a direct descendant of the firm which produced the Marmon Wasp and won the very first Indianapolis 500 with Ray Harroun in 1911, was represented in this year's race by John Andretti. The sponsorship was switched after Eric Bachelart failed to qualify Dale Coyne's Lola-Buick due to a variety of misfortunes.

• Jeff Sinden and Joe Kennedy, who run Team Menard on behalf of wealthy building supply merchant John Menard, bore the brunt of one of Nelson Piquet's practical jokes early in the month of May when an advertisement appeared in a local newspaper offering a Lear jet for sale at a knock-down price. The phone lines soon were ringing incessantly.

• Fittipaldi eschewed the traditional bottle of milk in Victory Lane, instead gaining refreshment from a flagon of orange juice produced from his own plantations in Brazil. He later relented and took a sip of the white beverage, although the following weekend Fittipaldi was roundly booed when he was introduced prior to the race in Milwaukee, situated on the edge of 'America's Dairyland'.

• Lola development engineer John Travis, working with the Budweiser King team of Kenny Bernstein, estimated that the warm and humid weather conditions prevalent through much of the first week of practice were reducing the cars' downforce by as much as 150 lb, or around 7.5 percent.

• Firestone confirmed in an announcement at Indianapolis that it will return to Indy Car competition on a full-time basis in 1995, following an extensive test and development program next season. Firestone withdrew from the series in 1974, following a bitter tire war with Goodyear.

• In recent years, the 'race pace' at Indianapolis frequently has been above 220 mph. Laps in the 214–220 mph range were the norm. But this year, even clear of traffic, the leaders rarely circulated at better than 210 mph. When there were slower cars to negotiate, the pace was around 200 mph and often below that mark. The action, though, was no less intense than before. Drivers, crews and fans alike agreed this was the most interesting Indianapolis 500 in years.

MILWAUKEE

Michael C. Brown

Nigel Mansell is a good student. His first encounter with a 'short' (one-mile) oval at Phoenix ended in a painful accident without him even starting the race. More recently, on his 'superspeedway' debut at Indianapolis, Mansell had lost his chance of victory with a moment's hesitation following a full-course caution late in the race.

Mansell clearly benefited from those experiences. In the Miller Genuine Draft 200, run over 200 laps of the demanding Milwaukee Mile, the Englishman drove a textbook race at the wheel of his Kmart/Texaco Havoline Lola-Ford/Cosworth to score a superb victory for Newman-Haas Racing.

Even a caution inside the final five laps failed to upset his concentration. Mansell calmly jumped ahead when the green flag waved with two laps remaining and held off the Duracell/Mobil 1/Sadia Lola-Ford/Cosworth of pole-winner Raul Boesel to the checkered flag.

'This makes up a little bit for Indy, because at the restart I was ready,' said Mansell. 'I bunched them up. I'm a quick learner. But I'll tell you, Raul still got too close for comfort.'

Boesel, ever the bridesmaid it seems, had to settle for second again, tying his best Indy Car result, while countryman Emerson Fittipaldi, fresh off his Indianapolis 500 victory one week earlier, finished a close third with his Marlboro Penske-Chevy. Bobby Rahal was the final unlapped finisher in a brand-new Miller Genuine Draft Lola-Chevy/C.

1st – MANSELL   **2nd – BOESEL**   **3rd – FITTIPALDI**

Main photo: **The start, with Boesel and Fittipaldi on the front row ahead of Tracy and Goodyear on row two, followed by Andretti, Brayton, Mansell, Gordon, Rahal and the rest.**

Inset left: **After coming close at Indy, Mansell was not to be denied in the 200-miler at Milwaukee. Ecstatic at his first oval win, Nigel throws his hat to the adoring crowd.**

Below: **Roberto Guerrero struggled home in seventh spot with the Budweiser King Lola.**

QUALIFYING

Boesel became the second driver in as many races – and the third in the five held thus far – to earn his maiden Indy Car pole. The Brazilian struggled to match the front-running pace in practice on Friday, but wholesale changes to his car's setup Saturday morning brought the desired improvement.

'The team and especially my engineer, Julian Robertson, did a great job,' praised Boesel after shattering the track record with a lap at 165.752 mph. 'This pole is very important. It gives a big boost to the whole team.'

Fittipaldi, comfortably fastest on Friday, was forced to abort his initial qualifying attempt due to a lack of boost pressure. After the problem had been solved, Fittipaldi returned to the back of the line-up and, under IndyCar rules, was allowed only a single lap instead of the normal two.

'I knew I had only one lap,' he said, 'but even if I had a second lap,

I wouldn't have matched Raul's time. He did a very good job.'

Canadians Scott Goodyear (Mackenzie Financial Lola-Ford) and Paul Tracy (Marlboro Penske) shared row two, followed by Mario Andretti (Kmart/Texaco Havoline Lola-Ford) and Scott Brayton (Amway/Northwest Airlines Lola-Ford), who last year posted a career-best third-place finish at Milwaukee.

Mansell and fellow track debu-

tant Robby Gordon (Copenhagen Lola-Ford) were next on the grid. Both men circulated within one-tenth of a second of earning a front-row berth, exemplifying just how competitive the Indy Car series has become.

'We're getting closer,' declared Gordon. 'We've found two seconds since yesterday, so I'm happy. Qualifying doesn't mean much, especially on a short oval. It's pretty easy to pass here. I'm really looking forward to tomorrow.'

Rahal qualified ninth, having spent all of practice desperately trying to dial in his newly acquired Lola.

Another noteworthy effort was posted by Adrian Fernandez. The Mexican rookie, last year's Indy Lights winner at Milwaukee, had never before driven an Indy car on an oval, and he blotted his copybook by spinning lightly into the wall on Saturday morning. Yet he still qualified comfortably ahead of his former PPG Cup champion teammates Danny Sullivan and Al Unser Jr. Indy pole-winner Arie Luyendyk (Target/Scotch Video Lola-Ford) also was embarrassed to be a lowly 22nd in the starting field.

RACE

There were four distinct phases to the Miller Genuine Draft 200, the first of which involved a tight, crowd-pleasing seven-car battle through the early stages of the race.

Boesel took off at the start like

he meant to continue. Fittipaldi, though, was equally determined not to let him get away. Goodyear also joined in the chase, while Gordon charged hard to make up four places inside the first couple of laps. Behind him came Tracy and the Newman-Haas pair, Andretti ahead of Mansell.

The first full-course caution came after only seven laps, when Stefan Johansson's miserable run of luck continued and his AMAX-backed Penske spun without warning into the wall at Turn Two.

Boesel continued to lead from the restart, only for Goodyear to move up and take over the lead on lap 46, swooping past on the outside at Turns Three and Four as they lapped the 14th-placed Pennzoil Lola of Teo Fabi.

Goodyear led handsomely through the first round of scheduled pit stops, which started on lap 66 when Tracy ducked in having moved into second place ahead of Boesel. Tracy took advantage of fresher tires to make rapid progress as the other leaders all made their pit stops, and on lap 83 he passed Goodyear with a typically brave move in traffic.

The two Canadians continued to lead past half-distance, until yet another strong run by Goodyear ended after 113 laps. This time a blown engine was the cause.

Most of the leaders pitted under the ensuing caution, leaving Gordon, who had stopped only 15 laps earlier, at the front of the pack

Michael C. Brown

After another strong oval performance, Raul Boesel *(right)* was just pipped by Mansell. The Brazilian – based in Miami, Florida – was still looking for that elusive first Indy Car win in his eighth year contesting the series.

Below: A pit stop for Scott Goodyear in Derrick Walker's Mackenzie Financial-backed Lola T93/00-Ford. The Canadian ran strongly in second place until engine failure sidelined him after 113 laps.

from Mansell, Tracy, Boesel and Fittipaldi.

Tracy, though, was on a mission, looking to erase the memory of his mistake at Phoenix. He immediately passed Mansell around the outside at Turn One on the restart, then dispensed with Gordon likewise in Turn Four to reassume the lead. Wow!

The leaders spread out somewhat over the next phase of the event, with Tracy running serenely out in front. Until lap 142, that is. Fernandez had spun in Turn Two after running solidly in

eighth place, and the unfortunate Tracy became entangled with the uncompetitive Luyendyk as they sought to avoid the Mexican's stricken car.

On came the caution lights again; and out went Tracy.

'Of course I'm disappointed, because my car was really running strong, but that's racing,' said Tracy philosophically.

Once again the leaders dived into the pits – all except Boesel, whose crew gambled that he might be able to make it to the finish with the fuel he already

had on board. It would be a close-run thing. Gordon, meanwhile, made a mistake and almost spun as he entered his pit. He lost a lap before resuming, effectively ending another brilliant challenge for the win.

Boesel soon put some distance between himself and the pursuing Mansell at the restart. Slowly but surely, though, as his own fuel load lightened and following another brief caution period, Mansell began to close in once more.

By now it had become apparent Boesel just might make it to the

finish without stopping again. So Newman-Haas team manager Jim McGee lost no time in informing Mansell of the situation.

'No problem,' replied the Englishman calmly over the radio.

By lap 180, Mansell was on Boesel's tail. His tires were in better shape than the Brazilian's. And two laps later he took advantage of a slower car, diving through into the lead on the exit of Turn Four. Mansell never looked back.

Boesel had one last hope when the caution flags came out again with just a handful of laps

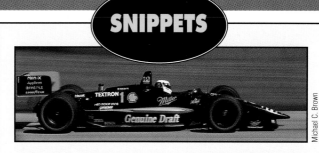

Michael C. Brown

SNIPPETS

• Bobby Rahal *(above)*, embarrassed at not being able to qualify his own R/H 001 chassis at Indy, appeared at Milwaukee with a pair of new Lolas. One was a brand-new car, chassis No. 34, while the spare had been purchased from Kenny Bernstein, who needed four cars for his three drivers at The Speedway but required only two for Roberto Guerrero for the remainder of the season.

• Raul Boesel's car featured air deflectors in front of the sidepods – *à la* Formula 1 McLaren. The non-standard aerodynamics had been formulated by British engineer Mike Clark following an exclusive five-day wind-tunnel test on behalf of Dick Simon Racing. Mansell's car sprouted similar appendages for the race.

• Willy T. Ribbs was delighted to finish 11th in his first-ever race on a one-mile oval. 'I like this place,' beamed Ribbs. 'I was having fun, especially on my second set of tires. I said to myself, "This is great! I'd like to go out there and run some more today." '

remaining, after Gordon's over-exuberant attempt to pass Rahal for fourth place ended in a spin. But Mansell wasn't flustered. He took off like a scalded cat when the green flag was waved to signal a two-lap dash to the end.

The two leaders were separated by only 0.514 second at the finish line, but it was enough. Mansell's first oval track win was in the bag.

'I thoroughly enjoyed it,' said a delighted Mansell, who extended his series lead to 18 points over Boesel. 'It's opened my eyes. It was very busy out there, and very

different to anything I've experienced before.'

Fittipaldi and Rahal also were on the same lap at the end of an action-packed race, while Unser Jr persevered to finish fifth, two laps off the pace after a weekend in which he was never happy with the Valvoline Lola's handling.

Brayton and Roberto Guerrero (Budweiser King Lola-Chevy/C) also were two laps in arrears, followed by Jimmy Vasser, who drove another sensible race in Jim Hayhoe's year-old Kodalux Processing/STP-backed Lola.

MILLER GENUINE DRAFT 200, MILWAUKEE MILE, WISCONSIN STATE FAIR PARK, MILWAUKEE, WISCONSIN • 6 June, 200 laps – 200.000 miles

Place	Driver	No.	Car	Q Speed (mph)	Q Time	Q Pos.	Laps	Time/Retirement	Ave. speed	Pts
1	**Nigel Mansell**	5	*Kmart/Texaco Havoline* Lola T93/00-Ford	160.414	22.442s	7	200	1h 48m 08.245s	110.970 mph	20
2	**Raul Boesel**	9	*Duracell/Mobil 1/Sadia* Lola T93/00-Ford	165.752	21.719s	1	200	1h 48m 08.759s	110.961	18
3	**Emerson Fittipaldi**	4	*Marlboro* Penske PC22-Chevy/C	161.057	22.352s	2	200	1h 48m 12.696s	110.894	14
4	**Bobby Rahal**	1	*Miller Genuine Draft* Lola T93/00-Chevy/C	157.912	22.798s	9	200	1h 48m 21.541s	110.743	12
5	**Al Unser Jr**	3	*Valvoline* Lola T93/00-Chevy/C	152.292	23.639s	18	198	Running		10
6	**Scott Brayton**	22	*Amway/Northwest Airlines* Lola T93/00-Ford	160.449	22.437s	6	198	Running		8
7	**Roberto Guerrero**	40	*Budweiser King* Lola T93/00-Chevy/C	157.234	22.896s	10	198	Running		6
8	**Jimmy Vasser**	18	*Kodalux Processing/STP* Lola T92/00-Chevy/A	155.351	23.173s	13	196	Running		5
9	**Teo Fabi**	8	*Pennzoil Special* Lola T93/00-Chevy/C	154.799	23.256s	14	195	Running		4
10	**Robby Gordon**	14	*Copenhagen Racing* Lola T93/00-Ford	160.391	22.445s	8	193	Running		3
11	**Willy T. Ribbs**	75	*Cosby/Service Merchandise* Lola T92/00-Ford	150.888	23.859s	21	193	Running		2
12	**Olivier Grouillard**	29	*Eurosport/Marlboro* Lola T92/00-Chevy/A	154.528	23.297s	15	191	Running		1
13	Hiro Matsushita	15	*Panasonic Special* Lola T93/00-Ford	150.134	23.979s	24	191	Running		
14	Ross Bentley	39	*AGFA/Rain-X* Lola T92/00-Chevy/A	150.212	23.966s	23	190	Running		
15	Buddy Lazier	20	*Viper/Applebee's* Lola T91/00-Buick	150.920	23.854s	20	187	Running		
16	Danny Sullivan	7	*Molson* Lola T93/00-Chevy/C	153.848	23.400s	17	186	Running		
17	Robbie Buhl	19	*Mi-Jack* Lola T91/00-Chevy/A	148.198	24.292s	25	184	Running		
18	Mario Andretti	6	*Kmart/Texaco Havoline* Lola T93/00-Ford	160.842	22.382s	5	176	Running		
19	Mike Groff	26	*Miller Genuine Draft* Rahal/Hogan 001-Chevy/C	153.989	23.378s	16	156	Electrical		
20	Paul Tracy	12	*Marlboro* Penske PC22-Chevy/C	160.867	22.379s	4	141	Accident		
21	Adrian Fernandez	11	*Tecate/Amway Mexico* Lola T93/00-Chevy/C	156.083	23.065s	12	139	Accident		
22	Arie Luyendyk	10	*Target/Scotch Video* Lola T93/00-Ford	150.856	23.864s	22	135	Accident		
23	Scott Goodyear	2	*Mackenzie Special* Lola T93/00-Ford	160.937	22.369s	3	113	Engine		
24	David Kudrave	50	*Andrea Moda/Agip* Lola T92/00-Chevy/A	152.248	23.646s	19	90	Engine		
25	Stefan Johansson	16	*AMAX Energy & Metals* Penske PC22-Chevy/C	156.674	22.978s	11	7	Accident		

Caution flags: Lap1, field out of formation; laps 7-18, accident/Johansson; laps 93-99, Kudrave/engine; laps 113-118, Goodyear/stalled; laps 141-151, accident/Luyendyk, Fernandez and Tracy; laps 160-163, Groff/slow on track; laps 194-197, accident/Gordon.

Lap leaders: Raul Boesel, 1-45 (45 laps); Scott Goodyear, 46-75 (30 laps); Robby Gordon, 76 (1 lap); Mike Groff, 77 (1 lap); Scott Goodyear, 78-82 (5 laps); Paul Tracy, 83-115 (33 laps); Robby Gordon, 116-119 (4 laps); Paul Tracy, 120-141 (22 laps); Raul Boesel, 142-181 (40 laps); Nigel Mansell, 182-200 (19 laps). *Totals:* Raul Boesel, 85 laps; Paul Tracy, 55 laps; Scott Goodyear, 35 laps; Nigel Mansell, 19 laps; Robby Gordon, 5 laps; Mike Groff, 1 lap.

Championship positions: **1** Mansell, 70 pts; **2** Boesel, 52; **3** Fittipaldi, 51; **4** Mario Andretti, 43; **5** Luyendyk, 37; **6** Rahal, 36; **7** Fabi, 34; **8** Al Unser Jr, 27; **9** Tracy, 22; **10** Vasser, 19; **11** Gordon, 17; **12** Guerrero, 16; **13** Brayton, 16; **14** Pruett, 12; **15** Cheever, 10; **16** Goodyear, 10; **17** Buhl, 8; **18** Smith, 7; **19** Sullivan, 5; **20** Kudrave, 5; **21** Matsushita, 5; **22** John Andretti, 3; **23** Johansson, 3; **24** Ribbs, 2; **25** Greco, 2; **26** Bentley, 1; **27** Al Unser, 1; **28** Grouillard, 1.

DETROIT

One week can seem like an eternity to a race car driver. Just ask Danny Sullivan. In the previous weekend's race on the Milwaukee Mile, Sullivan had been, shall we say, 'out to lunch' with his Molson-backed Galles Racing International Lola-Chevrolet Indy V8/C. He qualified poorly and ran even worse on raceday, running stone-cold last for much of the 200-lap distance. Afterward he and team owner Rick Galles had a heart-to-heart chat. Each was able to voice his misgivings. Sullivan claimed that all the team's efforts, engineering and otherwise, were geared toward Al Unser Jr; Galles questioned Sullivan's commitment and motivation.

The outcome was a far more assertive Sullivan when practice started on the attractive and demanding 2.1-mile circuit situated within Belle Isle Park.

Ultimately Sullivan qualified only tenth, yet by hook and crook he found himself leading on lap 48. Sullivan left no doubt as to his motivation as he successfully fought off challenges from Unser's Valvoline-liveried car and Robby Gordon's Copenhagen Lola in the closing stages, scoring his first victory since Long Beach last season.

Unser, meanwhile, was raging after a controversial late-race incident while challenging Sullivan for the lead. Emerson Fittipaldi also was furious after being (he thought unfairly) penalized for a starting infringement at the wheel of his Marlboro Penske. Nigel Mansell left in a huff, too, having crashed his Kmart/Texaco Havoline Lola-Ford while running fifth with ten laps remaining.

1st – SULLIVAN   **2nd – BOESEL**   **3rd – MARIO ANDRETTI**

Opposite page: **What a difference a week can make. Danny Sullivan, off the pace at Milwaukee, brought the Molson Lola home to an unexpected win in an incident-strewn race.**

Brits abroad. Nigel Mansell catches up with ex-Williams colleagues Peter Windsor *(centre)* and Sheridan Thynne. The 1993 season saw an unprecedented number of luminaries from Formula 1 going 'across the pond' to take a close look at the ever more appealing prospects available in Indy Car racing.

QUALIFYING

Mansell showed throughout practice and qualifying that he was the only driver capable of posting a serious challenge to the Penske-Chevrolet/C combination. Friday's opening qualifying session saw Mansell set second-best time behind Marlboro Racing Team Penske's young star Paul Tracy. Fittipaldi and Stefan Johansson – confirming the potential of Tony Bettenhausen's AMAX-sponsored PC22 – followed close behind. Yet Mansell promised there was more to come.

'I'm happy to be on the front row of the grid,' said Mansell on Friday afternoon. 'Invariably the second day is quicker, so I hope Paul is going to have to work hard to keep his pole.'

In fact, Tracy worked so hard he clipped a wall early in the final session, damaging his car's suspension beyond immediate repair. Fittipaldi also slid off with ten minutes remaining, leaving Mansell unopposed as he took his third pole of the season. The Englishman retained his 100 percent record on temporary circuits.

Fittipaldi, Tracy and Johansson lined up behind on the grid, followed by Bobby Rahal, who made excellent progress in dialing in his new Miller Genuine Draft Lola-Chevy/C.

The biggest surprise, however, was posted by ex-Formula 3000 star Andrea Montermini. The diminutive Italian set a superb seventh-best time the first day in the ex-Rahal Andrea Moda/Agip Lola-Chevy/A run by Antonio Ferrari's shoestring-budget Euromotorsport team, then improved one place more on Saturday.

'I'm very pleased,' agreed Montermini. 'To be there in sixth place I think is fantastic.'

Added crew chief John Weland: 'We have all the setups for Rahal from last year, so it's just a case of making the car comfortable for Andrea. We had a good basis to work from.'

Unser Jr improved his Friday best by more than two seconds to move up to seventh on the grid, while a 'flu-ridden Robby Gordon (Copenhagen Lola-Ford) was next despite missing most of Friday due to an accident. Mario Andretti was troubled by some engine woes and a fuel pickup problem in the second Newman-Haas car, but still managed to nip ahead of Sullivan, who slipped four places from Friday after running out of fuel.

RACE

The first note of discord in what was to prove a controversial race came even as the official starter, Jim Swintal, waved his green flag to get the 77-lap contest underway. Mansell led the field up toward the starting line in good order, but realized just as the flag came down that he had been jumped slightly by outside front row starter Fittipaldi.

Mansell threw his arm in the air, hoping to goad the flagman into displaying the yellow to signify a no-start. He was too late for that. Mansell's momentary distraction also allowed Tracy to charge around the outside and assume second place going into the first turn.

Mansell was fully aware of the predicament he faced, especially since the Belle Isle track is notoriously difficult for overtaking. He was not amused. He yelled over the radio for team manager Jim McGee to protest the start since, according to instructions issued at the drivers' briefing, the pole-sitter was supposed to lead across the start/finish line.

Out on the race track, the two Penskes quickly began to run away from Mansell, who in turn had his hands more than full in keeping a persistent Johansson at bay.

In race control, meanwhile, there was chaos for several laps as chief steward Wally Dallenbach, a veteran former racer himself, agonized over what to do. On the one hand, Mansell had a point. Fittipaldi did indeed lead across the line, and by a healthy margin – more than the one-and-a-half-car-lengths 'fudge factor' Dallenbach had alluded to in the briefing. Against that, once the green has been waved, the race is on.

Finally, to the consternation of Penske Racing and the utter amazement of the majority on pit lane, it was decreed that Fittipaldi had jumped the start. He was to be brought in for a stop-and-go penalty. Needless to say, the Brazilian was not happy. He resumed the race in sixth.

Teammate Tracy took over the running, while Mansell continued to fend off the attacks from an increasingly irate Johansson.

Main picture: Andrea Montermini was on the pace all weekend, qualifying sixth and finishing fourth in the race with Euromotorsport's Andrea Moda/Agip Lola T92/00. Montermini (car 50) holds off Arie Luyendyk (10) and Scott Goodyear *(part-hidden behind)*, while the lapped Buddy Lazier (20) stays well out of the battle.

Inset right: The 1992 Indy Lights 'Rookie of the Year' Adrian Fernandez took seventh place in the Amway Mexico-backed Galles Lola-Chevy.

Inset below right: The crashed Penskes of Johansson and Fittipaldi, just two of the casualties that littered the circuit.

'Sometimes blocking is just part of the game and I don't mind that,' said the Swede, 'but he would miss a [gear] shift and then cut right over in front of me. It was ridiculous.'

The first round of pit stops came on lap 21, after local driver Robbie Buhl had parked his year-old Mi-Jack Lola into a tire wall.

The order at the front remained unchanged, save for Fittipaldi falling farther back after running over a tire as he came into the pits. This just wasn't Emerson's day. A little later on, just to cap his miserable outing, Fittipaldi slid off deep into a tire barrier while disputing tenth place with Arie Luyendyk (Target/Scotch Video Lola-Ford). The yellows came out once again.

This time everyone save Rahal, who had been running fifth, dived for the pits. A faulty radio communication meant he hadn't heard the instruction to stop. The pit sequence also spelled disaster for race leader Tracy, who was adjudged to have exceeded the speed limit in pit lane.

All the breaks seemed to be going against the Penske team.

A lap or so after the restart, the battling Mansell and Johansson came together in a bizarre incident under a local yellow flag. Johansson slid out of the race altogether, while Mansell was obliged to pit to replace a punctured tire.

With Rahal also needing to stop for fuel and Tracy serving his stop-and-go penalty, the two Galles cars of Sullivan and Unser suddenly inherited the top two positions! They were followed by Robby Gordon, Raul Boesel (Duracell/Mobil 1/Sadia Lola-Ford) and Mario Andretti. Tracy, meanwhile, was down in ninth, and Montermini, the star of qualifying, had slipped to tenth after mistakenly stopping at the wrong pit stall.

Sullivan managed to edge out to an appreciable lead, only for Unser to whittle it down again. Soon it became apparent Sullivan

Mike Groff claimed 11th place in the Miller Genuine Draft Rahal/Hogan now abandoned by team owner Rahal in favor of his recently accquired Lola chassis.

Bottom: Al Unser Jr, aggrieved at his treatment at the hands of teammate Danny Sullivan, found no succor in his post-race appeal to IndyCar chief steward Wally Dallenbach.

was in trouble. His engine had lost its boost. It seemed only a matter of time before Unser would make the pass.

Sullivan, though, wasn't inclined to make things easy. Down on power he might have been, but on this track he reckoned he still had a chance.

After several unsuccessful attempts at making a pass, Unser drew alongside on the back straightaway on lap 69. Still Sullivan refused to give way. Finally, Unser was forced to run over

some marker cones which had been strategically positioned in place of a cement wall to afford the drivers a better line of sight to the following corner. Unfortunately for Unser, the drivers had been informed that to run over the cones would bring an automatic stop-and-go penalty.

It was inconsequential that he had been forced over the cones by his, er, teammate. And that the rule had been intended to prevent drivers from gaining an 'unfair' advantage. Which Unser clearly

didn't. He was simply trying to avoid contact.

A lap or two later, out came the black flag. A livid Unser was forced to pit. A late challenge by Gordon also came to naught as the youngster had his left-rear tire blow unexpectedly on the very last lap.

So it was that Sullivan emerged to score a quite incredible victory. Boesel picked his way through to a consistent second, mirroring his result of one year earlier, while Andretti claimed third. Montermi-

ni thrilled his team by annexing a magnificent fourth on the final lap at the expense of Rahal, who was forced to take evasive action as Gordon, virtually on three wheels, spun in front of him.

An irate Unser regarded sixth as no consolation whatever. Mexican Adrian Fernandez, in the Amway Mexico Lola, stayed out of trouble to take seventh, while Gordon, one tire flailing on the rim, struggled home eighth with a fine impression of the late, great Gilles Villeneuve.

SNIPPETS

• The 32-car entry represented the largest field (Indianapolis apart) since 35 cars turned up at Laguna Seca in 1989. As a further reminder of the current strength of the Indy Car scene, three teams – Galles Racing International, Dick Simon Racing and Walker Motorsport – ran three-car operations.

• Most drivers enjoyed the Belle Isle course, although everybody complained it was virtually impossible to pass. 'It's got a really good layout,' said Stefan Johansson *(below)*. 'It reminds me of Pau because of the park and because you have to trail into several of the corners on the brakes. It's a real drivers' circuit.'

• After the race chief steward Wally Dallenbach said he had heard complaints from several drivers about what he described as a growing problem of 'deliberate blocking' and that he was planning to confront the drivers about it. 'It was as bad as I've ever seen it today,' he said. 'I don't know whether it's been brought from Formula 1 or what, but we're going to do something about it.' *Above:* Olivier Grouillard makes it tough for Raul Boesel to pass.

ITT AUTOMOTIVE DETROIT GRAND PRIX, BELLE ISLE PARK CIRCUIT, DETROIT, MICHIGAN • 13 June, 77 laps – 161.700 miles

Place	Driver	No.	Car	Q Speed (mph)	Q Time	Q Pos.	Laps	Time/Retirement	Ave. speed	Pts
1	**Danny Sullivan**	7	*Molson* Lola T93/00-Chevy/C	104.356	1m 12.444s	10	77	1h 56m 43.678s	83.116 mph	21
2	**Raul Boesel**	9	*Duracell/Mobil 1/Sadia* Lola T93/00-Ford	104.234	1m 12.529s	11	77	1h 56m 55.884s	82.972	16
3	**Mario Andretti**	6	*Kmart/Texaco Havoline* Lola T93/00-Ford	104.486	1m 12.354s	9	77	1h 56m 59.249s	82.932	14
4	**Andrea Montermini**	50	*Andrea Moda/Agip* Lola T92/00-Chevy/A	104.823	1m 12.122s	6	77	1h 57m 01.031s	82.911	12
5	**Bobby Rahal**	1	*Miller Genuine Draft* Lola T93/00-Chevy/C	104.962	1m 12.026s	5	77	1h 57m 01.311s	82.908	10
6	**Al Unser Jr**	3	*Valvoline* Lola T93/00-Chevy/C	104.723	1m 12.191s	7	77	1h 57m 07.709s	82.796	8
7	**Adrian Fernandez**	11	*Tecate/Amway Mexico* Lola T93/00-Chevy/C	102.640	1m 13.655s	21	77	1h 57m 19.289s	82.696	6
8	**Robby Gordon**	14	*Copenhagen Racing* Lola T93/00-Ford	104.553	1m 12.308s	8	77	1h 58m 15.058s	82.046	5
9	**Paul Tracy**	12	*Marlboro* Penske PC22-Chevy/C	105.144	1m 11.902s	3	76	Tire		4
10	**Scott Goodyear**	2	*Mackenzie Special* Lola T93/00-Ford	102.116	1m 14.033s	22	76	Running		3
11	**Mike Groff**	26	*Miller Genuine Draft* Rahal/Hogan 001-Chevy/C	101.334	1m 14.605s	24	75	Accident		2
12	**Willy T. Ribbs**	75	*Cosby/Service Merchandise* Lola T92/00-Ford	100.596	1m 15.152s	25	75	Running		1
13	Hiro Matsushita	15	*Panasonic Special* Lola T93/00-Ford	100.362	1m 15.327s	27	74	Running		
14	Scott Brayton	22	*Amway/Northwest Airlines* Lola T92/00-Ford	102.969	1m 13.420s	17	74	Running		
15	Nigel Mansell	5	*Kmart/Texaco Havoline* Lola T93/00-Ford	106.627	1m 10.902s	1	68	Accident		1
16	Jimmy Vasser	18	*Kodalux Processing/STP* Lola T92/00-Chevy/A	103.568	1m 12.996s	14	65	Accident		
17	Arie Luyendyk	10	*Target/Scotch Video* Lola T93/00-Ford	103.724	1m 12.885s	13	58	Electrical		
18	Buddy Lazier	20	*Viper/Applebee's* Lola T91/00-Chevy/A	100.596	1m 15.152s	26	55	Accident		
19	Marco Greco	30	*Alfa Laval/Team Losi* Lola T92/00-Chevy/A	100.177	1m 15.466s	28	50	Accident		
20	Stefan Johansson	16	*AMAX Energy & Metals* Penske PC22-Chevy/C	105.082	1m 11.944s	4	44	Accident		
21	Eddie Cheever	99	*Say NO To Drugs* Penske PC21-Chevy/B	102.732	1m 13.589s	20	44	Accident		
22	Teo Fabi	8	*Pennzoil Special* Lola T93/00-Chevy/C	103.170	1m 13.277s	16	43	Accident		
23	Emerson Fittipaldi	4	*Marlboro* Penske PC22-Chevy/C	105.849	1m 11.422s	2	37	Accident		
24	Olivier Grouillard	29	*Eurosport/Marlboro* Lola T92/00-Chevy/A	103.455	1m 13.075s	15	24	Accident		
25	Scott Pruett	45	*Tobacco-Free America* Lola T91/00-Chevy/A	102.741	1m 13.583s	19	18	Accident		
26	Roberto Guerrero	40	*Budweiser King* Lola T93/00-Chevy/C	102.833	1m 13.517s	18	18	Accident		
27	Mark Smith	25	*Craftsman* Penske PC21-Chevy/B	104.187	1m 12.562s	12	17	Suspension		
28	Robbie Buhl	19	*Mi-Jack* Lola T92/00-Chevy/A	101.834	1m 14.238s	23	17	Accident		

Caution flags: Laps 20-24, accident/Buhl; laps 38-42, accident/Fittipaldi; laps 45-49, accident/Mansell and Johansson; laps 69-73, accidents/Vasser and Greco.

Lap leaders: Emerson Fittipaldi, 1-12 (12 laps); Paul Tracy, 13-38 (26 laps); Bobby Rahal, 39-46 (8 laps); Paul Tracy, 47 (1 lap); Danny Sullivan, 48-77 (30 laps). **Totals:** Danny Sullivan, 30 laps; Paul Tracy, 27 laps; Emerson Fittipaldi, 12 laps; Bobby Rahal, 8 laps.

Championship positions: 1 Mansell, 71 pts; **2** Boesel, 68; **3** Mario Andretti, 57; **4** Fittipaldi, 51; **5** Rahal, 46; **6** Luyendyk, 37; **7** Al Unser Jr, 35; **8** Fabi, 34; **9** Sullivan, 26; **10** Tracy, 26; **11** Gordon, 22; **12** Vasser, 19; **13** Guerrero, 16; **14** Brayton, 16; **15** Goodyear, 13; **16** Montermini, 12; **17** Pruett, 12; **18** Cheever, 10; **19** Buhl, 8; **20** Smith, 7; **21** Fernandez, 6; **22** Kudrave, 5; **23** Matsushita, 5; **24** John Andretti, 3; **25** Johansson, 3; **26** Ribbs, 3; **27** Greco, 2; **28** Groff, 2; **29** Bentley, 1; **30** Grouillard, 1; **31** Al Unser, 1.

PORTLAND

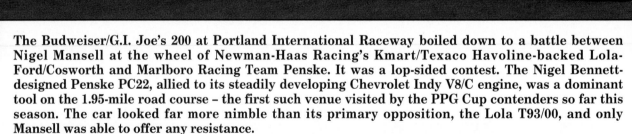

The Budweiser/G.I. Joe's 200 at Portland International Raceway boiled down to a battle between Nigel Mansell at the wheel of Newman-Haas Racing's Kmart/Texaco Havoline-backed Lola-Ford/Cosworth and Marlboro Racing Team Penske. It was a lop-sided contest. The Nigel Bennett-designed Penske PC22, allied to its steadily developing Chevrolet Indy V8/C engine, was a dominant tool on the 1.95-mile road course – the first such venue visited by the PPG Cup contenders so far this season. The car looked far more nimble than its primary opposition, the Lola T93/00, and only Mansell was able to offer any resistance.

The on-form Englishman won the pole with a sensational effort in qualifying but he was unable to resist the pressure on raceday and made one mistake at the chicane which enabled the Penske pair of Emerson Fittipaldi and Paul Tracy to move ahead.

'Nigel was running very strong,' noted Fittipaldi, playing down the effectiveness of his car. 'At one time I tried on the outside, he locked the wheels. I think that was the key moment of the race. I was able to get by him for the lead.'

Mansell later took advantage of changing weather conditions to regain second place from Tracy, but Fittipaldi was long gone. 'There's no disappointment in finishing second,' said Mansell. 'You can only do your best with what you have.'

| 1st – FITTIPALDI | 2nd – MANSELL | 3rd – TRACY |

by McMinnville, Oregon, yet still
he put many far more lavishly
equipped teams to shame, taking
advantage of circuit knowledge,
good preparation and solid engineering advice from the experienced Gordon Coppuck.

RACE

There was much speculation prior
to the start with Mansell and Fittipaldi sharing the front row, just
as they had in Detroit. This time
there was no controversy. Following an abnormally long pre-race
drivers' meeting in which the
starting procedure was discussed
at great length, Mansell made full
use of his inside front row berth
to out-accelerate Fittipaldi at the
green flag.

Mansell duly led into the
extremely tight Festival Curves
chicane and on around the opening lap. He was pursued by Fittipaldi, Johansson and Tracy. This
quartet quickly pulled out an
advantage over Andretti.

Mark Smith held sixth place in
the opening stages, maintaining
his speed from qualifying, but
sadly the rookie was out after
only a handful of laps due to a
broken gearbox casing.

The four leaders spent most of
the first 25 laps running in nose-
to-tail formation. Tracy by then
had taken advantage of some
slower traffic to move past
Johansson, which allowed teammate Fittipaldi to concentrate his
attention on race leader Mansell
instead of having to protect his
position ahead of the Swede.

Then, on lap 27, Mansell locked
up his brakes at the end of the
front straightaway. Fittipaldi
moved gratefully into the lead as
Mansell slid ignominiously into
the escape road.

'It was my mistake,' admitted
Mansell. 'I was driving like it was
qualifying to stay in front. When
you're on the limit and your
wheels lock up, you lose it.'

Mansell rejoined in fourth place
after his error, although that

QUALIFYING

The Penskes headed the time
sheets in the opening practice session on Friday morning, while
Stefan Johansson underlined the
potency of the PC22 by splitting
Fittipaldi and Tracy with Tony
Bettenhausen's similar privately
run AMAX-sponsored chassis.

'We've got a reasonably good
handle on it,' offered Johansson.
'We've lost our way a couple of
times [in terms of dialing in the
car to the circuit] but each time
we've managed to get it back
again.'

The Penskes looked especially
stable through the infield portion
which comprises a sequence of

long left- and right-handed corners, changing direction readily
and then displaying excellent
traction capabilities. The Lolas
looked sluggish by comparison,
their drivers having to manhan-
dle the cars through the turns.

Only Mansell was able to offer
any kind of a challenge. He was
having to work extremely hard,
but in the end his persistence
paid off with the pole and an
extra PPG Cup bonus point.

'The Penskes are working
incredibly well,' declared Mansell.
'We're sliding a bit too much. We
put a little more download in the
car, which helped, but we've got a
bit to learn.'

Fittipaldi wasn't able to make

the best use of his fresh tires and
wound up a tenth adrift of
Mansell, while, curiously, teammate Tracy remained a half-second off his veteran team leader's
pace all weekend.

Johansson, therefore, was able
to maintain position between the
two Marlboro cars, with Mario
Andretti a full second off his Newman-Haas teammate's time in
fifth position.

One of the most impressive
efforts in qualifying was posted
by rookie Mark Smith, who sat
sixth on the grid in Frank
Arciero's year-old Craftsman
Penske-Chevy/B. Admittedly,
Smith, a graduate of Super Vee
and Indy Lights, hails from near-

When the track began to dry out after a heavy mid-race shower, most drivers switched back to slick tires. Arie Luyendyk's Chip Ganssi-entered Target/Scotch Video Lola-Ford swings around the similar car of Mario Andretti and returns to the fray.

became third when Johansson's run ended after 37 laps with a broken transmission.

As the first round of pit stops unfolded, so the dark clouds which had been gathering to the west began to look more menacing. The first spots of rain came as the leaders were on their 41st lap.

Tracy was one of the first to stop for grooved tires. Fittipaldi followed him in a few laps later, allowing Mansell to regain the lead as he remained out on the track.

'To try to gain the edge, I had to stay on slicks as long as I could,' related Mansell.

For quite a while it looked as though his gamble might pay off. Even on the treacherous surface Mansell was able to lap fast enough to maintain an advantage over Fittipaldi. Finally, though, on lap 52, he gave up the struggle and pitted for wets. He rejoined the race in fourth place.

Fittipaldi was by now back in front, chased by Tracy and Bobby Rahal, who also stayed out on slicks with his Miller Genuine

Draft Lola-Chevy/C.

The rain ceased around lap 73, but the track remained extremely slippery. Fittipaldi, though, maintained his advantage. Tracy ran in second ahead of Mansell. Al Unser Jr, after a steady run in his Valvoline Lola-Chevy/C, was the only other driver on the lead lap.

A dry line began to emerge as the race entered its final 20 laps. The outcome remained in doubt since everyone still had to make one more pit stop for fuel. And

maybe tires.

Tracy was the first of the leaders to pit, on lap 84. Team owner Roger Penske decided the Canadian should remain on wet tires. Mansell followed him in next time around. The Englishman gambled once again, electing to switch to slicks in the hope he could catch the two Penskes on the fast-drying track.

Mansell did indeed move past Tracy on lap 91, and he was given one final hope of chasing down

Fittipaldi when the only full-course caution of the race came out just one lap later, so that Scott Brayton's stalled Amway/Northwest Airlines Lola-Ford could be removed to a safer location. Even so, when the green waved again to signify a six-lap dash to the finish, the two leaders were separated from each other by nine slower cars.

Try as he surely did, Mansell was unable to catch Fittipaldi.

'I knew there was one groove,' said Fittipaldi, referring to the solitary dry line which emerged on the race track in the final laps, 'and if you slid wide on a corner you could lose. I couldn't afford to make any mistakes.'

Mansell, as he suggested, was content with his hard-earned second place, which was enough to preserve his lead in the championship. Tracy, who stopped again for slicks under the caution, was the only other driver to complete the full distance. Rahal, Unser, who also stopped twice in the closing stages, and Andretti, who chose to stay on wets, were one lap down at the finish of another enthralling contest.

Paul Tracy remained on treaded tires at his final refueling stop and lost second place to Nigel Mansell.

SNIPPETS

• Team owner Norm Turley *(right),* who had terminated his agreement with Eddie Cheever *(below)* due to a lack of sponsorship, survived an attempt by a representative of Cheever to impound his equipment shortly before Friday qualifying at Portland. A few phone

calls settled the matter in Turley's favor and he was able to continue running Brian Till in his year-old Penske PC21. Till, who showed promise last season in an ex-Truesports chassis, ran well despite losing time with a spin.

• Adrian Reynard announced during the weekend that he would be challenging Lola's share of the Indy Car marketplace by producing his own chassis for next year. The car would be designed by Malcolm Oastler with input from Bruce Ashmore, who had announced the previous week he was leaving his post as chief designer for Lola Cars. Chip Ganassi was confirmed as Reynard's first customer.

• 'It's a weird feeling,' said new Reynard recruit Bruce Ashmore after noting the superiority of the Penske over his own Lola design during qualifying on Friday. 'I'm standing here thinking, "Cor, I'd better get these cars sorted out." But then I think, "Hang on a minute, they're the opposition now!" '

• Circuit owner Nicola Foulston headed a delegation from Brands Hatch in trying to persuade the Indy Car teams to stage a future event at the famous British venue.

• Johnny Unser, cousin of Al and son of the late Jerry, made a tentative Indy Car debut in one of Dale Coyne's year-old Chevy/A-powered Lolas. Sponsorship for the venture came from Ruger Firearms. Unser, who has contested the lackluster American Indy Car Series in recent years, made it to the finish in 18th place.

IndyCar photos

BUDWEISER/G.I. JOE'S 200, PORTLAND INTERNATIONAL RACEWAY, PORTLAND, OREGON • 27 June, 102 laps – 198.900 miles

Place	Driver	No.	Car	Q Speed (mph)	Q Time	Q Pos.	Laps	Time/Retirement	Ave. speed	Pts
1	Emerson Fittipaldi	4	*Marlboro* Penske PC22-Chevy/C	115.069	1m 01.007s	2	102	2h 03m 54.620s	96.312 mph	21
2	Nigel Mansell	5	*Kmart/Texaco Havoline* Lola T93/00-Ford	115.266	1m 00.902s	1	102	2h 03m 58.979s	96.255	17
3	Paul Tracy	12	*Marlboro* Penske PC22-Chevy/C	114.008	1m 01.575s	4	102	2h 04m 04.889s	96.179	14
4	Bobby Rahal	1	*Miller Genuine Draft* Lola T93/00-Chevy/C	111.777	1m 02.804s	15	101	Running		12
5	Al Unser Jr	3	*Valvoline* Lola T93/00-Chevy/C	112.783	1m 02.243s	9	101	Running		10
6	Mario Andretti	6	*Kmart/Texaco Havoline* Lola T93/00-Ford	113.379	1m 01.916s	5	101	Running		8
7	Raul Boesel	9	*Duracell/Mobil 1/Sadia* Lola T93/00-Ford	112.485	1m 02.408s	11	100	Running		6
8	Robby Gordon	14	*Copenhagen Racing* Lola T93/00-Ford	112.778	1m 02.246s	10	100	Running		5
9	Mike Groff	26	*Miller Genuine Draft* Rahal/Hogan 001-Chevy/C	112.232	1m 02.549s	12	100	Running		4
10	Arie Luyendyk	10	*Target/Scotch Video* Lola T93/00-Ford	111.865	1m 02.754s	14	99	Running		3
11	Jimmy Vasser	18	*Kodalux Processing/STP* Lola T92/00-Chevy/A	110.328	1m 03.628s	22	99	Running		2
12	Scott Goodyear	2	*Mackenzie Special* Lola T93/00-Ford	111.619	1m 02.892s	16	98	Out of fuel		1
13	Olivier Grouillard	29	*Eurosport/Marlboro* Lola T92/00-Chevy/A	110.429	1m 03.570s	21	98	Running		
14	Danny Sullivan	7	*Molson* Lola T93/00-Chevy/C	112.791	1m 02.239s	8	97	Running		
15	Ross Bentley	39	*AGFA/Rain-X* Lola T92/00-Chevy/A	107.978	1m 05.013s	26	97	Running		
16	Willy T. Ribbs	75	*Cosby/Service Merchandise* Lola T92/00-Ford	111.873	1m 02.750s	13	95	Running		
17	Scott Brayton	22	*Amway/Northwest Airlines* Lola T93/00-Ford	110.606	1m 03.469s	19	95	Running		
18	Johnny Unser	19	*Ruger Special* Lola T92/00-Chevy/A	105.286	1m 06.675s	28	93	Running		
19	Marco Greco	30	*Alfa Laval/Team Losi* Lola T92/00-Chevy/A	107.807	1m 05.116s	27	93	Running		
20	Lyn St James	90	*JC Penney/Nike* Lola T93/00-Ford	108.120	1m 04.928s	25	92	Running		
21	Hiro Matsushita	15	*Panasonic Special* Lola T93/00-Ford	110.514	1m 03.522s	20	87	Out of fuel		
22	Brian Till	99	*Say NO To Drugs* Penske PC21-Chevy/B	110.734	1m 03.395s	18	70	Spun off		
23	David Kudrave	50	*Andrea Moda/Agip* Lola T92/00-Chevy/A	110.011	1m 03.812s	23	64	Transmission		
24	Roberto Guerrero	40	*Budweiser King* Lola T93/00-Chevy/C	111.359	1m 03.039s	17	47	Accident		
25	Teo Fabi	8	*Pennzoil Special* Lola T93/00-Chevy/C	112.924	1m 02.166s	7	44	Engine		
26	Stefan Johansson	16	*AMAX Energy & Metals* Penske PC22-Chevy/C	114.241	1m 01.449s	3	37	Transmission		
27	Kevin Cogan	11	*Conseco* Lola T93/00-Chevy/C	108.642	1m 04.616s	24	21	Engine		
28	Jeff Wood	42	*Agip* Lola T91/00-DFS	105.026	1m 06.840s	29	13	Suspension		
29	Mark Smith	25	*Craftsman* Penske PC21-Chevy/B	112.973	1m 02.139s	6	6	Transmission		

Caution flags: Laps 91-95, Brayton/towed in.

Lap leaders: Nigel Mansell, 1-27 (27 laps); Emerson Fittipaldi, 28-33 (6 laps); Mario Andretti, 34 (1 lap); Emerson Fittipaldi, 35-48 (14 laps); Nigel Mansell, 49-52 (4 laps); Emerson Fittipaldi, 53-102 (50 laps). **Totals:** Emerson Fittipaldi, 70 laps; Nigel Mansell, 31 laps; Mario Andretti, 1 lap.

Championship positions: 1 Mansell, 88 pts; **2** Boesel, 74; **3** Fittipaldi, 72; **4** Mario Andretti, 65; **5** Rahal, 58; **6** Al Unser Jr, 45; **7** Tracy, 40; **8** Luyendyk, 40; **9** Fabi, 34; **10** Gordon, 27; **11** Sullivan, 26; **12** Vasser, 21; **13** Guerrero, 16; **14** Brayton, 16; **15** Goodyear, 14; **16** Montermini, 12; **17** Pruett, 12; **18** Cheever, 10; **19** Buhl, 8; **20** Smith, 7; **21** Fernandez, 6; **22** Groff, 6; **23** Kudrave, 5; **24** Matsushita, 5; **25** John Andretti, 3; **26** Ribbs, 3; **27** Johansson, 3; **28** Greco, 2; **29** Grouillard, 1; **30** Bentley, 1; **31** Al Unser, 1.

CLEVELAND

Paul Tracy was in total control of the Budweiser Cleveland Grand Prix, presented by Dairy Mart. The young Canadian won the 85-lap race around the temporary circuit comprising runways and taxiways at the Burke Lakefront Airport at a canter. His eventual margin of victory was 18.090 seconds.

Tracy, who qualified his Marlboro Penske-Chevrolet Indy V8/C on the pole at a new track record speed, was beaten away from the start by Nigel Mansell and was content to follow the reigning Formula 1 World Champion through the opening laps. Once into his stride, Tracy picked his moment, nipped through into the lead with a decisive maneuver on lap 15 and was never again seriously challenged. This was a thoroughly convincing, mature performance.

It was also the 75th Indy Car victory for Roger Penske, already the most successful car owner in Indy Car history.

Tracy was followed home by veteran teammate Emerson Fittipaldi, who ensured a one-two punch for Marlboro Racing Team Penske following an exciting duel with Mansell through the closing stages.

'It was a great race,' summarized Mansell after his third-place finish in the Kmart/Havoline Lola-Ford/Cosworth XB. 'The Penske is obviously a little bit better than the Lola at present, but outside of that it was fantastic. The Lola people have got to work real hard in developing the car because we need more aerodynamic download to compete on the same level.'

| 1st – TRACY | 2nd – FITTIPALDI | 3rd – MANSELL |

QUALIFYING

The Cleveland race track is one of the more difficult on the Indy Car calendar, for the simple reason that the wide-open spaces allow virtually no reference points from which the drivers can judge their turn-in points or apexes for the corners. Furthermore, an immediately effective setup was even more critical this year than usual since the meeting was restricted to just a two-day affair.

As in Portland, the combination of the Penske PC22 chassis and the Chevrolet Indy V8/C engine was the one to beat. Tracy and Fittipaldi topped the time sheets convincingly in the opening practice session on Saturday morning.

Nevertheless, despite not having seen the track before and with minimal time for improvement, Mansell was able to split the Penske pair. He was delighted.

'We wrung the neck of the Lola chassis as much as we could,' insisted Mansell. 'I couldn't go

Left: **The Marlboro Penskes were in the ascendancy at Cleveland with Paul Tracy scoring an emphatic win from his first pole position of the season.**

The distinctive chrome-yellow Pennzoil colors of Teo Fabi *(right)* **have not been seen as high on the grid as team boss Jim Hall would have wished in 1993; an eighth-place finish was one of the Italian driver's better results in an anonymous year.**

any quicker. I hustled the car and I ran off the road a few times, and I don't like doing that because we damaged the car a little bit.'

Mansell also damaged himself, caught out by a misaligned temporary staircase as he attempted to leap up into the interview room trailer right after qualifying. Mansell fell awkwardly and sustained a sprained wrist, which was to trouble him for several weeks ahead.

Tracy, meanwhile, secured the pole, his first of the season and the 101st for Penske Racing.

'Every point is critical,' said Tracy, who earned one PPG Cup bonus point. 'I need to get the season turned around. This is the halfway point in the season and I want to get up into the top three at the end of the season. That's my goal.'

Fittipaldi was the only other driver to dip below the one minute barrier. Stefan Johansson again ran well to place fourth in Tony Bettenhausen's AMAX-backed PC22, followed by Scott Goodyear, bouncing back after a poor showing in Portland with Derrick Walker's Mackenzie Financial Lola-Ford/Cosworth.

Next were the two Galles Lola-Chevrolets of Danny Sullivan and Al Unser Jr. And, incredibly, just as in Portland, they were separated by a scant 0.004 second – with Sullivan again marginally the faster!

Mark Smith (eighth) and Brian Till (13th) ran well with their year-old Penske PC21s, while Willy T. Ribbs again qualified strongly, 14th in his year-old Service Merchandise Lola-Ford.

RACE

Conditions on raceday were hot and humid, although the excellent viewing opportunities ensured a good-sized crowd. Tracy led the 29-car field toward the starter's rostrum in perfect order, only to lose valuable momentum as he accelerated through the

Raul Boesel's Duracell/Mobil 1/Sadia Lola T93/00-Ford lifts a wheel around the bumpy Cleveland airport circuit. Seventh place at the finish did little to help the Brazilian's fading championship challenge.

Getting back into the groove. Kevin Cogan *(bottom)* was checking out his fitness with the Conseco Lola after a long layoff, in preparation for a full season with the Galles team in 1994.

gears when his engine's 'pop-off' regulator valve unexpectedly opened to relieve momentary excess turbocharger boost pressure.

Mansell surged past in an instant to take the lead under braking for the sharp right-handed Turn One, followed by Tracy, Fittipaldi, Johansson and Sullivan. Behind, though, there was chaos as several cars became tangled together.

Bobby Rahal and Roberto Guerrero were out on the spot, their rival Miller Genuine Draft and Budweiser beer-backed cars perched incongruously one atop the other. Goodyear, Unser and Raul Boesel also were involved. All fell to the back of the pack.

The yellow flags waved as a result of the mêlée, so the remaining cars circulated under a full-course yellow while the mess was cleaned up.

Mansell maintained his advantage at the restart, whereupon he and Tracy quickly began to put some daylight between themselves and their pursuers.

Tracy never allowed Mansell a moment's rest. Finally, on lap 15, he made a better exit from Turn One, drew alongside Mansell as they accelerated toward Turn Two, then braved it out under braking and took advantage of his inside line to assume the lead.

It was a perfectly executed maneuver. And one to which Mansell was unable to respond.

Tracy quickly established a clear advantage, which he continued to extend for much of the remainder of the race.

'It's tough to be too far ahead,' commented Tracy, 'because it's difficult to keep your concentration at the level it needs to be. You have to be real careful in traffic. You have to be consistent.' Tracy was all those things this day. His second victory of the season was well deserved.

Mansell ran in a lonely second place through the middle stages. Later he came under increasing pressure from Fittipaldi. Their battle for position became a focal point as the race drew toward its conclusion.

By lap 66, the pair were running in nose-to-tail formation, the Brazilian looking for a way through.

Fittipaldi's chance came on lap 73, as they negotiated some slower cars in Turn Five. But Mansell didn't give up. Four laps later he

was able to return the favor, only to lose out again, for good, just a couple of laps later.

'I had an incredible battle with Nigel,' enthused Fittipaldi. 'Every time I thought I got rid of him he was back again! I think it was one of the best dices I ever had. It was a great race and I really enjoyed it.'

Johansson and Sullivan both lost ground after being assessed stop-and-go penalties for exceeding the 80 mph speed limit in pit lane during their first scheduled stops. Sullivan was delayed again later in the race when he collided with Galles teammate Unser Jr. The incident served to aggravate an already, shall we say, 'tense' atmosphere following their clash in Detroit.

A furious Sullivan continued to finish just out of the points, while an equally indignant Unser also recovered, only to retire late in the race due to an engine failure.

Teo Fabi moved up strongly to fourth place as a result of the penalties, posting his strongest performance of the season in Jim Hall's Pennzoil Lola-Chevy/C. Sadly, as Fabi was preparing to make his second scheduled pit stop on lap 61, his car ran out of fuel. He lost valuable time coasting into the pit lane, then several more seconds as his car was push-started. By the time he was back up to speed, Fabi had slipped to eighth.

Mario Andretti took over briefly in fourth in the second Kmart/Havoline Lola-Cosworth, only to relinquish the place to Johansson, who had driven hard to make up for his earlier penalty. Johansson moved ahead on lap 69 to score his best result of the season to date.

'Obviously we're pleased,' said Johansson, who drove with his right wrist strapped up following an incident during practice. 'It was a tough race. This is the worst track to have any kind of injury because it's so bumpy. I was having to steer left-handed virtually all the way around the race track.'

Andretti finished fifth, just ahead of Robby Gordon, who drove a good race in A.J. Foyt's similar Copenhagen Lola-Ford after being hampered in qualifying by a down-on-power engine. Gordon also had to contend with fading oil pressure in the closing stages. The engine held together long enough for him to stay ahead of a charging Boesel, who rose from 25th to sixth following the first-lap kerfuffle, then lost out again due to a puncture on lap 51.

Fabi's action-packed race also included a faulty shock absorber and clutch failure in the waning laps. He still held on for eighth ahead of Brian Till, who drove spiritedly in Norm Turley's Say NO To Drugs/Project Learning Penske PC21. Till was the highest-placed finisher running a year-old car.

SNIPPETS

Michael C. Brown

• Paul Tracy *(right)* earned the first pole position for the Chevrolet Indy V8/C engine, breaking a string of 11 straight for Ford which stretched back to the Vancouver race last season. (Tracy, incidentally, also was the last Chevy driver to claim a pole, at Road America in 1992.) The feat earned him a cool $100,000 under the Marlboro Pole Award scheme, which offers $10,000 plus a bonus of $15,000 should the pole-winner also win the race. If unclaimed, the bonus is rolled over to the next event, hence Tracy's windfall as no one had achieved the feat since Mansell at Surfers Paradise.

• Toyota top brass were given the royal treatment during the race weekend, courtesy of Roger Penske's team.

• Hard-trying Buddy Lazier took advantage of the first-lap shenanigans to move up from 23rd on the grid to a stunning eighth on the opening lap with his two-year-old Lola. Lazier ran strongly for a while before sliding briefly off the road and later retiring due to an electrical glitch.

BUDWEISER GRAND PRIX OF CLEVELAND, BURKE LAKEFRONT AIRPORT CIRCUIT, CLEVELAND, OHIO • 11 July, 85 laps – 201.365 miles

Place	Driver	No.	Car	Q Speed (mph)	Q Time	Q Pos.	Laps	Time/Retirement	Ave. speed	Pts
1	**Paul Tracy**	12	*Marlboro* Penske PC22-Chevy/C	144.139	59.168s	1	85	1h 34m 27.254s	127.913 mph	22
2	**Emerson Fittipaldi**	4	*Marlboro* Penske PC22-Chevy/C	143.072	59.609s	3	85	1h 34m 45.344s		16
3	**Nigel Mansell**	5	*Kmart/Texaco Havoline* Lola T93/00-Ford	143.569	59.403s	2	85	1h 34m 49.271s		14
4	**Stefan Johansson**	16	*AMAX Energy & Metals* Penske PC22-Chevy/C	141.178	1m 00.409s	4	84	Running		12
5	**Mario Andretti**	6	*Kmart/Texaco Havoline* Lola T93/00-Ford	139.757	1m 01.023s	11	84	Running		10
6	**Robby Gordon**	14	*Copenhagen Racing* Lola T93/00-Ford	136.774	1m 02.354s	20	84	Running		8
7	**Raul Boesel**	9	*Duracell/Mobil 1/Sadia* Lola T93/00-Ford	139.266	1m 01.238s	12	84	Running		6
8	**Teo Fabi**	8	*Pennzoil Special* Lola T93/00-Chevy/C	140.654	1m 00.634s	9	84	Running		5
9	**Brian Till**	99	*Say NO To Drugs* Penske PC21-Chevy/B	139.169	1m 01.281s	13	83	Running		4
10	**Arie Luyendyk**	10	*Target/Scotch Video* Lola T93/00-Ford	138.603	1m 01.531s	15	83	Running		3
11	**Olivier Grouillard**	29	*Eurosport/Marlboro* Lola T92/00-Chevy/A	137.513	1m 02.019s	17	82	Running		2
12	**Hiro Matsushita**	15	*Panasonic Special* Lola T93/00-Ford	136.640	1m 02.415s	21	81	Running		1
13	Kevin Cogan	11	*Conseco* Lola T93/00-Chevy/C	136.629	1m 02.420s	22	81	Running		
14	Danny Sullivan	7	*Molson* Lola T93/00-Chevy/C	140.902	1m 00.527s	6	80	Running		
15	Mark Smith	25	*Craftsman* Penske PC21-Chevy/B	140.670	1m 00.627s	8	79	Engine		
16	Ross Bentley	39	*AGFA/Rain-X* Lola T92/00-Chevy/A	132.686	1m 04.275s	25	79	Running		
17	Jeff Wood	42	*Agip* Lola T91/00-DFS	124.326	1m 08.597s	28	76	Running		
18	Scott Brayton	22	*Amway/Northwest Airlines* Lola T93/00-Ford	137.579	1m 01.989s	16	74	Running		
19	Al Unser Jr	3	*Valvoline* Lola T93/00-Chevy/C	140.893	1m 00.531s	7	73	Engine		
20	Scott Goodyear	2	*Mackenzie Special* Lola T93/00-Ford	140.996	1m 00.487s	5	67	Electrical		
21	Buddy Lazier	20	*Viper/Applebee's* Lola T91/00-Chevy/A	135.852	1m 02.777s	23	61	Electrical		
22	Marco Greco	30	*Alfa Laval/Team Losi* Lola T92/00-Chevy/A	No speed	No time	29	50	Turbo		
23	Lyn St James	90	*JC Penney/Nike* Lola T93/00-Ford	133.438	1m 03.913s	24	48	Suspension		
24	Robbie Buhl	19	*Mi-Jack* Lola T92/00-Chevy/A	132.445	1m 04.392s	26	39	Fire		
25	Christian Danner	50	*Andrea Moda/Agip* Lola T92/00-Chevy/A	136.833	1m 02.327s	19	35	Electrical		
26	Brian Bonner	28	*Applebee's/Office Depot* Lola T91/00-Chevy/A	130.358	1m 05.423s	27	17	Electrical		
27	Willy T. Ribbs	75	*Cosby/Service Merchandise* Lola T92/00-Ford	138.633	1m 01.518s	14	12	Suspension		
28	Bobby Rahal	1	*Miller Genuine Draft* Lola T93/00-Chevy/C	140.631	1m 00.644s	10	0	Accident		
29	Roberto Guerrero	40	*Budweiser King* Lola T93/00-Chevy/C	137.466	1m 02.040s	18	0	Accident		

Caution flags: Laps 1-4, accident/Rahal and Guerrero.

Lap leaders: Nigel Mansell, 1-14 (14 laps); Paul Tracy, 15-30 (16 laps); Nigel Mansell, 31 (1 lap); Paul Tracy, 32-60 (29 laps); Nigel Mansell, 61 (1 lap); Paul Tracy, 62-85 (24 laps).
Totals: Paul Tracy, 69 laps; Nigel Mansell, 16 laps.

Championship positions: 1 Mansell, 102 pts; **2** Fittipaldi, 88; **3** Boesel, 80; **4** Mario Andretti, 75; **5** Tracy, 62; **6** Rahal, 58; **7** Al Unser Jr, 45; **8** Luyendyk, 43; **9** Fabi, 39; **10** Gordon, 35; **11** Sullivan, 26; **12** Vasser, 21; **13** Guerrero, 16; **14** Brayton, 16; **15** Johansson, 15; **16** Goodyear, 14; **17** Montermini, 12; **18** Pruett, 12; **19** Cheever, 10; **20** Buhl, 8; **21** Smith, 7; **22** Fernandez, 6; **23** Groff, 6; **24** Matsushita, 6; **25** Kudrave, 5; **26** Till, 4; **27** John Andretti, 3; **28** Ribbs, 3; **29** Grouillard, 3; **30** Greco, 2; **31** Bentley, 1; **32** Al Unser, 1.

TORONTO

Local hero Paul Tracy waves the flag for a home victory. Teammate Emerson Fittipaldi *(opposite page)* made it a Penske one-two for the second weekend in a row and edged ahead of Nigel Mansell in the title chase.

It was a case of more of the same in the Molson Indy Toronto, round nine of the PPG Indy Car World Series, as the Marlboro Penske PC22-Chevrolet/C pair of Emerson Fittipaldi and Paul Tracy continued their display of superiority with a second straight one-two finish. This time they shared the honors as Fittipaldi took the pole and Tracy countered with another superlative performance on raceday.

It was a popular and emotional win for 24-year-old Tracy, who lives with his wife Tara and baby daughter Alysha just a few miles away from the 1.78-mile temporary circuit in Toronto's Exhibition Place.

'I just couldn't be happier for my team, my whole family and all my fans – and for Canada,' said a jubilant Tracy in Victory Lane.

Pit stops proved to be the deciding factor. Tracy regained the lead after his final stop and then pulled away as Fittipaldi encountered gearchange difficulties in the closing stages.

In the Penskes' wake, however, a thrilling battle developed between the improving Lola-Chevrolets of Danny Sullivan, Bobby Rahal and Al Unser Jr. The trio was covered by fractionally over one second after 103 laps of intense racing.

Nigel Mansell, meanwhile, was curiously off the pace all weekend with Newman-Haas Racing's Kmart/Texaco Havoline Lola-Ford/Cosworth. He simply was not a contender. Mansell crashed twice during practice, qualified a lowly (by his standards) ninth and retired from the race with a turbo wastegate failure.

Mansell's misery was compounded by the fact his first mechanical failure of the season enabled Fittipaldi to take over the lead in the PPG Cup point standings.

QUALIFYING

Tracy arrived in Toronto in a confident frame of mind. Fresh from his superb success in Cleveland just one week earlier, Tracy was hunting for glory again – this time in front of a fervently patriotic hometown crowd.

He had to give best to Stefan Johansson's AMAX Penske PC22 in the opening practice session on Friday morning, but Tracy redressed the balance in the afternoon's half-hour qualifying by clipping a half-second from his earlier best and eclipsing the previous track record. Even so he felt there was more to come.

'I still have some ideas where we can pick up some speed,' he confided: 'the fast turn in front of the pits and putting the power down a little better. We have some work to do on the car.'

Come Saturday afternoon, Tracy tried in vain to post an improvement. Nevertheless, his Friday time looked like standing . . . until the very last lap of the session when Fittipaldi punched in a

time two-tenths better than the Canadian's.

'It's tough to swallow,' said Tracy. 'I told Emerson this is my hometown, but he's a competitor just like everyone else. There was nothing I could do. It was a frustrating session. I couldn't go any quicker and I knew that's what I needed to do.'

Fittipaldi was delighted to earn his first pole of the season and the 14th of his Indy Car career. He had made some positive changes to his car following morning practice and knew he was in with a good chance to claim the pole after tailing Tracy early in the session.

'I could see I could be the same speed as Paul,' said Fittipaldi, 'and then I was very patient, waiting for the right time to go out on my new tires. Yesterday my car wasn't very good over the bumps and I wasn't able to take [the corner in front of the pits] flat [out]. It was much better today.'

A clutch of drivers fought to be 'best of the rest', with former

track record holder Bobby Rahal emerging on top after making excellent progress in development of his Miller Genuine Draft Lola-Chevy/C. Danny Sullivan (Molson Lola-Chevy/C), Johansson, Raul Boesel (Duracell/Mobil 1/Sadia Lola-Ford), Al Unser Jr (Valvoline Lola-Chevy/C), Arie Luyendyk (Target/Scotch Video Lola-Ford) and Mansell all were blanketed by a scant two-tenths, while Scott Goodyear (Mackenzie Financial Lola-Ford) and Teo Fabi (Pennzoil Lola-Chevy/C) also bettered the old lap record during a thrilling final session.

Andrea Montermini returned to Antonio Ferrari's Euromotorsport team and immediately made his presence felt by establishing the seventh-fastest time on Friday with his Agip/Andrea Moda Chevy/A-powered Lola T92/00. In fact, this was the same chassis, '02', with which Rahal qualified on pole and finished second last season.

Ultimately, the impressive Montermini slipped to 16th on the grid, one position behind series

debutant Bertrand Gachot who ran the '93 Lola-Ford previously handled by Lyn St James.

RACE

A record-sized crowd of 66,225 was drawn by perfect weather conditions and the prospect of a home victory for Tracy. Nevertheless it was Fittipaldi who duly took advantage of his inside front row grid position to seize the lead going into Turn One. Tracy dutifully followed in second, pursued by Rahal, Sullivan and Johansson.

Robby Gordon had qualified only 12th in A.J. Foyt's Copenhagen Lola-Ford, unable to find a clear lap, but the 24-year-old Californian charger made a typically sensational start to move up to sixth with a brave outside maneuver in Turn One.

'It was great,' declared Gordon, 'because everybody lined up behind each other and I just drove past them.'

The pace was slowed by two full-course cautions early in the race.

The first came on lap five, when Jeff Wood spun his outclassed two-year-old Cosworth DFS-powered Lola under braking for Turn Three and collected the wall. Then, shortly after the restart, the Chevy/A engine in Euromotorsport teammate Andrea Montermini's Lola expired as he crossed the start/finish line. Montermini promptly spun on his own oil at Turn One, whereupon several drivers behind him became tangled together, including Kevin Cogan, Willy T. Ribbs and Marco Greco. All lost at least one lap before they could resume.

The only significant place change in the early stages had come on lap nine, when Sullivan took advantage of a slight error by Rahal, nipping smartly past into third place at Turn Nine.

'He must have had a problem,' reported Sullivan. 'He slowed just enough to allow me to dive down underneath him under braking going into the turn.'

Following a handful of laps behind the pace car, the field was unleashed again with 15 laps in the books. Almost immediately the fans packed into grandstands in the start/finish area erupted as one to the sight – courtesy of three huge closed-circuit screens – of Tracy passing Fittipaldi for the lead under heavy braking into Turn Three at the end of Lakeshore Boulevard.

'I got off the previous corner real well,' recounted Tracy. 'I was able to draft down the straightaway. Emerson knew I was coming and he gave me room to race him. It was a clean pass.'

There was an enormous cheer as the hometown favorite scorched into view to complete lap 16, already pulling clear in the lead. Tracy quickly established a comfortable margin of around three seconds which he maintained until making his first pit stop on lap 39.

Fittipaldi held onto second despite stern pressure from Sullivan and Rahal, while Unser moved up to fifth on lap 34 when Johansson was forced out by a total electrical failure.

The first round of scheduled pit stops commenced shortly after the Swede's untimely demise. Tracy was among the first to dive into pit lane, but lost a few valuable seconds when he couldn't get the car into gear as it came down off the air jacks, service completed. The delay was critical. Fittipaldi, who pitted a lap later, swept past to regain the lead.

Once more, Tracy had to follow his senior. By lap 50, following another brief caution to remove Arie Luyendyk's stalled Lola, the first four cars remained in nose-to-tail formation. Fittipaldi was leading Tracy and the two Galles Racing International entries of

Sullivan and Unser. Rahal had slipped to fifth after a marginally slower pit stop.

The huge crowd was loving every moment of what was turning out to be a thrilling contest, fully living up to the promise shown by an exciting final period of qualifying on Saturday.

Tracy, of course, was the man they had come to cheer. Fittipaldi did manage to edge clear slightly during the middle stages of the race, his young teammate hindered slightly by a balky gearchange, but Tracy was able to close in again when the leader was held up while lapping some slower traffic.

On lap 73, as Fittipaldi went to put another lap on the wayward Hiro Matsushita's Lola-Ford, the Brazilian found himself pinched tight going into Turn Three. Fittipaldi brushed lightly against the wall. Thinking the impact may have been enough to damage a wheel rim, Fittipaldi wisely decided discretion was the better part of valor. It was almost time in any case for his second routine pit stop, so Fittipaldi peeled off directly into pit lane.

The stop was quite good, a little over 15 seconds for a full load of fuel and fresh Goodyear tires. Tracy's, three laps later, was sensational, almost three seconds faster.

So it was that Tracy found himself back in the lead. The crowd roared its approval once again.

By lap 80, Tracy had extended his advantage to almost six seconds, assisted by the fact Fittipaldi was encountering problems of his own. The gear linkage had started to come apart, making it difficult to shift.

Fittipaldi soon realized it would be impossible to challenge Tracy for the lead. Instead he concentrated on running a steady pace as he sought to maintain his advantage over the pursuing pack of Lola-Chevrolets. As the race entered its final stages, however, the gap began to dwindle.

For Nigel Mansell the weekend was a disaster, with two crashes in practice followed by retirement from the race with a turbo wastegate failure.

Fittipaldi cut his pace appreciably toward the end, finally crossing the line stuck in fifth gear when the linkage came apart in his hand on the very last lap. He just managed to hold position ahead of Sullivan, Rahal and Unser, all four cars crossing the line blanketed by just 2.2 seconds.

'I was pleased,' said Sullivan. 'It was a good race. It was clean and exciting. But we couldn't catch the Penskes.'

Gordon battled on for sixth, ruing a decision made following the morning warmup session to fit stiffer springs, while Boesel followed closely in seventh with his Lola-Ford. Mario Andretti finished one lap down in his similar car, as did Goodyear, who lost valuable ground due to an extra pit stop after erroneously believing he had picked up a puncture. Roberto Guerrero also was one lap adrift in his Budweiser Lola-Chevy/C.

The final point-paying positions also were under dispute all the way to the finish line, with Jimmy Vasser (Kodalux/STP Lola T92/00-Ford) just fighting off a last-corner passing attempt by Formula 1 veteran Bertrand Gachot, who drove a strong race on his Indy Car debut. Gachot had to make two extra pit stops, first when he was called in for a stop-and-go penalty for running over an air hose and later when his crew failed to properly connect the fuel hose.

Tracy, meanwhile, was basking in the glory, especially happy to have moved up to fourth in the standings, just three points shy of the consistent Boesel. He had driven another mature race. Car owner Roger Penske was clearly impressed.

'We had a really good race weekend,' acknowledged Penske. 'We had a really good car. It's a tremendous thing to have Paul win in his own town. He's doing a great job. Certainly he knows how to keep it on the race track.'

SNIPPETS

• Newman-Haas Racing tried all weekend in vain to find a balance for its pair of Lola-Fords. 'Pretty horrible, wasn't it?' admitted Nigel Mansell. 'A joke of a car and that's all there was to it. The only good news was that we had our first mechanical problem of the season and it coincided with an awful weekend. All we can do is just put it down to a case of "That's motor racing."'

• Bertrand Gachot thoroughly enjoyed his first experience of Indy Car racing, which included one brief test session earlier in the week. 'The car is fun to drive,' said Gachot. 'I just need to adapt my driving style to the turbo lag, which I'm not used to. I'm used to instant power, like a spark. I think the series has tremendously improved in competition. I was a bit surprised when I found myself 22nd [in the opening session], because in Formula 1 I'm not usually that far back!' *Right:* Gachot shadows Bobby Rahal's Miller Genuine Draft Lola during his impressive drive to 12th place with Dick Simon's T93/00.

• Several Lola-Chevy teams took advantage of some new front uprights which allowed them to run a little more camber, resulting in more grip through the tighter corners.

• Stefan Johansson delighted Tony Bettenhausen's crew by topping the time sheets in the opening session. On Saturday, though, after slipping to fifth on the grid, the ever-smiling Swede made an interesting observation: 'It's funny how expectations change,' he said. 'When we were fifth, everyone [on the team] was jumping up and down [with joy]. Now if we're outside the top three there are tears running down people's faces!'

Michael C. Brown

MOLSON INDY TORONTO, EXHIBITION PLACE CIRCUIT, TORONTO, ONTARIO, CANADA • 18 July, 103 laps – 183.340 miles

Place	Driver	No.	Car	Q Speed (mph)	Q Time	Q Pos.	Laps	Time/Retirement	Ave. speed	Pts
1	Paul Tracy	12	*Marlboro* Penske PC22-Chevy/C	109.544	58.497s	2	103	1h 53m 58.951s	96.510 mph	21
2	Emerson Fittipaldi	4	*Marlboro* Penske PC22-Chevy/C	109.997	58.256s	1	103	1h 54m 11.975s	96.326	17
3	Danny Sullivan	7	*Molson* Lola T93/00-Chevy/C	109.286	58.635s	4	103	1h 54m 13.151s	96.310	14
4	Bobby Rahal	1	*Miller Genuine Draft* Lola T93/00-Chevy/C	109.331	58.611s	3	103	1h 54m 13.744s	96.301	12
5	Al Unser Jr	3	*Valvoline* Lola T93/00-Chevy/C	109.033	58.771s	7	103	1h 54m 14.225s	96.294	10
6	Robby Gordon	14	*Copenhagen Racing* Lola T93/00-Ford	108.459	59.082s	12	103	1h 54m 45.750s	95.854	8
7	Raul Boesel	9	*Duracell/Mobil 1/Sadia* Lola T93/00-Ford	109.162	58.702s	6	103	1h 54m 46.069s	95.849	6
8	Mario Andretti	6	*Kmart/Texaco Havoline* Lola T93/00-Ford	108.205	59.221s	13	102	Running		5
9	Scott Goodyear	2	*Mackenzie Special* Lola T93/00-Ford	108.670	58.968s	10	102	Running		4
10	Roberto Guerrero	40	*Budweiser King* Lola T93/00-Chevy/C	108.006	59.330s	14	102	Running		3
11	Jimmy Vasser	18	*Kodalux Processing/STP* Lola T92/00-Ford	107.555	59.579s	17	101	Running		2
12	Bertrand Gachot	90	*CAPA* Lola T93/00-Ford	107.959	59.356s	15	101	Running		1
13	Brian Till	99	*Say NO To Drugs* Penske PC21-Chevy/B	107.475	59.623s	18	101	Running		
14	Teo Fabi	8	*Pennzoil Special* Lola T93/00-Chevy/C	108.601	59.005s	11	100	Running		
15	Kevin Cogan	11	*Conseco* Lola T93/00-Chevy/C	104.967	1m 01.048s	23	98	Running		
16	Hiro Matsushita	15	*Panasonic Special* Lola T93/00-Ford	103.662	1m 01.816s	26	88	Running		
17	Johnny Unser	19	*Ruger Special* Lola T92/00-Chevy/A	102.167	1m 02.721s	28	87	Gearbox		
18	Willy T. Ribbs	75	*Cosby/Service Merchandise* Lola T92/00-Ford	105.990	1m 00.458s	21	86	Accident		
19	Scott Brayton	22	*Amway/Northwest Airlines* Lola T93/00-Ford	107.376	59.678s	19	62	Flat tire		
20	Nigel Mansell	5	*Kmart/Texaco Havoline* Lola T93/00-Ford	108.920	58.832s	9	55	Wastegate		
21	Marco Greco	30	*Alfa Laval/Team Losi* Lola T92/00-Chevy/A	104.462	1m 01.343s	24	46	Halfshaft		
22	Arie Luyendyk	10	*Target/Scotch Video* Lola T93/00-Ford	109.029	58.773s	8	44	Fuel pressure		
23	Mark Smith	25	*Craftsman* Penske PC21-Chevy/B	105.740	1m 00.602s	22	40	Gearbox		
24	Stefan Johansson	16	*AMAX Energy & Metals* Penske PC22-Chevy/C	109.175	58.695s	5	34	Electrical		
25	Ross Bentley	39	*AGFA/Rain-X* Lola T92/00-Chevy/A	103.275	1m 02.048s	27	28	Gearbox		
26	Scott Pruett	45	*Pro Formance/Spirit* Lola T91/00-Chevy/A	106.948	59.917s	20	25	Engine		
27	Andrea Montermini	50	*Andrea Moda/Agip* Lola T92/00-Chevy/A	107.888	59.395s	16	10	Engine/spin		
28	Jeff Wood	42	*Agip* Lola T91/00-DFS	101.695	1m 03.012s	29	3	Accident		
DNS	Olivier Grouillard	29	*Eurosport/Marlboro* Lola T92/00-Chevy/A	104.200	1m 01.493s	25		Accident in practice		

Caution flags: Laps 5-7, accident/Wood; laps 11-14, accident/Montermini; laps 45-48, Luyendyk/stopped on course.

Lap leaders: Emerson Fittipaldi, 1-15 (15 laps); Paul Tracy, 16-38 (23 laps); Emerson Fittipaldi, 39-72 (34 laps); Paul Tracy, 73-103 (31 laps). **Totals:** Paul Tracy, 54 laps; Emerson Fittipaldi, 49 laps.

Championship positions: 1 Fittipaldi, 105 pts; 2 Mansell, 102; 3 Boesel, 86; 4 Tracy, 83; 5 Mario Andretti, 80; 6 Rahal, 70; 7 Al Unser Jr, 55; 8 Luyendyk, 43; 9 Gordon, 43; 10 Sullivan, 40; 11 Fabi, 39; 12 Vasser, 23; 13 Guerrero, 19; 14 Goodyear, 18; 15 Brayton, 16; 16 Johansson, 15; 17 Montermini, 12; 18 Pruett, 12; 19 Cheever, 10; 20 Buhl, 8; 21 Smith, 7; 22 Fernandez, 6; 23 Groff, 6; 24 Matsushita, 6; 25 Kudrave, 5; 26 Till, 4; 27 John Andretti, 3; 28 Ribbs, 3; 29 Grouillard, 3; 30 Greco, 2; 31 Bentley, 1; 32 Al Unser, 1; 33 Gachot, 1.

MICHIGAN

The fickle wind masquerading as this year's PPG Indy Car World Series switched direction again for the Marlboro 500 at Michigan International Speedway.

Emerson Fittipaldi arrived at the two-mile high-banked oval on an emotional high after recently taking over as the new PPG Cup points leader. Teammate Paul Tracy was on the crest of a wave following two straight victories. Both men were expected to be front-runners. Nigel Mansell, meanwhile, was coming off a diabolical weekend in Toronto. And he was unnerved by his first experience of Roger Penske's super-fast, super-bumpy oval. 'Daunting' and 'dangerous' were among the words he used to describe the place. Some of the others were barely printable.

By the end of the weekend, Mansell was back on top of the points table following a sensational and hard-earned triumph. Ford Motor Company and Cosworth Engineering were celebrating the first 500-mile race victory for their XB engine, ending a long string of disappointments which included failure at Indianapolis earlier in the season.

Their joy was compounded by the fact Mansell's Newman-Haas teammate Mario Andretti, who had qualified on the pole at a new closed-circuit world record speed, finished in second place.

'It's a wonderful weekend,' declared team co-owner Carl Haas. 'Being one-two on the grid and finishing the same way in the race and setting new records, it's one of those races you dream about. I'll probably still be pinching myself tomorrow.'

The Penskes? Well, neither was close to the pace in qualifying. They moved up into contention during the early stages of the race, but Tracy retired with a blown engine and Fittipaldi ran into handling difficulties and finished out of the points.

Not even a painful wrist and a splitting headache could deny Mansell victory in the Marlboro 500, which he described as the toughest race he'd ever won.

1st – MANSELL

2nd – ANDRETTI

3rd – LUYENDYK

QUALIFYING

Mario Andretti seems to have a special affinity for Michigan International Speedway. He was on pole position for the track's very first Indy Car race 25 years ago at an average speed of 183.670 mph. Last year he was on the pole again, lapping at a new track record of 230.150 mph in the Kmart/Havoline Lola-Ford owned by Carl Haas and Paul Newman.

This time, in near-perfect conditions, sunny and not too warm, the 53-year-old grandfather did the trick again. Andretti achieved the feat by establishing a new closed-course world record at an average speed of 234.275 mph. He was also fastest through the front

straightaway speed trap at almost 242 mph.

'I held my breath and hoped the setup [of the car] would hold because I trimmed it out [aerodynamically] pretty good,' said an excited Andretti after securing the 66th pole of his career and his sixth at MIS.

It came at the expense of Mansell, who had set the pace earlier in the one-at-a-time session. The Englishman, on his very first visit to Michigan, had been fastest in each of the timed practice sessions on Friday and Saturday morning, turning a best lap of 233.057 mph. He proceeded to circulate even faster during qualifying, stopping the clocks at 233.462 mph and leaving Andretti with a tough task ahead of him.

'I didn't think I could match that,' admitted Andretti, 'because I hadn't done that [speed] in practice. But it all came together in qualifying. We took a chance on the settings and it worked. I surprised myself, to be honest.'

Mansell was surprised and a little disappointed to be beaten to the pole by his teammate but he was reasonably content given the fact he was struggling to come to grips with the enormous speed and the bumpy track surface.

'I'm not comfortable,' he declared. 'I ran some laps on full [fuel] tanks and I was certainly hurting inside the car. I've never had such a headache in my life.'

Arie Luyendyk, the pole-winner at Indianapolis in May, again showed his superspeedway

prowess by annexing third place on the grid with Chip Ganassi's Target/Scotch Video Lola-Ford, while Raul Boesel, in fourth, was pleased with the consistency of Dick Simon's similar Duracell/Mobil 1/Sadia-backed car.

Paul Tracy was fastest of the Chevrolet contingent, clearly no match for the Fords on this high-speed track. Tracy would start fifth with a best lap at 227.468 mph.

RACE

Mirroring their impressive display in practice and qualifying, the two Newman-Haas drivers were able to continue that dominance on raceday in front of a large and enthusiastic crowd.

Michael C. Brown

Left: Raul Boesel's car is hosed with water from behind the pit wall to the left to wash away any fuel overflow during a refueling stop. Meanwhile the tires are changed once more in this marathon race which lasted more than 2¹/₂ hours.

Ford-powered Lolas took the first five places. *Below:* Fifth-placed Scott Goodyear in the Mackenzie Financial car heads Arie Luyendyk, who took a fine third in Chip Ganassi's similar Target/Scotch Video machine.

always knew he had the ability. He's been fast everywhere. He's a fast learner, that's for sure.'

Andretti did manage to unlap himself in the waning stages, and when the yellow lights came on with less than 40 laps to go, signifying a blown turbo on Marco Greco's Alfa Laval/Team Losi Lola-Chevy/A, Andretti had one last hope of catching Mansell. It didn't last long. Both cars made their final pit stops for fuel under the full-course caution, whereupon Mansell, despite a severe headache and feeling sick inside the car, retained his superiority by driving away to a clear victory. He took the chequered flag 9.434 seconds ahead of his teammate.

'I'm tired and I had a tough time out there,' said an exhausted but elated Mansell after having to be helped from his car in Victory Lane. 'This track is tough on machinery, it's tough on the drivers and it just was a complete new experience from every aspect. I've never been in a race like this. For sure this is one of the greatest victories of my career. Very special.'

Andretti, his car running a little loose in the closing stages, was

happy to finish second.

Boesel looked set for third place until making a pit stop just a couple of laps before the final caution. He lost a lap in the process, while Luyendyk was able to maintain his track position when he pitted under the yellow.

'The car never missed a beat all day,' said Luyendyk. 'There were a few guys that were stronger than I was, but that's what happens in a 500-mile race. Finishing third here and second at Indy gives me a couple of good finishes but I would trade them both for a win.'

Boesel, unlucky again, finished fourth to maintain third place in the point standings behind Mansell and Fittipaldi, who moved up strongly from a lowly 15th on the grid to run fourth on lap 40. But then Fittipaldi fell off the pace when his Penske's handling suddenly deteriorated. The team worked hard to relieve his problems, but by then the damage was done. He finished a distant 13th, no fewer than 13 laps behind the winner.

Goodyear overcame inconsistent handling to claim fifth, his best finish of the season so far, while Fabi was hampered by a lack of boost pressure on his way to sixth.

Michael C. Brown

Andretti immediately took off into the lead, while Mansell showed his inexperience on the ovals as Luyendyk ducked into second place going into Turn One. It didn't last long. In fact, Mansell redressed the balance on lap three, motoring by on the long back straightaway and setting his sights on the race leader.

Andretti led Mansell by as much as five seconds as the two leaders began to encounter slower traffic inside the first 20 laps, but soon the Englishman started to close. By lap 27 he had reduced the deficit to just a car length or so. Next time around, Mansell drove side-by-side with Andretti through Turn Two before completing the pass superbly in Turns Three and Four.

'We were wheel to wheel,' explained Mansell, 'and to do that on this sort of a track, at those speeds, you have to be with a classy driver. That's Mario. It was fun out there.'

Mansell soon began to stretch out his advantage. Officially he relinquished the lead for only one lap, during a scheduled pit stop, throughout the remainder of the race. Mansell put a lap on Andretti right before the halfway point, after the veteran had lost ground with a miscue in pit lane, but even then he didn't relax, lapping consistently at between 222 and 225 mph. Andretti was left gasping in his wake.

'It was very impressive,' said Andretti of Mansell's performance, 'but I'm not surprised. I

Mario Andretti was 'super-quick' all weekend, taking pole with a shattering lap at 234.275 mph and second place in the race behind Newman-Haas teammate Mansell. *Below:* Andretti gazes ahead intently during a pit stop as fine adjustments are made to the front wings of his Kmart/Texaco Havoline Lola.

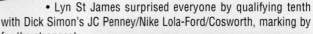

SNIPPETS

• Rick Galles *(right)* confirmed that Academy Award-winning actor Gene Hackman and Steve Hilbert, chairman of insurance specialists Conseco, had joined him on the board of Galles Racing International.

• Danny Sullivan withdrew from the event after picking up a severe stomach bug. Mansell, who played golf with Sullivan earlier in the week, also was sick on Friday night and had to contend with the after-effects all weekend.

Michael C. Brown

• Lyn St James surprised everyone by qualifying tenth with Dick Simon's JC Penney/Nike Lola-Ford/Cosworth, marking by far the strongest performance to date for last year's Indy 500 Rookie of the Year. St James also ran solidly among the top 12, in company with the likes of Al Unser Jr and Robby Gordon, until electrical problems ended her race.

IndyCar

• Both Newman-Haas Lolas were fitted with the latest Ford/Cosworth motors, featuring a revised inlet system and new camshafts, which were said to generate an extra 40 horsepower. It showed.

• Willy T. Ribbs was delighted to finish tenth on his maiden appearance at Michigan. 'Our first set of tires was a disaster,' he said. 'After we put some downforce in the car it was great, but by that time we'd lost too much ground. When the car's working good, this place is like driving down the freeway. And when it's not working well, it's like a moto-cross track.'

MARLBORO 500, MICHIGAN INTERNATIONAL SPEEDWAY, BROOKLYN, MICHIGAN • 1 August, 250 laps – 500.000 miles

Place	Driver	No.	Car	Q Speed (mph)	Q Time	Q Pos.	Laps	Time/Retirement	Ave. speed	Pts
1	Nigel Mansell	5	Kmart/Texaco Havoline Lola T93/00-Ford	233.462	30.840s	2	250	2h 39m 24.131s	188.203 mph	21
2	Mario Andretti	6	Kmart/Texaco Havoline Lola T93/00-Ford	234.275	30.733s	1	250	2h 39m 33.565s	188.018	17
3	Arie Luyendyk	10	Target/Scotch Video Lola T93/00-Ford	229.743	31.339s	3	249	Running		14
4	Raul Boesel	9	Duracell/Mobil 1/Sadia Lola T93/00-Ford	229.562	31.364s	4	248	Running		12
5	Scott Goodyear	2	Mackenzie Special Lola T93/00-Ford	227.408	31.661s	6	247	Running		10
6	Teo Fabi	8	Pennzoil Special Lola T93/00-Chevy/C	225.536	31.924s	8	246	Running		8
7	Roberto Guerrero	40	Budweiser King Lola T93/00-Chevy/C	224.204	32.114s	11	245	Running		6
8	Al Unser Jr	3	Valvoline Lola T93/00-Chevy/C	219.370	32.821s	17	245	Running		5
9	Bobby Rahal	1	Miller Genuine Draft Lola T93/00-Chevy/C	222.100	32.418s	16	243	Running		4
10	Willy T. Ribbs	75	Cosby/Service Merchandise Lola T92/00-Ford	223.852	32.164s	13	243	Running		3
11	Scott Brayton	22	Amway/Northwest Airlines Lola T93/00-Ford	226.134	31.839s	7	241	Running		2
12	David Kudrave	42	Andrea Moda/Agip Lola T92/00-Chevy/A	215.697	33.380s	19	239	Running		1
13	Emerson Fittipaldi	4	Marlboro Penske PC22-Chevy/C	222.524	32.356s	15	237	Running		
14	Hiro Matsushita	15	Panasonic Special Lola T93/00-Ford	224.045	32.136s	12	231	Running		
15	Robby Gordon	14	Copenhagen Racing Lola T92/00-Ford	224.815	32.026s	9	229	Engine		
16	Ross Bentley	39	AGFA/Rain-X Lola T92/00-Chevy/A	205.468	35.042s	23	222	Running		
17	Olivier Grouillard	29	Eurosport/Marlboro Lola T92/00-Chevy/A	214.326	33.594s	20	184	Engine		
18	Marco Greco	30	Alfa Laval/Team Losi Lola T92/00-Chevy/A	212.020	33.959s	21	163	Engine		
19	Paul Tracy	12	Marlboro Penske PC22-Chevy/C	227.468	31.653s	5	114	Engine		
20	Jeff Wood	50	Andrea Moda/Agip Lola T91/00-DFS	207.188	34.751s	22	52	Handling		
21	Buddy Lazier	20	Leader Cards Lola T92/00-Buick	217.935	33.037s	18	43	Oil pressure		
22	Lyn St James	90	JC Penney/Nike Lola T93/00-Ford	224.208	32.113s	10	39	Electrical		
23	Stefan Johansson	16	AMAX Energy & Metals Penske PC22-Chevy/C	223.632	32.196s	14	36	Accident		
WDN	Adrian Fernandez	7	Molson Lola T93/00-Chevy/C	214.354	33.589s					

Caution flags: Laps 38-45, accident/Johansson; laps 119-127, Tracy/engine; laps 205-211, Greco/engine.

Lap leaders: Mario Andretti, 1-27 (27 laps); Nigel Mansell, 28-82 (55 laps); Arie Luyendyk, 83 (1 lap); Nigel Mansell, 84-250 (167 laps). **Totals:** Nigel Mansell, 222 laps; Mario Andretti, 27 laps; Arie Luyendyk, 1 lap.

Championship positions: 1 Mansell, 123 pts; **2** Fittipaldi, 105; **3** Boesel, 98; **4** Mario Andretti, 97; **5** Tracy, 83; **6** Rahal, 74; **7** Al Unser Jr, 60; **8** Luyendyk, 57; **9** Fabi, 47; **10** Gordon, 43; **11** Sullivan, 40; **12** Goodyear, 28; **13** Guerrero, 25; **14** Vasser, 23; **15** Brayton, 18; **16** Johansson, 15; **17** Montermini, 12; **18** Pruett, 12; **19** Cheever, 10; **20** Buhl, 8; **21** Smith, 7; **22** Fernandez, 6; **23** Kudrave, 6; **24** Groff, 6; **25** Matsushita, 6; **26** Ribbs, 6; **27** Till, 4; **28** John Andretti, 3; **29** Grouillard, 3; **30** Greco, 2; **31** Bentley, 1; **32** Al Unser, 1; **33** Gachot, 1.

NEW HAMPSHIRE

Photos: Steve Swope

Nigel Mansell celebrated his 40th birthday in grand style. The reigning Formula 1 World Champion emerged victorious after a thrilling battle with Marlboro Penske teammates Paul Tracy and Emerson Fittipaldi which lasted throughout the New England 200 at New Hampshire International Speedway.

Make no mistake, this was a magnificent contest. The three major protagonists had nothing but praise for each other in the post-race press conference, while veteran broadcaster and publisher Chris Economaki stated he had seen no better race in his 60 years of covering the sport.

Tracy led for most of the distance, only for Mansell to pull off a sensational pass around the outside line at Turn One with just four laps remaining. The Englishman sped to victory by less than half a second over Tracy's Penske-Chevrolet Indy V8/C.

'If you've got to be 40, this is the way to do it,' grinned an excited Mansell after capturing his fourth victory of the season, his third on the ovals and his second in as many weekends with his Kmart/Havoline Lola-Ford/Cosworth. 'This was pure racing at its best. I've been in some races in the past; I've been wheel to wheel at 200 mph with Ayrton Senna and it doesn't come close to what happened today.'

Mansell's stunning success extended his lead in the PPG Cup standings to 25 points over Fittipaldi, who finished third.

Main picture: The Union Jack flies high over New England as Nigel Mansell fans up in the stands watch their hero down on the track continue to take the PPG Indy Car World Series by storm, winning yet another race on an oval.

QUALIFYING

Mansell added another point to his championship tally by securing pole position on Bob Bahre's state-of-the-art 1.058-mile oval. He earned the top spot with a lap in 22.504 seconds, for an average speed of 169.247 mph.

It was Mansell's fifth pole of the season in just ten starts (he failed to race at Phoenix after crashing in practice) and his first on an oval. Thus far no one else had earned the pole more than once.

'That was the most exhilarating, frustrating, demanding qualifying that I've ever gone through,' declared Mansell, who had been the ninth driver to set a time and then had to sit and watch while all the other contenders took their turn at trying to topple his Lola-Ford/Cosworth from the premier position.

'You have to wait a long time. I've never experienced anything like that. Milwaukee [his only other start on a one-mile oval] was different because I only qualified seventh, so I didn't pay attention too much.'

Mansell, though, had to play second fiddle during practice to Raul Boesel. The Brazilian had set the pace from the outset in Dick Simon Racing's similar Duracell/Mobil 1/ Sadia Lola-Ford, but after completing his two warmup laps in preparation for qualifying, he felt he couldn't match his earlier best of 22.291 seconds (170.867 mph). And rather than accept an unrepresentative time, Boesel elected to wave off his qualifying attempt.

A half-hour or so later, after making a couple of minor tweaks to the setup of his car, Boesel returned to the qualifying line. His final warmup lap was a superb 22.447s. It would have been good enough for the pole. Mansell was concerned.

'I was saying, "Slow down, slow down," ' quipped Mansell later. 'And he did!'

Sure enough, when the clocks were ticking officially, Boesel could manage only a 22.510s, good for 169.207 mph. Mansell's time would stand – by a scant 0.006 second.

'To tell the truth I felt inside the car it wasn't a good lap,' said Boesel, 'and that the warmup lap was better. The car picked up a push on the second lap. We made an adjustment to the car just before we went out. I guess it was good for one lap, not two laps. Of course I'm disappointed because we were fastest all week and the car just didn't handle the way it should for qualifying.'

The second row of the grid was all Canadian, with Scott Goodyear improving from eighth in morning practice with Derrick Walker's Mackenzie Financial Lola-Ford to sneak ahead of Paul Tracy's Penske-Chevy/C. Tracy, though, was content, especially as Emerson Fittipaldi languished far back in 13th, complaining of a lack of turbo boost and, therefore, horsepower.

Roberto Guerrero qualified strongly in fifth, the most competitive showing to date for Kenny Bernstein's Budweiser Lola-Chevy/C, while the top 11 drivers – all the way down to Jimmy Vasser's Kodalux/STP Lola-Ford/Cosworth, once again fastest of the year-old cars – were within six-tenths of the pole time.

RACE

Mansell took advantage of his inside position to take the lead at the start, chased initially by Boesel and the two Canadians, Goodyear and Tracy, who immediately became embroiled in a no-holds-barred battle over third place.

Tracy drew alongside several times but Goodyear was in a feisty mood. He carried a little more straightline speed than his rival and refused to give up without a fight. Finally, on lap 15, Tracy moved ahead for good. Three laps later, another bold

Steve Swope

maneuver enabled him to slip ahead of Boesel at Turn One. Then he set his sights on Mansell.

The Englishman had set off at a fast pace. Little by little, though, Tracy began to inch closer. By lap 40 he was on Mansell's tail. Next time around, Tracy took advantage of some slower traffic to take over the lead.

Boesel was in third place at this stage, followed by Guerrero, who was enjoying his best run of the season. Goodyear, struggling as his car lost its balance, had slipped back to a distant fifth.

Soon he would come under attack from Fittipaldi, who had started 13th. The Brazilian gained only two places in the first 30 laps and came close to being lapped by the flying Mansell and Tracy. But as soon as he realized his predicament, Fittipaldi sprung to life.

Suddenly, he was charging toward the front. On lap 43 he relegated Goodyear to sixth. On lap 57 he moved up one more place at the expense of Boesel. Another seven laps and Guerrero, too, had fallen prey. Now only Tracy and Mansell lay ahead.

This threesome remained in control for the remainder of the afternoon.

The first major incident of the race came on lap 66. It involved David Kudrave, who had moved up from 20th on the grid to a strong 13th in Antonio Ferrari's year-old Agip/Andrea Moda Lola-Chevy/A. Not far ahead of him were former champions Mario

Andretti (Kmart/Havoline Lola-Ford/Cosworth) and Al Unser Jr (Valvoline Lola-Chevy/C). But then Kudrave's day came to a premature end when he spun into the wall in Turn Four.

When the yellow flags waved, Mansell ducked immediately into the pits for service. Tracy's crew was not so quick to react. He completed a full lap under caution before taking on service himself. The delay enabled Mansell to regain the lead.

Guerrero's crew also erred during the caution, calling him in too early. He was caught behind the pace car, almost a full lap down to the leaders.

When the green flag waved again to start lap 75, only five cars remained on the lead lap. Mansell jumped into a clear lead, chased by the Penskes. Fittipaldi looked to have the strongest car at this stage of the race as he caught and passed his teammate on lap 85, diving through on the inside at Turn One. Before long he had closed right up on Mansell . . . taking Tracy along with him.

The crowd then was treated to a heart-stopping battle as the three leaders weaved their way through slower traffic. On lap 94, Tracy became tired of running in third. He repassed Fittipaldi in traffic, then scorched past Mansell in Turn One.

'I learned from these guys today,' admitted Mansell. 'You can race in a different way on the ovals to how you race on the road courses. It's the most thorough-

bred racing I've ever been involved with in my life.'

Through the middle portion of the race, Tracy continued to maintain a slender advantage over Mansell and Fittipaldi. It was cut and thrust. For most of the time all three were separated by little more than a second.

Boesel continued to hold down fourth but was unable to challenge the leaders. On lap 120, he was put a lap down by the flying Tracy. Next time around he was spinning into the barriers on the exit of Turn Three.

'There were a lot of cars in front,' explained Boesel, 'and suddenly my car was losing downforce, I think from the turbulence of the air, and I spun. I hit the wall.'

It was the first time this year Boesel had failed to finish in the points. The yellow flags waved again to warn of the mishap, and all the leaders took the opportunity to make their second scheduled pit stops for fuel and tires. This time it was Mansell's turn for a slight delay, caused by a cross-threaded wheel nut. He fell to third place. Guerrero, his nearest pursuer, was by now a lap behind and in no position to challenge.

Mansell refused to allow the inconvenience to worry him. When the green flags waved again on lap 131, he immediately set off after the Penskes. On lap 143, the three leaders were blanketed by a scant 0.38 second as they flashed across the start/finish line. This was building into a classic contest.

There was one more lull in the action when Goodyear and Andretti clashed on the exit of Turn Four and brought out the final caution of the day. But it didn't affect the battle for the lead, which raged stronger than ever when the green flags signified a restart.

Mansell slipped ahead of Fittipaldi on lap 174 with a decisive move into Turn Three. Tracy was determined not to capitulate so easily. He drove hard and without the hint of an error.

'I think it was one of the best races of the year,' said Tracy, with masterful understatement.

On lap 191, Mansell found a chink in Tracy's armor, taking advantage of traffic in Turn One and regaining the lead going onto the back straightaway. But Tracy wasn't giving up yet. When Mansell also encountered traffic on the entry to Turn Three, Tracy drove brilliantly around the outside of him in Turn Three. Tracy drove brilliantly around the outside to reclaim the top position. Wow!

'It was just a question of learning where to be,' said Mansell. 'Paul anticipated the next move. It was like a chess game. I forgot the next corner was coming up and Paul just blew past me on the outside. It was a great move.'

Now it was Mansell's turn. On lap 197, as Tracy hesitated for a split-second, Mansell called upon every ounce of bravery by driving around the outside of him in Turn One. It was a move indicative of an oval track veteran – and yet Mansell was taking part in only

Left: **The rolling start of the New England 200 with Nigel Mansell and Raul Boesel** *(left)* **heading the 25-car field toward Turn One.**

his fourth-ever oval track race.

'Paul was on the inside and I went to the outside,' explained Mansell calmly, 'and I had the momentum in my favor.'

Try as he did, Tracy was unable to respond. He had to settle for second place.

'It feels good that I've been able to lead on the one-mile ovals this year, but I haven't been able to win one yet,' said the young Canadian. 'It's disappointing. But that was a great race. It was definitely a tough battle all race long. I enjoyed it.'

Fittipaldi concurred. 'It was great to watch,' he said. 'They did

a fantastic drive. The last segment of the race my car was a little bit loose. I had to be a bit cautious in traffic, so I couldn't challenge the other two.'

Guerrero maintained his strong showing to claim fourth, unlucky to have lost a lap early in the race. Robby Gordon also was one lap behind, less than four seconds adrift of Guerrero at the checkered flag after a sensible drive in his Copenhagen Lola-Ford. Scott Brayton was delighted to finish sixth, equaling his best result of the year in the Amway/Northwest Airlines Lola-Ford/Cosworth.

• Former F1 racers Mauricio Gugelmin and Roberto Moreno, plus Le Mans winner Andy Wallace were among the ranks of underemployed drivers snooping around the paddock area in search of work.

• Nigel Mansell padded his coffers by virtue of winning the Marlboro Pole Award, worth $10,000, and then scooping the bonus pool of $45,000, unclaimed for the past three races, for taking the race victory as well.

• The crowd was slightly down compared to the track's first Indy Car event a year ago. The deficit was put down to cool weather conditions as well as a clashing NASCAR Winston Cup stock car race at Watkins Glen, situated only a few hours' drive to the west.

• Paul Tracy *(right)* perhaps provided the best summation of the tense closing stages. 'The last ten laps were white-knuckle, let's-get-on-with-it racing,' he declared. 'It was serious racing.'

Michael C. Brown

NEW ENGLAND 200, NEW HAMPSHIRE INTERNATIONAL SPEEDWAY, LOUDON, NEW HAMPSHIRE • 8 August, 200 laps – 211.600 miles

Place	Driver	No.	Car	Q Speed (mph)	Q Time	Q Pos.	Laps	Time/Retirement	Ave. speed	Pts
1	Nigel Mansell	5	Kmart/Texaco Havoline Lola T93/00-Ford	169.247	22.504s	1	200	1h 37m 33.033s	130.148 mph	21
2	Paul Tracy	12	Marlboro Penske PC22-Chevy/C	167.788	22.700s	4	200	1h 37m 33.487s	130.138	17
3	Emerson Fittipaldi	4	Marlboro Penske PC22-Chevy/C	164.096	23.211s	13	200	1h 37m 41.830s	129.953	14
4	Roberto Guerrero	40	Budweiser King Lola T93/00-Chevy/C	167.089	22.795s	5	199	Running		12
5	Robby Gordon	14	Copenhagen Racing Lola T93/00-Ford	162.550	23.432s	14	199	Running		10
6	Scott Brayton	22	Amway/Northwest Airlines Lola T93/00-Ford	165.507	23.013s	7	198	Running		8
7	Bobby Rahal	1	Miller Genuine Draft Lola T93/00-Chevy/C	165.209	23.054s	9	197	Running		6
8	Al Unser Jr	3	Valvoline Lola T93/00-Chevy/C	162.318	23.465s	15	197	Running		5
9	Jimmy Vasser	18	Kodalux Processing/STP Lola T92/00-Ford	164.937	23.092s	11	194	Running		4
10	Brian Till	99	Say NO To Drugs Penske PC21-Chevy/B	158.795	23.986s	21	194	Running		3
11	Mike Groff	26	Miller Genuine Draft Rahal/Hogan 001-Chevy/C	162.264	23.473s	16	194	Running		2
12	Olivier Grouillard	29	Eurosport/Marlboro Lola T92/00-Chevy/A	160.056	23.797s	19	192	Running		1
13	Hiro Matsushita	15	Panasonic Special Lola T93/00-Ford	157.784	24.139s	22	191	Running		
14	Stefan Johansson	16	AMAX Energy & Metals Penske PC22-Chevy/C	164.707	23.125s	12	190	Running		
15	Willy T. Ribbs	75	Cosby/Service Merchandise Lola T92/00-Ford	161.614	23.567s	17	190	Running		
16	Teo Fabi	8	Pennzoil Special Lola T93/00-Chevy/C	165.082	23.072s	10	185	Running		
17	Marco Greco	30	Alfa Laval/Team Losi Lola T92/00-Chevy/A	155.617	24.475s	24	183	Running		
18	Johnny Unser	19	Ruger Special Lola T92/00-Chevy/A	156.947	24.268s	23	163	Running		
19	Scott Goodyear	2	Mackenzie Special Lola T93/00-Ford	167.863	22.690s	3	140	Accident		
20	Mario Andretti	6	Kmart/Texaco Havoline Lola T93/00-Ford	166.970	22.811s	6	137	Accident		
21	Raul Boesel	9	Duracell/Mobil 1/Sadia Lola T93/00-Ford	169.207	22.510s	2	120	Accident		
22	Danny Sullivan	7	Molson Lola T93/00-Chevy/C	165.267	23.046s	8	94	Handling		
23	David Kudrave	42	Andrea Moda/Agip Lola T92/00-Chevy/A	160.050	23.798s	20	63	Accident		
24	Jeff Wood	50	Andrea Moda/Agip Lola T91/00-DFS	155.350	24.518s	25	55	Engine		
25	Arie Luyendyk	10	Target/Scotch Video Lola T93/00-Ford	161.505	23.583s	18	32	Handling		

Caution flags: Laps 1-3, accident/Greco and Wood; laps 66-73, accident/Kudrave; laps 121-131, accident/Boesel; laps 144-156, accident/Goodyear and Andretti.

Lap leaders: Nigel Mansell, 1-40 (40 laps); Paul Tracy, 41-68 (28 laps); Nigel Mansell, 69-94 (26 laps); Paul Tracy, 95-196 (102 laps); Nigel Mansell, 197-200 (4 laps). *Totals:* Paul Tracy, 130 laps; Nigel Mansell, 70 laps.

Championship positions: **1** Mansell, 144 pts; **2** Fittipaldi, 119; **3** Tracy, 100; **4** Boesel, 98; **5** Mario Andretti, 97; **6** Rahal, 80; **7** Al Unser Jr, 65; **8** Luyendyk, 57; **9** Gordon, 53; **10** Fabi, 47; **11** Sullivan, 40; **12** Guerrero, 37; **13** Goodyear, 28; **14** Vasser, 27; **15** Brayton, 26; **16** Johansson, 15; **17** Montermini, 12; **18** Pruett, 12; **19** Cheever, 10; **20** Buhl, 8; **21** Groff, 8; **22** Till, 7; **23** Smith, 7; **24** Fernandez, 6; **25** Kudrave, 6; **26** Matsushita, 6; **27** Ribbs, 6; **28** Grouillard, 4; **29** John Andretti, 3; **30** Greco, 2; **31** Bentley, 1; **32** Al Unser, 1; **33** Gachot, 1.

ROAD AMERICA

The Texaco/Havoline 200 at Road America was all about Paul Tracy. The 24-year-old Canadian led all the way from pole position in his Marlboro Penske PC22-Chevrolet/C and was never seriously challenged in the 50-lap race.

Tracy's only trouble was the legacy of a high-speed crash on Friday, caused by a rear toe-link failure. Tracy had been fortunate to escape with nothing worse than heavy bruising to his right ankle, although he was hindered when it became inflamed in the closing stages of the race.

'It wasn't so much the movement, but the strapping on it was so tight I began to lose feeling,' said Tracy. 'Luckily I had a good lead so I was able to back off a bit.'

PPG Cup points leader Nigel Mansell was no match for Tracy but nevertheless drove strongly to a distant second place in his Kmart/Havoline Lola-Ford/Cosworth XB. Mansell duly strengthened his lead in the championship over fifth-placed finisher Emerson Fittipaldi, who lost time with a stop-and-go penalty after exceeding the speed limit in pit lane.

Mansell's teammate, Mario Andretti, was heading toward a clear third-place finish until his engine fell sick with less than five laps remaining. Andretti's misfortune allowed defending PPG Cup champion Bobby Rahal to annex third place in his Miller Genuine Draft Lola-Chevy/C.

No one, though, could hold a candle to Tracy.

| 1st – TRACY | 2nd – MANSELL | 3rd – RAHAL |

Main photo: Paul Tracy kicks up the dust as he makes the break from the pack at the restart. The Marlboro Penske driver was never seriously challenged despite the handicap of an ankle injury sustained in a practice crash.

Nigel Mansell *(inset)* took a distant second place, but consolidated his position as PPG Cup points leader.

QUALIFYING

Paul Tracy battled hard to earn his second successive pole at Road America and his second of the season. Still suffering the effects of his crash the day before, he underwent intense therapy on Saturday morning to prepare him for final qualifying.

'I had ultra-sound to loosen my ankle and a massage for my neck,' he said. 'If it wasn't for those guys [in the IndyCar medical unit], I'm sure I wouldn't be able to drive.'

Nigel Mansell, who was fastest on the first day, slipped to second on the grid but was nevertheless content with his effort.

'We had a couple of great runs and I think I optimized the car,' he said. 'I'm very happy with my time. There's no doubt the Penske car is good but I'd like to say Paul did a great job. I think he set a marvelous time. I've no complaints at all.'

Mario Andretti took a deep breath and improved his time on his very last lap to annex third on the grid in his sister car.

'I came in [to the pits] to make a change [to the setup] and have another stab at it,' declared the 53-year-old veteran. 'I knew I had one lap to go and it paid off.'

Andretti's effort nosed out Raul Boesel, who was rightly pleased with his performance since his Dick Simon Racing Duracell/Mobil 1/Sadia Lola still was not privy to the latest Ford/Cosworth engines. Boesel was consistently quick through the corners, confirmed by independent split times in the Carousel, while on the critical straightaways, which make up a large proportion of the four-mile track, his Lola was generally four or five mph slower than the Newman-Haas entries.

Tracy's teammate, Emerson Fittipaldi, set the fifth-best time after overcoming more boost problems, while Al Unser Jr made a quantum leap forward in Rick Galles' Valvoline Lola-Chevy/C, moving up from 11th to sixth in the final session.

'We've steadily been improving the car to try and get around the corners better,' said Unser, whose record at Road America included second-place finishes in each of the previous two races. 'We've been nibbling at some things and it has helped the car all the way around.'

RACE

Any thoughts of Tracy being caught were cast aside even before the end of the opening lap. The youngster took the lead at the start and apart from running slightly wide at the second corner he never put a wheel wrong.

He was able to pull away handsomely in the early stages, with Mansell heading the vain pursuit ahead of Andretti, Boesel and Robby Gordon, who made another of his patented fast getaways from eighth on the grid in A.J. Foyt's Copenhagen Lola-Ford.

Arie Luyendyk also made progress, up from 11th to sixth in the Target/Scotch Video Lola-Ford. Fittipaldi followed, despite being handicapped right away by a down-on-power engine.

'I just put the throttle [pedal] down and everybody went by me,' lamented Fittipaldi. 'My boost was so low I had no power.'

Teammate Tracy, meanwhile, was driving away from everyone . . . at least until lap six, when his six-second lead was trimmed to nothing by a full-course caution.

Rookie Adrian Fernandez had crashed heavily at the Turn 11 kink – the same place that claimed Tracy on Friday. The Mexican's Conseco Lola-Chevy/C sustained heavy front-end damage, although once again the driver was fortunate and escaped with only a bruised knee and a slight concussion.

The interruption was but a minor inconvenience to Tracy. His advantage once again grew by a second per lap for the first four laps after the restart, whereupon

Photos: Michael C. Brown

Olivier Grouillard is about to feel a Genuine Draft as Bobby Rahal's Miller machine chases down the Eurosport/Marlboro Lola to put a lap on the Frenchman early in the race.

Mansell was able to hold station until the first round of pit stops, which began on lap 19.

By the time everyone was back up to speed, Mansell had slipped some nine seconds behind Tracy. Boesel ran between them, in second, but only as the result of having made his first stop during the earlier caution. He, uniquely among the leaders, was planning to make three stops.

Luyendyk ran fourth after passing Gordon under braking for Canada Corner, only to spin at Turn Five on lap 30 as he attempted to lap Hiro Matsushita's Panasonic Lola-Ford. Luyendyk lost out once again to Gordon, and thereafter his car was troubled by oversteer, the result of clipping a barrier as he rejoined the track.

The two Newman-Haas cars continued serenely in second and third places, quite unable to match Tracy, while Rahal had moved up to fourth after a typically consistent performance.

'We tested well here but qualifying was disappointing,' said Rahal, who started only tenth. 'In the race, the car was as good as it has been all year.'

Tracy duly settled into a comfortable pace, and apart from nursing his numb right foot, was able to cruise home to a superb victory, his fourth of the season. Mansell crossed the line more than 27 seconds adrift in second place.

'We didn't have any problems at all,' stated Mansell. 'The car worked absolutely beautifully. It's just that it wasn't quick enough to keep up with the Penske.'

The unlucky Andretti succumbed to an engine failure four laps from the finish, which allowed Rahal to make his first visit to the podium since finishing second at Long Beach in April.

'We couldn't run with Nigel or Paul but we could keep up with everyone else,' said Rahal. 'That's about as fast as we could ask for today.'

Boesel, ruing his team's three-stop strategy, slowed toward the finish but maintained fourth in the race and the PPG Cup standings, followed by a disappointed Fittipaldi.

Luyendyk was headed for fifth until suffering a blown right-rear tire just a couple of laps from the finish. He pitted and crossed the line in eighth, only to be penalized an additional 25 seconds for running over an air hose during that final unscheduled stop. He was classified a disgruntled ninth.

SNIPPETS

Michael C. Brown

• The notorious 'kink', situated midway along one of the longest straightaways, is negotiated foot-to-the-floor by the quickest drivers in ideal circumstances. The ensuing corner, Turn 12, is known as Canada Corner, because in the track's early days the regular clean-up crews discovered much of the debris emanated from north of the border. Following Tracy's accident, however, fellow Canadian Scott Goodyear, who crashed in the same place last year, suggested the kink should be renamed Canada Corner.

• Eddie Cheever *(above)* returned to the fray at the wheel of the same Dick Simon Lola-Ford used previously by Lyn St James and Bertrand Gachot. Cheever qualified 15th but ran rather better in the race after a problem with the front shock absorbers had been diagnosed. In the closing stages he enjoyed a close tussle for position with Scott Goodyear until they made contact in Turn Five. Cheever's car lost its nosecone but he was able to limp home in sixth, the last runner to complete the full distance.

• Christian Danner, making only his second Indy Car start of the season, lost more than half a minute during his first stop when the air jacks failed on his Agip/Andrea Moda Lola T92/00-Chevy/A. Danner was obliged to complete the entire race without a change of tires, so 11th place represented a fine effort.

• Mike Groff qualified his regular Rahal/Hogan car but, following the detection of a major crack in the chassis, he started the race in Rahal's backup Lola T93/00-Chevy/C.

IndyCar

• Immediately after the race, Bill Stokkan, chairman and chief executive officer of Championship Auto Racing Teams, the sanctioning body for IndyCar racing, announced he will not stand for re-election when his current term expires at the end of 1994.

TEXACO/HAVOLINE 200, ROAD AMERICA CIRCUIT, ELKHART LAKE, WISCONSIN • 22 August, 50 laps – 200.000 miles

Place	Driver	No.	Car	Q Speed (mph)	Q Time	Q Pos.	Laps	Time/Retirement	Ave. speed	Pts
1	Paul Tracy	12	*Marlboro* Penske PC22-Chevy/C	134.072	1m 47.405s	1	50	1h 41m 20.689s	118.408 mph	22
2	Nigel Mansell	5	*Kmart/Texaco Havoline* Lola T93/00-Ford	133.516	1m 47.852s	2	50	1h 41m 48.148s	117.875	16
3	Bobby Rahal	1	*Miller Genuine Draft* Lola T93/00-Chevy/C	131.450	1m 49.547s	10	50	1h 42m 00.207s	117.643	14
4	Raul Boesel	9	*Duracell/Mobil 1/Sadia* Lola T93/00-Ford	133.059	1m 48.223s	4	50	1h 42m 12.446s	117.408	12
5	Emerson Fittipaldi	4	*Marlboro* Penske PC22-Chevy/C	132.985	1m 48.283s	5	50	1h 42m 20.845s	117.248	10
6	Eddie Cheever	90	*Menard/Immobiliser* Lola T93/00-Ford	130.536	1m 50.314s	15	50	1h 43m 12.493s	116.270	8
7	Scott Brayton	22	*Amway/Northwest Airlines* Lola T93/00-Ford	131.293	1m 49.678s	13	49	Running		6
8	Teo Fabi	8	*Pennzoil Special* Lola T93/00-Chevy/C	130.386	1m 50.441s	16	49	Running		5
*9	Arie Luyendyk	10	*Target/Scotch Video* Lola T93/00-Ford	131.419	1m 49.573s	11	49	Running		4
10	Scott Goodyear	2	*Mackenzie Special* Lola T93/00-Ford	131.836	1m 49.227s	7	49	Running		3
11	Christian Danner	50	*Andrea Moda/Agip* Lola T92/00-Chevy/A	130.538	1m 50.313s	14	49	Running		2
12	Willy T. Ribbs	75	*Cosby/Service Merchandise* Lola T92/00-Ford	128.266	1m 52.267s	22	48	Running		1
13	Hiro Matsushita	15	*Panasonic Special* Lola T93/00-Ford	129.199	1m 51.456s	21	48	Running		
14	Buddy Lazier	20	*Financial World* Lola T91/00-Buick	121.196	1m 58.816s	28	48	Running		
15	Mario Andretti	6	*Kmart/Texaco Havoline* Lola T93/00-Ford	133.118	1m 48.175s	3	47	Engine		
16	Olivier Grouillard	29	*Eurosport/Marlboro* Lola T92/00-Chevy/A	124.362	1m 55.791s	25	47	Spun off		
17	Ross Bentley	39	*AGFA/Rain-X* Lola T92/00-Chevy/A	123.635	1m 56.472s	27	47	Running		
18	Mike Groff	26	*Miller Genuine Draft* Lola T93/00-Chevy/C	130.007	1m 50.763s	18	44	Engine		
19	Robbie Buhl	19	*Simon/Mi-Jack* Lola T92/00-Chevy/A	126.381	1m 53.941s	23	44	Electrical		
20	Robby Gordon	14	*Copenhagen Racing* Lola T93/00-Ford	131.703	1m 49.337s	8	43	Overheating		
21	Stefan Johansson	16	*AMAX Energy & Metals* Penske PC22-Chevy/C	120.145	1m 50.646s	17	39	Gearbox		
22	Brian Till	99	*Say NO To Drugs* Penske PC21-Chevy/B	129.401	1m 51.282s	20	34	Halfshaft		
23	Roberto Guerrero	40	*Budweiser King* Lola T93/00-Chevy/C	131.357	1m 49.625s	12	33	Engine		
24	Mark Smith	25	*Craftsman* Penske PC21-Chevy/B	131.515	1m 49.493s	9	30	Engine		
25	Al Unser Jr	3	*Valvoline* Lola T93/00-Chevy/C	132.331	1m 48.818s	6	21	Gearbox		
26	Danny Sullivan	7	*Molson* Lola T93/00-Chevy/C	120.740	1m 50.991s	19	15	Engine		
27	Jeff Wood	42	*Andrea Moda/Agip* Lola T91/00-DFS	120.059	1m 59.941s	29	12	Gearbox		
28	Marco Greco	30	*Alfa Laval/Team Losi* Lola T92/00-Chevy/A	123.787	1m 56.329s	26	6	Gearbox		
29	Adrian Fernandez	11	*Conseco* Lola T93/00-Chevy/C	125.332	1m 54.895s	24	3	Accident		

* 25-second penalty for pit lane infringement

Caution flags: Lap 1, field out of formation; laps 5-8, accident/Fernandez.

Lap leaders: Paul Tracy, 1-50 (50 laps). **Totals:** Paul Tracy, 50 laps.

Championship positions: 1 Mansell, 160 pts; **2** Fittipaldi, 129; **3** Tracy, 122; **4** Boesel, 110; **5** Mario Andretti, 97; **6** Rahal, 94; **7** Al Unser Jr, 65; **8** Luyendyk, 61; **9** Gordon, 53; **10** Fabi, 52; **11** Sullivan, 40; **12** Guerrero, 37; **13** Brayton, 32; **14** Goodyear, 31; **15** Vasser, 27; **16** Cheever, 18; **17** Johansson, 15; **18** Montermini, 12; **19** Pruett, 12; **20** Buhl, 8; **21** Groff, 8; **22** Till, 7; **23** Smith, 7; **24** Ribbs, 7; **25** Fernandez, 6; **26** Kudrave, 6; **27** Matsushita, 6; **28** Grouillard, 4; **29** John Andretti, 3; **30** Greco, 2; **31** Danner, 2; **32** Bentley, 1; **33** Al Unser, 1; **34** Gachot, 1.

VANCOUVER

The first half of the season had been pretty much disastrous for Al Unser Jr, but in recent races he had been creeping gradually closer to his rightful position toward the front of the field. Finally, in the Molson Indy Vancouver, all the pieces fell into place at the right time to enable him to score a well-earned victory in Galles Racing International's Valvoline Lola T93/00-Chevrolet Indy V8/C.

'I'm really happy,' declared Unser after taking his first win since Indianapolis in 1992. 'It's been a long time without winning a race. This year it's been a pretty long struggle.'

Unser was able to run a consistently fast pace, and once Paul Tracy's Marlboro Penske PC22-Chevy/C was hobbled by a faulty alternator, he had only last year's PPG Cup champion Bobby Rahal to beat.

Passing, however, is notoriously difficult on the fast and bumpy 1.648-mile temporary circuit centered upon the imposing BC Place Stadium on the outskirts of downtown Vancouver. So Unser bided his time, then took advantage of a superior pit strategy. He gained the lead during the second round of stops before romping home to the 19th Indy Car victory of his career.

Rahal, slightly miffed after leading most laps, followed in second place with his Miller Genuine Draft Lola-Chevy/C, while Stefan Johansson (AMAX Penske-Chevy/C) usurped Scott Goodyear, whose Mackenzie Financial Lola-Ford/Cosworth was hobbled by a failing gearbox, for third place in the closing stages.

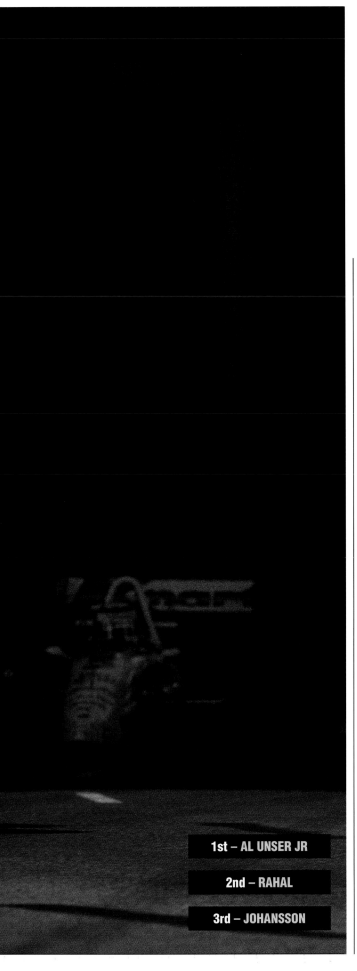

Out of the shadows. Al Unser Jr took his first win of the year with Galles Racing International's Valvoline Lola-Chevy/C. Here he exits the tunnel ahead of Nigel Mansell's Kmart/Texaco Havoline Lola-Ford.

1st – AL UNSER JR

2nd – RAHAL

3rd – JOHANSSON

QUALIFYING

If there was anything to be learned from practice and qualifying it was the fact that for the first time this season there was virtually nothing to choose between the three primary engine/chassis combinations. Bobby Rahal topped the time sheets in Friday's opening practice with his Lola-Chevy/C and Paul Tracy's Penske-Chevy/C gained the provisional pole that same afternoon, while on Saturday Nigel Mansell and Scott Goodyear shared the sessional honors in their Lola-Ford/Cosworths.

Ultimately, and to the delight of the Canadian crowd, it was Goodyear who emerged with the pole for Derrick Walker's team. But it was a close-run thing.

'We bounced off every curb in the place but it seemed to work,' said Goodyear after earning his second pole of the year.

Rahal, who lost time the first day with a cracked cylinder liner, and Mansell (Kmart/Havoline Lola-Ford/Cosworth) were within a tenth of a second of Goodyear's best. Tracy slipped to fourth on the grid but explained he had been unable to extract the best from his car.

'It was just a question of traffic,' he confided. 'I think there was a lot more to come.'

Unser Jr also was quietly confident after setting the fifth-fastest time in qualifying. Robby Gordon was close to the pace, too, despite having to run A.J. Foyt's '92 Copenhagen Lola-Ford after clipping a wall and destroying the '93 car's bell-housing during the first session on Friday.

The first seven drivers were separated by a scant half-second, including young Italian Andrea Montermini, who once again displayed his talents in Antonio Ferrari's under-financed Agip/Andrea Moda '92 Lola-Chevy/A. The next seven cars also were blanketed by less than four-tenths.

RACE

Gorgeous weather, a perfect British Columbia setting and a Canadian driver on the pole ensured a record-sized crowd was gathered for the 102-lap race. The first attempt at a start was aborted when Rahal jumped ahead into the first corner, but at the second time of asking everyone accelerated away cleanly and Goodyear was able to maintain his advantage.

Gordon, as usual, made a blinding start to scorch around the outside of Unser at Turn One. He also usurped Mansell in Turn Two, although sadly his race was short-lived, ended by a broken driveshaft as he accelerated out of the final hairpin.

By that time the yellow flags already were waving as the result of several incidents on a fraught opening lap. Arie Luyendyk (Target/Scotch Video Lola-Ford), Olivier Grouillard (Eurosport/Marlboro Lola-Chevy/A) and Scott Brayton (Amway/Northwest Airlines Lola-Ford) were rendered *hors de combat*, while Willy T. Ribbs (Service Merchandise Lola-Ford) continued only after a lengthy delay.

The restart came with seven laps already on the board, and it wasn't long before Tracy began to move toward the front. He took over second place when Rahal locked up his brakes going into the final hairpin turn on lap ten, and three laps later drew alongside Goodyear under acceleration out of the same corner.

Not this time, thank you, said Scott, who held the inside advantage going into Turn One.

Next time around, Goodyear emulated Rahal's mistake and slid wide on the exit of Turn Ten. Before he knew it he was in third place, which soon became fourth when Unser moved ahead a couple of laps later.

Tracy's lead lasted only one lap, before he, too, erred by going too deep into the hairpin. In a flash,

Photos: Michael C. Brown

Stefan Johansson *(above)* finally got a few breaks in Tony Bettenhausen's AMAX Penske PC22-Chevy/C, snatching a third-place finish away from Scott Goodyear on the penultimate lap when the Canadian encountered gearbox difficulties.

Below: **Scott Goodyear (2)** makes contact lapping Roberto Guerrero (40), happily without mishap. Paul Tracy (12) holds a watching brief behind.

Rahal was able to draw alongside and gain the lead as they sped past the pit area.

Mansell, meanwhile, was clearly in trouble, having waved Unser through as early as lap 12.

'I just had no grip,' said the PPG Cup leader. 'I needed to finish the race so there was no point in holding him up.'

On lap 23, Tracy's hopes of victory were dashed when his engine cut dead. An alternator failure was to blame.

The Penske was towed in under a full-course caution while everyone else made their first scheduled pit stops. Tracy resumed after a lengthy delay but could manage no better than 13th place. No points this day.

Rahal and Unser joined battle when the green flags flew again, and soon they began to draw away from Goodyear. Johansson had taken advantage of a good pit stop to move up to fourth ahead of Raul Boesel (Duracell/Mobil 1/Sadia Lola-Ford) and Emerson Fittipaldi (Marlboro Penske-Chevy/C), while Mansell's miserable day worsened as he fell all the way back to tenth after stalling his engine.

The crowd's interest, however, was focused on the battle for the lead.

'I looked in my mirror and saw Unser lurking,' said Rahal. 'That's always a bad sign when you see him in the mirror, because you know he's running strong.'

Both men kept a wary eye on their fuel consumption, always a critical factor in Vancouver with the constant acceleration out of tight corners, but it was a good, clean fight.

'I couldn't pass him in a legitimate way,' said Unser. 'I would've had to force the issue and risk taking us both out, so I tried to pressure him and hope he'd make a mistake.'

None came. Instead, the pass was made during the second round of routine pit stops. Rahal ducked in for service on lap 65. Unser was able to stretch his fuel load two more laps, during which he pulled out the decisive margin.

Tires, as well as fuel consumption and excellent pit work, were the critical factors, as Unser's two extra laps on hot rubber enabled him to make his own pit stop on lap 67 without relinquishing the lead.

'I really need to thank my guys [on the crew],' said Unser. 'They made the pass. That's teamwork and that's how you win races.'

The remaining laps saw Rahal unable to make inroads into Unser's advantage. Goodyear, meanwhile, was having trouble with third and fifth gears, which allowed Johansson to take over third place a couple of laps from the end. In fact, Goodyear was lucky to make the finish, losing third altogether on the final lap.

Good pit work by the Newman-Haas crew enabled Andretti and Mansell to move from eighth and ninth to fifth and sixth after their final stops, with Fittipaldi dropping to seventh ahead of Teo Fabi, who drove a consistent race in his Pennzoil Lola-Chevy/C. Boesel slipped to ninth after stalling the engine during his second pit stop.

SNIPPETS

• With Nigel Mansell struggling to find speed during practice on Saturday morning, Willy T. Ribbs thought he was in deep trouble after tangling with the Formula 1 World Champion and forcing him into the backup Lola. Ribbs assumed it was his mistake, having not seen Mansell approaching, and later went to apologize. Ribbs, though, was surprised at Mansell's reaction. 'There he was, in the middle of his debrief, and I thought he'd be mad,' related Ribbs. 'But he jumped up, a big grin on his face, gave me a big bear-hug and said, "Sorry, it was my fault, I braked too late. And thanks very much, because the backup car was much better." I couldn't believe it!'

Michael C. Brown

Michael C. Brown

• Bobby Rahal displayed his most competitive form of the season and had no problems setting fastest time in the race morning warmup. 'It's easy,' said Rahal. 'I was attacking the corners but I wasn't having to hold my breath.'

• Canadian Prime Minister Kim Campbell gave the time-honored command to fire up the engines prior to the race.

• Scott Goodyear was delighted with the handling of his car after a switch to three-way adjustable Penske shock absorbers. He was also using a revised undertray and other aerodynamic tweaks for the first time. 'It just seems like it's given the car more grip and improved stability,' he noted, 'and it's much more consistent.'

MOLSON INDY VANCOUVER, BC PLACE, VANCOUVER, BRITISH COLUMBIA, CANADA • 29 August, 102 laps – 168.000 miles

Place	Driver	No.	Car	Q Speed (mph)	Q Time	Q Pos.	Laps	Time/Retirement	Ave. speed	Pts
1	Al Unser Jr	3	*Valvoline* Lola T93/00-Chevy/C	109.604	54.112s	5	102	1h 49m 52.452s	91.794 mph	20
2	Bobby Rahal	1	*Miller Genuine Draft* Lola T93/00-Chevy/C	110.171	53.851s	2	102	1h 50m 03.651s	91.638	17
3	Stefan Johansson	16	*AMAX Energy & Metals* Penske PC22-Chevy/C	108.644	54.608s	11	102	1h 50m 26.789s	91.318	14
4	Scott Goodyear	2	*Mackenzie Special* Lola T93/00-Ford	110.293	53.791s	1	102	1h 50m 35.008s	91.205	13
5	Mario Andretti	6	*Kmart/Texaco Havoline* Lola T93/00-Ford	108.229	54.817s	14	102	1h 50m 39.545s	91.143	10
6	Nigel Mansell	5	*Kmart/Texaco Havoline* Lola T93/00-Ford	110.128	53.872s	3	101	Running		8
7	Emerson Fittipaldi	4	*Marlboro* Penske PC22-Chevy/C	108.739	54.560s	10	101	Running		6
8	Teo Fabi	8	*Pennzoil Special* Lola T93/00-Chevy/C	108.900	54.479s	9	101	Running		5
9	Raul Boesel	9	*Duracell/Mobil 1/Sadia* Lola T93/00-Ford	108.971	54.444s	8	101	Running		4
10	Danny Sullivan	7	*Molson* Lola T93/00-Chevy/C	107.838	55.016s	15	100	Running		3
11	Roberto Guerrero	40	*Budweiser King* Lola T93/00-Chevy/C	107.485	55.196s	18	100	Running		2
12	Hiro Matsushita	15	*Panasonic Special* Lola T93/00-Ford	104.453	56.790s	22	96	Running		1
13	Paul Tracy	12	*Marlboro* Penske PC22-Chevy/C	109.946	53.961s	4	93	Running		
14	Dominic Dobson	17	*Winning Spirit* Galmer G92B-Chevy/A	102.694	57.771s	23	85	Running		
15	Jeff Wood	42	*Andrea Moda/Agip* Lola T91/00-DFS	99.694	57.510s	25	74	Gearbox		
16	Willy T. Ribbs	75	*Cosby/Service Merchandise* Lola T92/00-Ford	107.764	55.054s	16	49	Running		
17	Ross Bentley	39	*AGFA/Rain-X* Lola T92/00-Chevy/A	104.612	56.712s	21	46	Gearbox		
18	Jimmy Vasser	18	*Kodalux Processing/STP* Lola T92/00-Ford	108.364	54.749s	12	40	Accident		
19	Andrea Montermini	50	*Andrea Moda/Agip* Lola T92/00-Chevy/A	109.312	54.274s	7	32	Header		
20	Marco Greco	30	*Alfa Laval/Team Losi* Lola T92/00-Chevy/A	102.331	57.976s	24	32	Gearbox		
21	Johnny Unser	19	*Ruger Special* Lola T92/00-Chevy/A	98.920	59.976s	26	24	Gearbox		
22	Mark Smith	25	*Craftsman* Penske PC21-Chevy/B	108.230	54.816s	13	16	Gearbox		
23	Robby Gordon	14	*Copenhagen Racing* Lola T92/00-Ford	109.444	54.209s	6	2	Halfshaft		
24	Scott Brayton	22	*Amway/Northwest Airlines* Lola T93/00-Ford	107.369	55.256s	19	2	Suspension		
25	Arie Luyendyk	10	*Target/Scotch Video* Lola T93/00-Ford	107.633	55.120s	17	1	Accident		
26	Olivier Grouillard	29	*Eurosport/Marlboro* Lola T92/00-Chevy/A	105.254	56.367s	20	1	Accident		

Caution flags: Lap 1, field out of formation; laps 2-6, accident/Grouillard, Luyendyk and Brayton; laps 23-27, Tracy/tow; laps 42-45, accident/Vasser.

Lap leaders: Scott Goodyear, 1-13 (13 laps); Paul Tracy, 14 (1 lap); Bobby Rahal, 15-64 (50 laps); Al Unser Jr, 65-102 (38 laps). *Totals:* Bobby Rahal, 50 laps; Al Unser Jr, 38 laps; Scott Goodyear, 13 laps; Paul Tracy, 1 lap.

Championship positions: **1** Mansell, 168 pts; **2** Fittipaldi, 135; **3** Tracy, 122; **4** Boesel, 114; **5** Rahal, 111; **6** Mario Andretti, 107; **7** Al Unser Jr, 85; **8** Luyendyk, 61; **9** Fabi, 57; **10** Gordon, 53; **11** Goodyear, 44; **12** Sullivan, 43; **13** Guerrero, 39; **14** Brayton, 32; **15** Johansson, 29; **16** Vasser, 27; **17** Cheever, 18; **18** Montermini, 12; **19** Pruett, 12; **20** Buhl, 8; **21** Groff, 8; **22** Smith, 7; **23** Till, 7; **24** Matsushita, 7; **25** Ribbs, 7; **26** Fernandez, 6; **27** Kudrave, 6; **28** Grouillard, 4; **29** John Andretti, 3; **30** Greco, 2; **31** Danner, 2; **32** Bentley, 1; **33** Al Unser, 1; **34** Gachot, 1.

MID-OHIO

Emerson Fittipaldi underscored the significance of patience during the Pioneer Electronics 200 at the Trueman family's scenic Mid-Ohio Sports Car Course.

The Brazilian never put a wheel wrong, in contrast to a number of his rivals. He also withstood several determined challenges before emerging from an entertaining 89-lap race with his third victory of the season in Roger Penske's Marlboro Penske-Chevrolet Indy V8/C.

Fittipaldi's triumph kept alive his slim championship hopes, since points leader Nigel Mansell finished an angry 12th in his Kmart/Texaco Havoline Lola-Ford/Cosworth following a first-corner contretemps while disputing the lead with Paul Tracy.

Raul Boesel (Duracell/Mobil 1/Sadia Lola-Ford), Al Unser Jr (Valvoline Lola-Chevy/C) and Scott Goodyear (Mackenzie Financial Lola-Ford) all ran in second place at one time or another, only for Robby Gordon (Copenhagen Lola-Ford) to emerge with the position after by far the most mature drive of his short career on the Indy Car scene.

'Robby did a hell of a job,' praised team owner A.J. Foyt, who holds the all-time record with 67 Indy Car victories to his name. 'I give a lot of credit to him. When you're running against guys like Emerson and all the big guys, any finish in the top five is a hell of a job.'

Emerson Fittipaldi *(left)* was back in business with a resolute performance. Once again the Chevy/C-powered Marlboro Penske was in its element on a road course.

Michael C. Brown

1st – FITTIPALDI

2nd – GORDON

3rd – GOODYEAR

After qualifying in a lowly 15th spot, Robby Gordon drove his best Indy Car race to date to claim second place in the Copenhagen Racing Lola T93/00-Ford, mightily impressing his boss A.J. Foyt in the process.

Below: Mauricio Gugelmin, another refugee from F1, appeared in Indy Car racing for the first time with the Dick Simon-entered Lola previously handled this year by Lyn St James, Bertrand Gachot and Eddie Cheever.

Michael C. Brown

QUALIFYING

Paul Tracy led the way through most of practice and qualifying, only for Nigel Mansell to steal the pole on the very last lap of a thrilling final half-hour session.

'I just hung it all out there,' said Mansell after a typically spectacular effort. 'Nobody's holding back. It was the end of the session and I was going for it.

'The team has worked really hard. We've made some progress with the car. I'm very pleased.'

Penske teammates Tracy and Fittipaldi both topped the timing sheet briefly, but ultimately had to be content with second and third on the grid. Tracy, in particular, reckoned he might have been able to post a faster time had he not run out of fuel on what should have been his quickest lap.

The top three championship contenders held a significant advantage over the rest of the field, which was led on this occasion by Boesel. Goodyear and Unser shared identical times, just a gnat's whisker adrift of the Brazilian, with Teo Fabi (Pennzoil Lola-Chevy/C) and Arie Luyendyk (Target/Scotch Video Lola-Ford) both showing competitively also.

Behind them, Jimmy Vasser posted another fine effort in Jim Hayhoe's Kodalux Processing/STP Lola T92/00-Ford/Cosworth. Vasser was reaping the benefits of working with an engineer, Ian Ashdown, for the first time since

switching to the Ford-powered car in Toronto and found a significant amount of time after disconnecting the rear sway-bar.

'We're happy to be in the top ten,' said Vasser, who qualified ahead of such luminaries as Mario Andretti, Stefan Johansson, Bobby Rahal and Danny Sullivan. 'We tried a lot of things today and we learned a lot.'

Mauricio Gugelmin became the latest Formula 1 refugee to try his hand on the PPG Cup scene, setting 12th-best time in Dick Simon's trusty ex-St James/Gachot/Cheever Lola-Ford, which carried support from Hollywood American Blend cigarettes.

RACE

Mansell and Tracy topped the times again in the traditional race morning warmup, while Vasser again turned some heads by recording the third-fastest lap a little more than one-tenth away from Mansell's best.

Weather conditions were cool and overcast when the 28 starters assembled on the grid in front of the pit area. The threat of rain seemingly had passed. By the end of the race, indeed, the heavy clouds had been replaced by a clear, blue sky.

The starting signal was given midway down the long back straightaway, as usual at Mid-Ohio, since the pit straight is considered too short for safety.

Michael C. Brown

Mansell made an aggressive start, accelerating clear as the green flags waved, only for Tracy to make a move for the lead under braking for the first corner – Turn Five.

The pair raced side-by-side into the right-handed corner, with Tracy emerging ahead following a light clash of wheels.

'I was keying in on Nigel at the start of the race,' said Tracy, who claimed he barely felt the contact. 'I've always been able to take the outside line going into the Esses

so, based on my starting position, that's what I did.

'I got ahead of Nigel and I guess his left-front tire tagged my right-rear, and I didn't see him after that.'

Mansell, though, saw plenty of Tracy. 'He chopped right across in front of my car,' declared an irate Mansell, whose car sustained suspension damage. 'I mean, it's very unprofessional, isn't it? He just took me out.'

Worse, a couple of corners later, as he fought to keep his damaged

steed under control, he came into contact with Arie Luyendyk. That impact tore a front wing from Mansell's car.

Both headed for the pits. Mansell resumed, two laps down after repairs had been made, only to be called in for a stop-and-go penalty after illegally passing the pace car in his haste to rejoin the action.

Following a full-course caution while various pieces of debris were cleared away, Tracy rocketed away into the lead and left Fit-

tipaldi to cope with the advances of a string of cars comprising Boesel, Unser Jr, Goodyear and Fabi.

'My car was a little loose and I think I was driving too conservatively,' said Fittipaldi. 'My car was a little slow on the back straight and I had to defend my position. My biggest concern was to finish the race.'

Several times Boesel drew alongside his compatriot on the main straight, but he was unable to make the pass stick. And soon, once his Penske had burned off

some of its fuel load, Fittipaldi began to edge clear.

Tracy, though, was long gone. By lap 20 he had stretched his advantage to over 15 seconds. Two laps later he was parked against the tire wall, deep in the sand trap at Turn 11, having simply braked too late while coming up to lap a couple of slower cars. It was, sadly, an error born out of inexperience and impatience.

'My Marlboro Penske was perfect today and I feel terrible for the crew,' said a chastened Tracy.

The caution flags came out again while the car was retrieved, and at the restart Fittipaldi had his work cut out to maintain the lead.

Goodyear passed Unser brilliantly on the outside at Turn One, then tried to do the same to Fittipaldi at the end of the back straight. He looked to have the pass completed, but ran too deep into the corner and slid wide. Unser slipped gratefully back through into second place, then took his turn at trying to pass

131

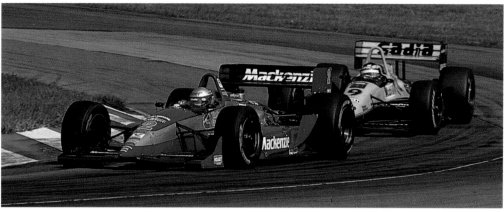

Right: Scott Goodyear leads Raul Boesel. The pair finished third and fourth respectively, though the Canadian driver had earlier made a determined bid for the lead before traction problems forced him to abandon his chase of Fittipaldi.

Below: Mike Groff spins his black Miller Genuine Draft machine and Scott Pruett takes to the grass on the infield in avoidance. Brian Till (99) checks his mirrors and sees the rest of the pack – Hiro Matsushita (15), Robbie Buhl (19), Marco Greco (30), Willy T. Ribbs (75), Buddy Lazier (20), David Kudrave (50) and Olivier Grouillard (29) – taking evasive action.

Fittipaldi. Again to no avail.

Once, Unser drew alongside as they crested the rise at Turn Six, but Fittipaldi was wise to that maneuver and unceremoniously edged Unser over the curb and onto the grass. Unser snaked down the edge of the track as he fought to regain control, then lost his front wings as he snagged Goodyear's right-rear wheel.

As Unser made for the pits and repairs, completed with remark-able speed by Owen Snyder's crew, Goodyear redoubled his attempts to pass Fittipaldi. Again the veteran remained in control.

Goodyear kept the pressure on all the way through to the second round of pit stops, made between laps 58 and 60, but thereafter could not keep pace.

'We just didn't have any traction,' related Goodyear. 'The car was very, very loose. We just had to try to survive.'

Fittipaldi romped clear by the finish, leaving Goodyear under siege from Gordon, who had moved steadily through the field. Gordon made a decisive pass into Turn Five on lap 77, but Boesel, close behind despite losing time on each of his pit stops, never was able to find a way past the Canadian and had to settle for fourth place at the finish.

Luyendyk crossed the line hard on their heels, having driven through the field in style after his first-lap delay. Brian Till also followed closely, and impressively, in Norm Turley's Say NO To Drugs/Project Learning Penske PC21, albeit several laps down after losing time when the car had become jammed in first gear.

'If we couldn't make up any places, at least I could show people I'm worthy,' said Till chirpily.

Bobby Rahal's Miller Genuine Draft Lola completed the top six.

SNIPPETS

• Bobby Rahal was in Las Vegas the day before practice commenced to hear official confirmation that American Honda will enter the PPG Cup series in 1994. Rahal will run a pair of Honda-powered Lolas in the colors of Miller Genuine Draft beer.

• John Paul Jr was slated to drive Tim Duke's Pro Formance Lola T91/00-Chevy/A but realized after the first session he was too tall to drive the car comfortably. Paul graciously gave up the seat to Scott Pruett, who qualified solidly in 20th.

• Eddie Cheever *(right)* was hired to replace Roberto Guerrero following a string of disappointing races for Kenny Bernstein's Budweiser King Lola-Chevy/C. Cheever, though, qualified a disastrous 21st and then sat in the pits at the start while the crew worked vainly on an electrical problem.

• With only 28 pit spaces available, three entrants were left without a race. Dominic Dobson made the cut in his PacWest Galmer but did not start due to a catastrophic gearbox failure on Sunday morning. Olivier Grouillard took his place on the grid.

Michael C. Brown

PIONEER ELECTRONICS 200, MID-OHIO SPORTS CAR COURSE, LEXINGTON, OHIO • 12 September, 89 laps – 200.250 miles

Place	Driver	No.	Car	Q Speed (mph)	Q Time	Q Pos.	Laps	Time/Retirement	Ave. speed	Pts
1	Emerson Fittipaldi	4	*Marlboro* Penske PC22-Chevy/C	118.113	1m 08.579s	3	89	1h 56m 59.188s	102.217 mph	21
2	Robby Gordon	14	*Copenhagen Racing* Lola T93/00-Ford	116.084	1m 09.777s	15	89	1h 57m 15.857s	101.975	16
3	Scott Goodyear	2	*Mackenzie Special* Lola T93/00-Ford	117.177	1m 09.126s	5	89	1h 57m 19.745s	101.918	14
4	Raul Boesel	9	*Duracell/Mobil 1/Sadia* Lola T93/00-Ford	117.209	1m 09.107s	4	89	1h 57m 20.278s	101.911	12
5	Arie Luyendyk	10	*Target/Scotch Video* Lola T93/00-Ford	116.582	1m 09.479s	8	89	1h 57m 21.155s	101.898	10
6	Bobby Rahal	1	*Miller Genuine Draft* Lola T93/00-Chevy/C	116.274	1m 09.663s	14	89	1h 57m 34.896s	101.700	8
7	Mario Andretti	6	*Kmart/Texaco Havoline* Lola T93/00-Ford	116.464	1m 09.549s	10	89	1h 57m 52.722s	101.443	6
8	Al Unser Jr	3	*Valvoline* Lola T93/00-Chevy/C	117.177	1m 09.126s	6	89	1h 57m 57.956s	101.368	5
9	Scott Brayton	22	*Amway/Northwest Airlines* Lola T93/00-Ford	115.458	1m 10.155s	18	88	Running		4
10	Jimmy Vasser	18	*Kodalux Processing/STP* Lola T92/00-Ford	116.477	1m 09.541s	9	88	Running		3
11	Willy T. Ribbs	75	*Cosby/Service Merchandise* Lola T92/00-Ford	114.266	1m 10.887s	22	88	Running		2
12	Nigel Mansell	5	*Kmart/Texaco Havoline* Lola T93/00-Ford	118.372	1m 08.428s	1	87	Running		2
13	Hiro Matsushita	15	*Panasonic Special* Lola T93/00-Ford	113.866	1m 11.136s	23	87	Running		
14	Robbie Buhl	19	*Mi-Jack* Lola T92/00-Chevy/A	113.194	1m 11.559s	24	87	Running		
15	Scott Pruett	45	*Pro Formance* Lola T91/00-Chevy/A	114.494	1m 10.746s	20	87	Running		
16	Olivier Grouillard	29	*Eurosport/Marlboro* Lola T92/00-Chevy/A	111.384	1m 12.722s	29	85	Running		
17	Brian Till	99	*Say NO To Drugs* Penske PC21-Chevy/B	115.142	1m 10.348s	19	83	Running		
18	Marco Greco	30	*Alfa Laval/Team Losi* Lola T92/00-Chevy/A	112.364	1m 12.087s	25	77	Gearbox		
19	Mark Smith	25	*Craftsman* Penske PC21-Chevy/B	116.390	1m 09.594s	13	69	Gearbox		
20	Buddy Lazier	20	*Financial World* Lola T91/00-Buick	112.005	1m 12.318s	26	69	Running		
21	Mauricio Gugelmin	90	*Hollywood* Lola T93/00-Ford	116.403	1m 09.586s	12	69	Header		
22	Mike Groff	26	*Miller Genuine Draft* Lola T93/00-Chevy/C	115.918	1m 09.877s	17	30	Accident		
23	David Kudrave	50	*Andrea Moda/Agip* Lola T92/00-Chevy/A	111.710	1m 12.509s	28	24	Gearbox		
24	Teo Fabi	8	*Pennzoil Special* Lola T93/00-Chevy/C	116.601	1m 09.467s	7	23	Electrical		
25	Paul Tracy	12	*Marlboro* Penske PC22-Chevy/C	118.138	1m 08.564s	2	21	Accident		
26	Stefan Johansson	16	*AMAX Energy & Metals* Penske PC22-Chevy/C	116.459	1m 09.552s	11	18	Gearbox		
27	Danny Sullivan	7	*Molson* Lola T93/00-Chevy/C	116.068	1m 09.787s	16	7	Oil pressure		
28	Eddie Cheever	40	*Budweiser King* Lola T93/00-Chevy/C	114.493	1m 10.746s	21	7	Electrical		
DNS	Dominic Dobson	17	*Winning Spirit* Galmer G92B-Chevy/A	111.748	1m 12.484s	27		Transmission		

Caution flags: Laps 1-4, accident/Mansell and Tracy; laps 25-30, accident/Tracy.

Lap leaders: Paul Tracy, 1-20 (20 laps); Emerson Fittipaldi, 21-89 (69 laps). *Totals:* Emerson Fittipaldi, 69 laps; Paul Tracy, 20 laps.

Championship positions: **1** Mansell, 170 pts; **2** Fittipaldi, 156; **3** Boesel, 126; **4** Tracy, 122; **5** Rahal, 119; **6** Mario Andretti, 113; **7** Al Unser Jr, 90; **8** Luyendyk, 71; **9** Gordon, 69; **10** Goodyear, 58; **11** Fabi, 57; **12** Sullivan, 43; **13** Guerrero, 39; **14** Brayton, 36; **15** Vasser, 30; **16** Johansson, 29; **17** Cheever, 18; **18** Montermini, 12; **19** Pruett, 12; **20** Ribbs, 9; **21** Buhl, 8; **22** Groff, 8; **23** Smith, 7; **24** Till, 7; **25** Matsushita, 7; **26** Fernandez, 6; **27** Kudrave, 6; **28** Grouillard, 4; **29** John Andretti, 3; **30** Greco, 2; **31** Danner, 2; **32** Bentley, 1; **33** Al Unser, 1; **34** Gachot, 1.

NAZARETH

Before the season, Indy Car insiders were predicting Nigel Mansell would have a tough time adapting to the altogether different world of oval track racing. Especially, they said, on the demanding one-mile ovals.

Mansell must have taken the comments to heart. Admittedly, he didn't make the field at Phoenix due to a high-speed crash in practice, but thereafter he remained unbeaten.

The Englishman's final success, in the Bosch Spark Plug Grand Prix at Nazareth Speedway, was perhaps his most impressive. His pit stops were perfect. His Kmart/Texaco Havoline Lola-Ford/Cosworth XB never missed a beat. And Mansell drove flawlessly throughout an all-action 200-lap race uninterrupted by caution flags.

'It was just an incredible race,' said Mansell. 'I learned some more today and I just think these one-mile ovals are so much fun – racing at its best.'

The stunning performance also assured Mansell of the PPG Indy Car World Series championship crown, his tally of 191 points unbeatable with only one race remaining.

Mansell thereby became the first driver ever to claim Formula 1 and Indy Car championships in successive seasons – and technically he held both crowns simultaneously, since Alain Prost did not clinch the 1993 Formula 1 title until the following week.

| 1st – MANSELL | 2nd – GOODYEAR | 3rd – TRACY |

Photos: Michael C. Brown

The advertising boards stepping down alongside the track give an indication of the elevation changes of the Nazareth tri-oval. Mansell, Andretti, Boesel and Fittipaldi do battle, having put Brian Till a lap down in his Say NO To Drugs Penske.

Inset left: No problems for Nigel Mansell at a refueling stop. In the background, Paul Newman looks on.

QUALIFYING

Actually there was none. Steady rain on Saturday saw to that. And since this was scheduled only as a two-day affair, practice time was limited to a pair of half-hour sessions on Sunday morning.

Mansell, fortunately, had taken advantage of an official CART-sanctioned test at Roger Penske's quirky little three-cornered oval immediately following the race at New Hampshire. He was quick then, so knew he had a good setup from which to work.

The all-too-brief practice brought few surprises. Raul Boesel, who has shone especially on the short ovals this year, ended up fastest in Dick Simon's Duracell/Mobil 1/Sadia Lola-Ford/Cosworth at 19.749 seconds, an average speed of 182.288 mph.

Mansell was content to be second quickest, especially as he had to step out of his primary Lola after a water leak manifested itself just a few minutes after practice began. There followed an example both of his talent and the expertise of his Tom Wurtz-led crew when Mansell hopped aboard the spare car and within a few more minutes had posted the quickest time thus far! His best of 19.894 seconds in the 5X machine was beaten only by Boesel.

Mansell returned to his originally scheduled race car for the final part of the second session and also set the fifth-fastest time, fractionally slower than his teammate – and hometown hero – Mario Andretti.

Paul Tracy, who has run thousands of miles of testing at Nazareth, was ahead of the two Newman-Haas cars in his Marlboro Penske PC22-Chevy/C. Afterward, during final preparations for the race, a spark plug became jammed, so the crew was obliged to hurriedly change the engine.

Both Mansell and Tracy were ready to go in their primary cars for the race, with Mansell on pole

as the grid was decided according to championship positions. Fittipaldi, who still harbored hopes of claiming the PPG Cup title, would start alongside on row one. Boesel and Tracy were on the second row ahead of Bobby Rahal (Miller Genuine Draft Lola-Chevy/C) and Andretti.

RACE

Cool but dry conditions prevailed for the race, which began only at the second attempt after several cars had been caught out of position first time around. Mansell was among them, having edged clearly ahead of Fittipaldi. The green was given at the start of the second lap, even though Mansell lagged slightly behind.

'I probably tried to get too much of a jump on the Penskes at the first start,' admitted Mansell, 'and then the second time I was a bit too conservative.'

Fittipaldi accelerated instantly ahead, followed around the outside line by teammate Tracy. Within three laps, Boesel also had found a way past Mansell.

'It was a nightmare for the first 10 or 20 laps,' declared Mansell. 'I was wondering what was happening. Paul, Emerson and Raul were going off into the distance and I thought, "I'm not enjoying this; I'd better get on with the program."'

'The car was pushing,' he continued, 'and sometimes you can alter your lines [through the corners] a little bit and improve the handling; and I did just that. The car came back into balance and I had a great race from there on.'

No question about that. Mansell zipped past Boesel on lap 27 and quickly closed the gap to Fittipaldi, who had relinquished the lead to teammate Tracy on lap 11. Mansell took over second place in Turn Three on lap 45, and two laps later took advantage of some slower traffic to out-maneuver Tracy entering Turn One.

Mansell was the fastest man on the track, and was never again

Scott Goodyear enhanced his reputation with yet another fine oval performance in the Mackenzie Financial Lola-Ford.

Below: **Bobby Rahal picked up sixth place, but his Lola-Chevy/C was unable to match the pace of the leaders.**

seriously challenged as he roared on to victory.

Tracy had begun to struggle several laps before being passed by Mansell, his car having developed a dangerous oversteer characteristic. Wisely, Tracy decided to make an early pit stop in the hope of alleviating the problem. It worked. He lost a lap and was out of sync with the rest of the field on pit stops for the remainder of the race, but he was able to run competitively.

Fittipaldi, despite a similar complaint, opted to remain out on the track until it was time for his first scheduled pit stop on lap 70. By then he had fallen to fourth place behind Scott Goodyear, who had emerged as Mansell's closest challenger in Derrick Walker's Mackenzie Financial Lola-Ford, and Arie Luyendyk, who had

moved up well in the similar Target/Scotch Video entry.

'The car was really good,' said Luyendyk. 'I was having fun. I could run really good into Turn Two; I was passing all sorts of people there.'

By half-distance, 100 laps, Mansell led Goodyear by around eight seconds. The Canadian chased hard and on a couple of occasions closed to within striking distance, only for Mansell to edge away again. Finally, Goodyear began to experience the same 'loose' characteristic that had hobbled so many others.

'I was just hanging onto it at the end,' said Goodyear. 'Any time I was in traffic, I was just dirt-tracking it.'

Luyendyk's car also lost its edge and began pushing into the corners. Then, later, the right-front

wing adjuster broke off, inducing dire oversteer as the front wings exerted more than the optimum amount of downforce. Luyendyk was unable to defend his position. He slipped back to eighth at the finish ahead of Boesel, whose car also was a nightmare to drive.

Robby Gordon, meanwhile, had moved into contention after starting ninth in his Copenhagen Lola-Ford. He took fourth place on lap 115, at the expense of Fittipaldi, and 15 laps later demoted Luyendyk.

Tracy also was making progress, and as the race drew toward its conclusion, he began to close on Gordon for third place. Gordon, though, was blissfully unaware, since for many laps a glitch with the official scoring system had erroneously shown Tracy one lap adrift of the Californian.

Just three laps from the end, Tracy made a move on Gordon as they sped into Turn Three. Gordon tried to respond but it was too late. Tracy was gone. Both were two laps behind the leaders at the checkered flag.

Fittipaldi also completed 198 laps, although fifth place was not enough to prevent Mansell from clinching the title.

'The car was really strong the first 20 laps, then it went really loose,' explained Fittipaldi. 'We made some changes at the pit stops and the car was better, but it was not consistent enough to run with Nigel.

'I would like to congratulate Nigel [on winning the championship]. He did a beautiful job.'

Or as Paul Newman so succinctly described his driver's title-winning performance: 'Wow!'

SNIPPETS

• Mauricio Gugelmin had a fraught time in his first-ever oval track race. The Brazilian had looked impressive in his midweek rookie test and turned the 11th-fastest time on Sunday morning. That was the good news. Unfortunately, having to start 25th, he soon found out how difficult overtaking can be at Nazareth. Gugelmin was unable to find a way past Ross Bentley and was lapped by countryman Fittipaldi for the first time on his eighth lap! Inside 50 laps he was seven laps behind the leaders. The F1 veteran soldiered on as best he could before finally parking his Hollywood American Blend Lola-Ford.

• Michael Andretti, who, like his father Mario, lives within earshot of the track, confirmed at a press conference hosted by Chip Ganassi that he would be rejoining the PPG Cup trail in 1994, developing and racing Ganassi's new Reynard. McLaren's Ron Dennis flew in on Concorde for the announcement.

• The following day, Nigel Mansell (pictured above with Paul Newman and Carl Haas) confirmed he had signed a two-year contract to remain in the Indy Car series with Newman-Haas Racing.

• Incredibly, 23 out of the 26 starters were running at the end of the fastest race ever run on a one-mile oval, with Mansell averaging no less than 158.685 mph – inclusive of two pit stops.

• The Rick Mears Night of Champions charity softball event, held midweek at nearby Reading, Pennsylvania, saw the Indy Car drivers lose 8-3 to a strong team of NHRA drag racing stars.

BOSCH SPARK PLUG GRAND PRIX, NAZARETH SPEEDWAY, NAZARETH, PENNSYLVANIA • 19 September, 200 laps – 200.000 miles

Place	Driver	No.	Car	Q Speed (mph)	Q Time	Pos.	Laps	Time/Retirement	Ave. speed	Pts
1	Nigel Mansell	5	Kmart/Texaco Havoline Lola T93/00-Ford	—	—	1	200	1h 15m 37.273s	158.685 mph	21
2	Scott Goodyear	2	Mackenzie Special Lola T93/00-Ford	—	—	10	200	1h 15m 56.539s	158.015	16
3	Paul Tracy	12	Marlboro Penske PC22-Chevy/C	—	—	4	198	Running		14
4	Robby Gordon	14	Copenhagen Racing Lola T93/00-Ford	—	—	9	198	Running		12
5	Emerson Fittipaldi	4	Marlboro Penske PC22-Chevy/C	—	—	2	198	Running		10
6	Bobby Rahal	1	Miller Genuine Draft Lola T93/00-Chevy/C	—	—	5	196	Running		8
7	Stefan Johansson	16	AMAX Energy & Metals Penske PC22-Chevy/C	—	—	14	196	Running		6
8	Arie Luyendyk	10	Target/Scotch Video Lola T93/00-Ford	—	—	8	195	Running		5
9	Raul Boesel	9	Duracell/Mobil 1/Sadia Lola T93/00-Ford	—	—	3	194	Running		4
10	Eddie Cheever	40	Budweiser King Lola T93/00-Chevy/C	—	—	15	192	Running		3
11	Teo Fabi	8	Pennzoil Special Lola T93/00-Chevy/C	—	—	11	191	Running		2
12	Mark Smith	25	Craftsman Penske PC21-Chevy/B	—	—	19	189	Running		1
13	Mario Andretti	6	Kmart/Texaco Havoline Lola T93/00-Ford	—	—	6	188	Running		
14	David Kudrave	42	Andrea Moda/Agip Lola T92/00-Chevy/A	—	—	21	186	Running		
15	Scott Brayton	22	Amway/Northwest Airlines Lola T93/00-Ford	—	—	13	186	Running		
16	Brian Till	99	Say NO To Drugs Penske PC21-Chevy/B	—	—	18	185	Running		
17	Robbie Buhl	19	Mi-Jack Lola T92/00-Chevy/A	—	—	17	184	Running		
18	Olivier Grouillard	29	Eurosport/Marlboro Lola T92/00-Chevy/A	—	—	22	183	Running		
19	Willy T. Ribbs	75	Cosby/Service Merchandise Lola T92/00-Ford	—	—	16	181	Running		
20	Danny Sullivan	7	Molson Lola T93/00-Chevy/C	—	—	12	179	Running		
21	Hiro Matsushita	15	Panasonic Special Lola T93/00-Ford	—	—	20	176	Running		
22	Ross Bentley	39	AGFA/Rain-X Lola T92/00-Chevy/A	—	—	24	170	Running		
23	Marco Greco	30	Alfa Laval/Team Losi Lola T92/00-Chevy/A	—	—	23	163	Running		
24	Mauricio Gugelmin	18	Hollywood Lola T93/00-Ford	—	—	25	145	Handling		
25	Al Unser Jr	3	Valvoline Lola T93/00-Chevy/C	—	—	7	75	Engine		
26	Buddy Lazier	20	Financial World Lola T91/00-Buick	—	—	26	57	Suspension		

Grid arranged according to championship standings due to rain

Caution flags: Lap 1, field out of formation.

Lap leaders: Nigel Mansell, 1 (1 lap); Emerson Fittipaldi, 2-10 (9 laps); Paul Tracy, 11-46 (36 laps); Nigel Mansell, 47-200 (154 laps). **Totals:** Nigel Mansell, 155 laps; Paul Tracy, 36 laps; Emerson Fittipaldi, 9 laps.

Championship positions: 1 Mansell, 191 pts; **2** Fittipaldi, 166; **3** Tracy, 136; **4** Boesel, 130; **5** Rahal, 127; **6** Mario Andretti, 113; **7** Al Unser Jr, 90; **8** Gordon, 81; **9** Luyendyk, 76; **10** Goodyear, 74; **11** Fabi, 59; **12** Sullivan, 43; **13** Guerrero, 39; **14** Brayton, 36; **15** Johansson, 35; **16** Vasser, 30; **17** Cheever, 21; **18** Montermini, 12; **19** Pruett, 12; **20** Ribbs, 9; **21** Buhl, 8; **22** Smith, 8; **23** Groff, 8; **24** Till, 7; **25** Matsushita, 7; **26** Fernandez, 6; **27** Kudrave, 6; **28** Grouillard, 4; **29** John Andretti, 3; **30** Greco, 2; **31** Danner, 2; **32** Bentley, 1; **33** Al Unser, 1; **34** Gachot, 1.

1st – TRACY

2nd – FITTIPALDI

3rd – LUYENDYK

LAGUNA SECA

Photos: Michael C. Brown

Paul Tracy has endured a few disappointments, made a few mistakes this year. He has also posted some quite excellent drives. One such came in the season finale at Laguna Seca Raceway, where he scored an emphatic victory in the Makita 300/Toyota Monterey Grand Prix.

Tracy led for all but three laps *en route* to his fifth win, which tied him with new champion Nigel Mansell and secured third place in the final PPG Cup standings.

The young Canadian took charge right away from his pole-winning teammate Emerson Fittipaldi. The pair of identical Marlboro Penske PC22-Chevrolets were never again seriously threatened in the 84-lap contest.

Danny Sullivan ran strongly until his Molson Lola-Chevy/C was sidelined by a broken exhaust header.

Arie Luyendyk also drove a fine race, finishing third in Chip Ganassi's Target/Scotch Video Lola-Ford/Cosworth, while Mansell's sizzling season fizzled out as his Kmart/Texaco Havoline Lola-Ford came into contact with two other cars before retiring to the pits.

QUALIFYING

Back on a road course, so it must be Penske country, right? Sure enough, Tracy lost no time in getting up to speed in his PC22, while Fittipaldi, a little more circumspect at first, gradually moved up into contention before grabbing the pole with yet another of his patented last-lap charges on Saturday afternoon.

'I think we gained a little more downforce today because of the cooler weather,' said a delighted Fittipaldi, 'but I think we lost a bit of grip due to the track being a bit more slippery.'

The overall trend, however, was a tad faster, and Fittipaldi responded admirably to beat Tracy, the provisional pole-winner on Friday, by a scant 0.041

second. The Brazilian's effort at 1m 10.976s represented a new track record at 112.296 mph, some two-tenths underneath Michael Andretti's year-old standard.

'It was really a great lap,' said Fittipaldi after taking the 15th pole of his Indy Car career. 'The car is very well balanced.'

Tracy was following Fittipaldi on the track right at the end of the session but ran out of time to post an improvement of his own. He had to make do with a place alongside on the front row.

'It was disappointing,' he admitted, 'but where we're starting [on the grid] is a good spot, the car is good and I'm looking forward to the race.'

Mansell was unable to better his time from Friday, hindered by a broken clutch in the final session, while Sullivan and Luyendyk both maintained their excellent form of the day before to take fourth and fifth on the grid.

'The team has done a really good job of getting a grip on the handling of the Lola chassis, and it shows, because suddenly we're a lot more competitive,' said Luyendyk, who learned at Nazareth he is being replaced next season by Michael Andretti. 'It's bittersweet [to be so far up the grid] because obviously I would like to stay with the team.'

Mauricio Gugelmin impressed in qualifying eighth with his Hollywood American Blend Lola-Ford, while Bobby Rahal rued the fact if he had been a little over one-tenth faster in the Miller Genuine Draft Lola-Chevy/C, he would have been fifth on the grid instead of tenth.

'It's tough when the top ten cars are six-tenths apart and we're the tenth car,' said Rahal. 'On a 2.2-mile course, six-tenths can be just a missed shift. It just shows how competitive this series is right now.'

Even Robby Gordon, using his '92 Copenhagen Lola-Ford again after crashing the '93 car in practice, and Scott Brayton (Amway/Northwest Airlines Lola-Ford), 14th and 15th on the grid, were only fractionally more than one second away from Fittipaldi's pole-winning time, while the final qualifier, Dominic Dobson's newly Chevy/C-powered Skycell Galmer G92B, recorded a best of 1m 14.138s. One year ago, that would have been good enough for 17th place on the grid.

RACE

Thick fog enshrouded the track Sunday morning. The veil lifted briefly in time for a belated warmup session, then quickly descended again. The officials had no option but to postpone the Firestone Indy Lights race until after the main event, which itself was delayed 45 minutes.

It was decidedly cool, too, as the 29 qualifiers assembled in front of the pits. Finally, the order was given to fire up the engines. Stefan Johansson's AMAX Penske was in the pits at that time, requiring a fresh fuel pump, but was present and correct for the green flag.

The start was clean, with Tracy immediately getting the jump on Fittipaldi. He led the pack up over the slightly left-handed crest, nominally entitled Turn One, then downhill again toward the heavy braking area at Turn Two.

Mansell tucked in behind, but it soon became apparent he could not match the Penskes' pace. Sullivan, Luyendyk, Mario Andretti (Kmart/Texaco Havoline Lola-Ford), Johansson and Gugelmin all followed dutifully in grid order.

Very little had changed by lap 20. Tracy had pulled out a breathing space over his teammate and was maintaining the gap at around three seconds. Mansell had lost almost a second per lap in third place. He in turn remained under pressure from Sullivan and Luyendyk. Johansson had moved up to sixth, leaving Andretti to fend off a dicing Rahal and Scott Goodyear (Mackenzie Financial Lola-Ford), both of whom had out-fumbled Gugelmin at Turn 11 on the 17th lap.

As the first round of pit stops approached, Luyendyk found a way past Sullivan, only to lose the place again due to a faster stop by Sullivan's 'Ziggy' Harcus-led crew. Mansell found himself back in fifth once the stops were complete, followed by Johansson and Goodyear.

Tracy also pulled out a distinct advantage over Fittipaldi, although this diminished quickly when Tracy came upon a knot of slower cars.

At the same time, Sullivan's fine run in third place ended abruptly after 43 laps with a broken exhaust header.

'I guess it wasn't our day,' reflected Sullivan. 'We couldn't stay with the Penskes but we were the best of the rest.'

Luyendyk, who had shadowed Sullivan since the earlier pit stops, took over the position and remained well clear of Johansson. The Swede had taken over fourth place on lap 44, when Mansell came together with series debutant Scott Sharp's Rain-X/AMAX Penske PC22 in Turn 11.

'I really thought I gave him enough room,' reckoned the newly crowned Trans-Am champion with ample justification. Sharp rejoined the race, but only after a lengthy pit stop to fit a new rear wing.

Mansell also continued, after losing another place to Goodyear, only to come into smart contact with Mark Smith's Craftsman Penske-Chevy/B at Turn One on lap 71. This time the Englishman headed for the pits, his Lola sporting right-side damage. Mansell immediately alighted and was taken to the infield care center. Then he vented his spleen.

'My wrist took a good twist and bang inside the car,' reported Mansell. 'It's a sorry situation when you are overtaking people who are much slower than you and this is what happens.' Exit one irate PPG Cup champion.

By this juncture, the proceedings had been enlivened somewhat at the sharp end of the field. Tracy had again encountered a large group of cars – in this instance those of Al Unser Jr (Valvoline Lola-Chevy/C), Johansson, after a slow second pit stop, and Rahal. They were all

Michael C. Brown

embroiled in a splendid scrap over sixth place and were not about to make life easy for Tracy, whether he was the race leader or not.

Within a matter of laps, Fittipaldi suddenly was right back on Tracy's tail, anxiously looking for a way past.

'I was struggling with the traffic,' admitted Tracy, 'and I didn't want to put a foot wrong, so I was being careful. Emerson caught up in a hurry.'

Tracy had something else to worry about, too, having inadvertently unclasped his seat belt buckle while maneuvering through the tight Turn 11 hairpin.

'It was horrible,' he said. 'I never realized how hard it is to drive [without the belts]. It's almost impossible to keep yourself in the car, especially here with all the elevation change and everything.'

Tracy contemplated making a pit stop – and decided he certainly would do if Fittipaldi were to find a way past. But he didn't. Instead Fittipaldi made an error, caught out while trying to lap the ever-present Hiro Matsushita's Panasonic Lola-Ford in Turn Five on lap 79.

Tracy duly ran away to take another well-earned victory, while Fittipaldi recovered from his spin to finish a distant second. Afterward he quipped he might dig into his pocket and buy Matsushita a Christmas present – a large rear-view mirror!

Luyendyk, Goodyear and Unser, all of whom posted solid performances, were the only other unlapped finishers. Johansson claimed sixth, his progress hindered by a loose piece of carbon fiber which rattled around inside the footbox, while farther back Adrian Fernandez was the top rookie finisher, 12th, after a most promising drive through from 24th on the grid in Rick Galles' Conseco Lola-Chevy/C.

Michael C. Brown

SNIPPETS

Michael C. Brown

• Kenny Bernstein announced the previous week that Scott Goodyear will drive his Budweiser King Lola for the next two seasons. At Goodyear's insistence, Ford/Cosworth engines will be used instead of the present Chevrolet/Ilmors. Derrick Walker also confirmed Goodyear's place will be taken by Robby Gordon *(left)*, with backing from Valvoline and Cummins Diesel.

• Bridgestone/Firestone verified the fact veteran team owner U.E. 'Pat' Patrick will return following a two-year sabbatical. The reformed Patrick Racing will run a concerted test program for Firestone in 1994, prior to re-entering the PPG Cup series in 1995.

• Dick Simon owned no fewer than six cars among the 34 which attempted to qualify. Aside from the regular entries for Raul Boesel and Scott Brayton, plus Jimmy Vasser and Mauricio Gugelmin, he also ran a year-old (ex-Lyn St James) Lola-Ford in the colors of

Kinko's Copiers for Didier Theys and leased a '92 Lola-Chevy/A (the same car taken to third place at Phoenix by Vasser) to Joe Kennedy and Jeff Sinden. The car was run under the Paragon Motorsports banner for former Super Vee/Toyota Atlantic runner John C. Brooks, who had procured backing from the popular TV show 'Lifestyles of the Rich and Famous'. Predictably, without proper testing, he was unable to qualify.

• Mario Andretti confirmed over the weekend he will remain with Newman-Haas Racing one more season, then hang up his helmet. Andretti's tally of 52 Indy Car victories is second only to A.J. Foyt with 67.

Michael C. Brown

MAKITA 300/TOYOTA MONTEREY GRAND PRIX, LAGUNA SECA RACEWAY, MONTEREY, CALIFORNIA • 3 October, 84 laps – 185.976 miles

Place	Driver	No.	Car	Q Speed (mph)	Q Time	Pos.	Laps	Time/Retirement	Ave. speed	Pts
1	**Paul Tracy**	12	*Marlboro* Penske PC22-Chevy/C	112.232	1m 11.017s	2	84	1h 44m 58.169s	106.303 mph	21
2	**Emerson Fittipaldi**	4	*Marlboro* Penske PC22-Chevy/C	112.296	1m 10.976s	1	84	1h 45m 25.660s	105.841	17
3	**Arie Luyendyk**	10	*Target/Scotch Video* Lola T93/00-Ford	111.433	1m 11.527s	5	84	1h 45m 44.338s	105.529	14
4	**Scott Goodyear**	2	*Mackenzie Special* Lola T93/00-Ford	111.282	1m 11.623s	9	84	1h 46m 00.729s	105.257	12
5	**Al Unser Jr**	3	*Valvoline* Lola T93/00-Chevy/C	110.758	1m 11.962s	12	84	1h 46m 09.991s	105.104	10
6	Stefan Johansson	16	*AMAX Energy & Metals* Penske PC22-Chevy/C	111.327	1m 11.594s	7	83	Running		8
7	Bobby Rahal	1	*Miller Genuine Draft* Lola T93/00-Chevy/C	111.225	1m 11.660s	10	83	Running		6
8	Teo Fabi	8	*Pennzoil Special* Lola T93/00-Chevy/C	111.146	1m 11.711s	11	83	Running		5
9	Mario Andretti	6	*Kmart/Texaco Havoline* Lola T93/00-Ford	111.362	1m 11.572s	6	83	Running		4
10	Robby Gordon	14	*Copenhagen Racing* Lola T92/00-Ford	110.700	1m 12.000s	14	83	Running		3
11	Raul Boesel	9	*Duracell/Mobil 1/Sadia* Lola T93/00-Ford	110.706	1m 11.996s	13	82	Fuel pickup		2
12	Adrian Fernandez	11	*Conseco* Lola T93/00-Chevy/C	108.387	1m 13.536s	24	82	Running		1
13	Mauricio Gugelmin	90	*Hollywood* Lola T93/00-Ford	111.301	1m 11.611s	8	82	Running		
14	Eddie Cheever	40	*Budweiser King* Lola T93/00-Chevy/C	109.184	1m 12.999s	19	82	Running		
15	Didier Theys	23	*Kinko's* Lola T92/00-Ford	108.700	1m 13.325s	22	81	Running		
16	Robbie Buhl	19	*Mi-Jack* Lola T92/00-Chevy/A	108.288	1m 13.604s	25	81	Running		
17	Mark Smith	25	*Craftsman* Penske PC21-Chevy/B	109.642	1m 12.695s	17	81	Running		
18	Dominic Dobson	17	*Skycell* Galmer G92B-Chevy/C	107.507	1m 14.138s	29	80	Running		
19	Hiro Matsushita	15	*Panasonic Special* Lola T93/00-Ford	107.733	1m 13.983s	27	80	Running		
20	Olivier Grouillard	29	*Eurosport/Marlboro* Lola T92/00-Chevy/A	107.509	1m 14.137s	28	80	Running		
21	Jimmy Vasser	18	*Kodalux Processing/STP* Lola T92/00-Ford	110.135	1m 12.369s	16	79	Spin		
22	Scott Sharp	33	*Rain-X/AMAX* Penske PC22-Chevy/C	108.438	1m 13.502s	23	78	Running		
23	Nigel Mansell	5	*Kmart/Texaco Havoline* Lola T93/00-Ford	111.730	1m 11.336s	3	71	Accident		
24	Scott Brayton	22	*Amway/Northwest Airlines* Lola T93/00-Ford	110.683	1m 12.011s	15	61	Engine		
25	Scott Pruett	45	*Pro Formance* Lola T91/00-Chevy/A	109.298	1m 12.923s	18	55	Engine		
26	Christian Danner	50	*Andrea Moda/Agip* Lola T92/00-Chevy/A	108.190	1m 13.671s	26	54	Transmission		
27	Danny Sullivan	7	*Molson* Lola T93/00-Chevy/C	111.646	1m 11.390s	4	43	Header		
28	Willy T. Ribbs	75	*Cosby/Service Merchandise* Lola T92/00-Ford	108.863	1m 13.215s	21	31	Transmission		
29	Brian Till	99	*Say NO To Drugs* Penske PC21-Chevy/B	109.135	1m 13.032s	20	28	Header		

Caution flags: No full-course yellow flags.

Lap leaders: Paul Tracy, 1-26 (26 laps); Emerson Fittipaldi, 27-29 (3 laps); Paul Tracy, 30-84 (55 laps). **Totals:** Paul Tracy, 81 laps; Emerson Fittipaldi, 3 laps.

Championship positions: 1 Mansell, 191 pts; 2 Fittipaldi, 183; 3 Tracy, 157; 4 Rahal, 133; 5 Boesel, 132; 6 Mario Andretti, 117; 7 Al Unser Jr, 100; 8 Luyendyk, 90; 9 Goodyear, 86; 10 Gordon, 84; 11 Fabi, 64; 12 Sullivan, 43; 13 Johansson, 43; 14 Guerrero, 39; 15 Brayton, 36; 16 Vasser, 30; 17 Cheever, 21; 18 Montermini, 12; 19 Pruett, 12; 20 Ribbs, 9; 21 Buhl, 8; 22 Smith, 8; 23 Groff, 8; 24 Fernandez, 7; 25 Till, 7; 26 Matsushita, 7; 27 Kudrave, 6; 28 Grouillard, 4; 29 John Andretti, 3; 30 Greco, 2; 31 Danner, 2; 32 Bentley, 1; 33 Al Unser, 1; 34 Gachot, 1.

FIRESTONE INDY LIGHTS CHAMPIONSHIP

The Firestone Indy Lights Championship has enjoyed the most successful season in its somewhat checkered history. The fields have been larger than ever before, the teams and drivers have shown a greater commitment and the standard of competition has improved immeasurably.

Two factors have been primarily responsible for this overdue growth. First, the decision to replace the aging March/Wildcat chassis with the far more up-to-date Lola T93/20, and second, the advent of a brand new race team, Tasman Motorsports Group.

Steve Horne is the man behind the Tasman team, and equally gifted 23-year-old Bryan Herta has been the main beneficiary.

New Zealand-bred Horne was the man to whom the late Jim Trueman turned when he decided to go Indy Car racing with Bobby Rahal in 1982. Their Truesports team was a winner virtually from its inception.

Horne led the way to an Indy Lights title, a pair of PPG Indy Car World Series championships, and one Indianapolis 500 victory, elevating Rahal from a merely ambitious open-wheel racer to one of the sport's most successful heroes.

Along the way Horne graduated from being chief mechanic/team manager to co-owner. Midway through 1992, however, following a few less successful seasons, he left to pursue his own dreams. Tasman was the result.

Horne installed Herta as his new team leader, the youngster having already won the Barber Saab Pro Series title prior to impressing during his rookie Indy Lights season with Landford Racing in 1992. Herta repaid the faith shown in him in spades.

The Tasman team dominated the season in no uncertain terms, and while Herta was kept on his toes by aggressive English teammate Steve Robertson, the young American's own determination, poise and self-control – not to mention pace – were enough to ensure he emerged a deserving champion.

Herta broke Paul Tracy's 1990 record by earning no less than eight pole positions during the 12-race season (whereas Tracy earned his tally of seven from 14 races). His worst starting position was third on the grid at Long Beach and Milwaukee. Herta led more than 50 percent of the season's total laps and emerged victorious seven times in his MyLifeCard Lola T93/20-Buick.

He should have won twice more, too. He led at Phoenix until suffering a blown tire on the very last lap, while at Portland he had the field covered until running into more tire problems.

No doubt about it, 23-year-old Herta has emerged as a very bright prospect for the future. He has achieved everything expected of him and plans to graduate into the Indy Car series next year with the Tasman team.

Herta's primary challengers this season all spent their formative years in the sport in Europe, exemplifying once more the growing appeal of the series.

Frenchman Franck Freon started the year as a firm title favorite but rarely matched Herta's pace due to a distinct lack of finance – and therefore testing – in John

Main photo: Star of the season in Firestone Indy Lights was undoubtedly Bryan Herta, who claimed eight pole positions and seven victories in the 12-race series.

Left: Robbie Groff switched teams midseason but a win continued to elude him, though he was a regular front-runner.

Bottom: An international rostrum at Long Beach with Britain's Steve Robertson flanked by Frenchman Franck Freon *(left)* and Bryan Herta of the United States. The championship attracted drivers from many countries.

build on the experience he gained this season and will be a hot favorite to claim the crown.

Portugal's Pedro Chaves made good progress during the year with Brian Stewart Racing. He never did get to grips with the ovals but his Castrol/Fly to Porto car was always a threat on the road courses. He finished just two points shy of Robertson in the chase for Rookie of the Year honors.

For the third straight season, Robbie Groff endured a mixed bag of fortunes. He quit the Bradley Motorsports fold at midseason and switched instead to Andreas Leberle's AL Motorsport camp, albeit with little noticeable effect on his results. Groff, whose brother Mike won the Indy Lights crown in 1989 and started half a dozen PPG Cup races with Rahal/Hogan Racing this season, was always up among the top half-dozen. His best result was a second place at New Hampshire.

If there was an award for the Most Improved Driver it would surely go to Nick Firestone, who made impressive progress under the tutelage of Peter Jacobs at

Dick Simon Racing. A great grandson of automotive tire pioneer Harvey S. Firestone, Nick switched to Indy Lights after a disappointing season of British Formula 3000 in 1992 and came on strong in the later races with his Mirachem/NOW Lola.

The turning point for Firestone came at Milwaukee, where he led the race until being passed by Herta. His confidence boosted, Firestone became more and more competitive once he had undertaken a few test days. He ran well at Vancouver, in between a couple of spins, and chased Herta to the checkered flag at Nazareth.

Sweden's Fredrik Ekblom marked himself as a major talent despite a minimal budget in Cary Agapiou's Petro Globe/ZW Motorsports car. The highlight of his year was a second-place finish at Portland, although he would undoubtedly have achieved more had he been able to conduct a test program.

Fellow Scandinavian Harald Huysman capped a largely disappointing year with a third-place finish at New Hampshire. Huys-

man, who started the season with Tasman Motorsports, had looked on course for a victory at Phoenix until being one of many to be hobbled by a blistered tire, but later quit the team abruptly following his third major accident of the season. He switched to Leading Edge for the final few races but by then his confidence had been badly eroded.

Canadian teenager Greg Moore marked himself as a young man with a bright future, while four-time motor cycle World Champion Eddie Lawson impressed everyone with his skill and commitment in his first taste of four-wheel competition. Lawson's achievements have made him a huge star in his own sport, yet you'd never know it. He remains a humble, sincere character who is set on carving a new career for himself. His performances at Vancouver, where he qualified and finished third, and at Laguna Seca, where he rounded off the season by being beaten only by Herta, were quite remarkable given his level of experience. Lawson, most definitely, is a man to watch.

Martin Racing's Entrepreneur Magazine/Aldus Software Lola. He qualified on the front row only once, with a typically bold effort at Long Beach, but he was consistent and proved to be a strong racer who rarely made a mistake. He was one of only two drivers to break the Tasman stranglehold on Victory Lane, moving to the front at Portland when Herta and Pedro Chaves were obliged to make pit stops to change blistered tires.

Robertson finished third in points with Tasman's Crane & Shovel Sales entry. The tempestuous Englishman was blindingly quick in his rookie season but also made several mistakes. He won three times and earned three poles, although each time he started at the front his race ended in disaster. Next year he is set to

Michael C. Brown

SCCA PLAYER'S TOYOTA ATLANTIC CHAMPIONSHIP

Forsythe-Green Racing was as dominant in the SCCA Player's Toyota Atlantic Championship as was the Tasman team in Indy Lights. The partnership of wealthy businessman Gerry Forsythe and team manager/co-owner Barry Green had been successful before, notably in the Can-Am championship and in the 1983 Indy Car series, when Teo Fabi finished a close second in the PPG Cup standings in a sensational rookie season unmatched until Nigel Mansell appeared on the scene this year.

Forsythe and Green renewed their association with the sole intention of preparing for a return to the Indy Car series in 1994. Judging by their success this year, they will be instantly successful.

The team's pair of Player's-backed Ralt RT40s were always immaculately prepared, the class of the field. But drivers Claude Bourbonnais and Jacques (son of Gilles) Villeneuve made too many errors and ended up losing the championship to fellow Canadian David Empringham's Motomaster/Canaska Racing Ralt.

All three drivers marked themselves as prodigious talents. Bourbonnais showed a quite startling turn of pace, finally earning the opportunity to display his worth after several years of struggling to match the impression he created in his formative years in Formula Ford 2000. He won seven races and would have taken the title had he not been served with a dubious penalty in the season-opener at Phoenix. By the same token, he would have won had it not been for crashes at Road Atlanta and Halifax, or if his engine hadn't failed while running second in the final race at Laguna Seca. If, if, if . . .

Villeneuve also ran strongly, taking seven poles from the 15 races and winning five times. Empringham, meanwhile, was superbly consistent. He won only once, at Trois Rivières, but earned ten podium finishes, despite the fact his team had neither the resources nor the depth of experience assembled by Barry Green. His triumph was surely earned against the odds. And was well-deserved.

No one else, frankly, was in the same class. Jamie Galles showed well on sporadic appearances in the Vital Hair Care Ralt, while Jeff Barker (Lynx Racing Ralt), Colin Trueman (Red Roof Inns Ralt), an improving Peter Faucetta (Newport Ralt), Steve O'Hara (O'Hara Financial Services Ralt) and Bert Hart (Simpson Ralt) starred from time to time. Frenchman Patrick LeMarie also came on strong at the end of the season.

Veteran Ron Tauranac's Ralt design became the dominant equipment this year, finally eclipsing David Bruns' Swift DB-4 design, although yet another Canadian, Trevor Seibert, displayed his talents by posting some dogged efforts in his Dyno Max/STP Swift, including a fine victory in Halifax and a pole in Vancouver.

Top: **David Empringham's consistency in the Motomaster/Canaska Racing Ralt beat off the title challenge of the very fast but sometimes erratic Claude Bourbonnais in Forsythe-Green Racing's Player's-backed Ralt.**

144